From This Day Forward

Commitment, Marriage, and Family in Lesbian and Gay Relationships

Gretchen A. Stiers

St. Martin's Griffin
New York

*To my parents, Tom and Brenda Stiers, whose love and support
continues to make all the difference in life
and
To Silvana Solano, for always*

*Dedicated to the memory of
Julie Ann Lam,
who lived life every day.
August 18, 1958–January 14, 2000*

FROM THIS DAY FORWARD
© Gretchen A. Stiers, 1999. All rights reserved. Printed in the United States of
America. No part of this book may be used or reproduced in any manner
whatsoever without written permission except in the case of brief quotations
embodied in critical articles or reviews. For information, address St. Martin's
Press, 175 Fifth Avenue, New York, N.Y. 10010.

ISBN 0-312-22964-x

Library of Congress Cataloging-in-Publication Data

Stiers, Gretchen A., 1962-
    From this day forward : commitment, marriage, and family in
lesbian and gay relationships / Gretchen A. Stiers.
    p.   cm.
    Includes bibliographical references and index.
    ISBN 0-312-17542-6 (cloth)   0-312-22964-x (pbk)
    1. Same-sex marriage--United States.   I. Title.
HQ76.3.U5S76 1999
306.84'8'0973--dc21   98-45783
                                                           CIP

Design by Acme Art, Inc.

First published in hardcover in the United States of America in 1998
First St. Martin's Griffin edition: May 2000
10 9 8 7 6 5 4 3 2 1

CONTENTS

List of Tables v

Acknowledgments vii

Preface to the Paperback Edition: Our Common Humanity ix

Preface xiii

PART I:
LESBIAN AND GAY RELATIONSHIPS

1. Our Love Is Here to Stay: Lesbian and Gay
   Relationships in the 1990s 3

2. As Long as I Have a Heart:
   On the Meaning of Love in Lesbian and
   Gay Relationships 25

3. The Power of Two: On the Meaning of Commitment
   and Marriage in Lesbian and Gay Relationships. 45

PART II:
LESBIAN AND GAY COMMITMENT
CEREMONIES

4. For Richer, For Poorer?: Same-Sex Ceremonies
   as Rites of Passage 71

5. Going to the Chapel and I'm Going to Get _____?:
   Same-Sex Ceremonies and the Politics of Naming. 105

6. Church Bells May Ring: Same-Sex Ceremonies as
   Acts of Accommodation and Resistance. 125

PART III:
SAME-SEX MARRIAGES
AND LEGAL ISSUES

7. A Change Is Gonna Come: The Movement to
Legalize Lesbian and Gay Marriages. 161

Appendix I: Fieldwork and Methods 191

Appendix II: Demographic Characteristics of Sample. 199

Notes 205

Bibliography. 211

Index 231

LIST OF TABLES

TABLE 2.1 Qualities Important in a Love Relationship 30

TABLE 3.1 Meanings of Commitment. 50

TABLE 3.2 Length Committed to Partner 54

TABLE 3.3 Think of Self as Being Married 57

TABLE 3.4 Use Term "Marriage" to Describe
Same-Sex Relationship (by Age) 62

TABLE 3.5 Use Term "Marriage" to Describe
Same-Sex Relationship
(by Feminist Identification) 65

TABLE 4.1 Had or Would Consider Having a
Same-Sex Ceremony (by Age). 102

TABLE 4.2 Had or Would Consider Having a
Same-Sex Ceremony
(by Previous Marital Status) 103

TABLE 7.1 Should Same-Sex Marriages Be Legalized? 164

TABLE 7.2 Reasons for Legalizing Same-Sex Marriages 165

TABLE 7.3 Would You Marry Legally? 170

TABLE 7.4 Should Marriage Be a Priority? 177

TABLE 7.5 Should Domestic Partnership Legislation
Be a Priority? 183

ACKNOWLEDGMENTS

I WOULD LIKE TO THANK all of the lesbians and gay men who generously gave their time to participate in this study. I am grateful to them for sharing their lives with me and for helping me to better understand lesbian and gay relationships. Without their assistance, this book would not have been possible. I also wish to thank many of my colleagues and friends who supported me throughout the process of writing this book.

I originally began the study this book is based on while I was a graduate student in the Ph.D. program at the University of Massachusetts–Amherst, where my dissertation committee was exceptionally supportive of this work. The dissertation chair, Naomi Gerstel, helped me to form the original ideas behind this book, and provided many insightful comments on how to make my drafts more comprehensible. My teacher, Michael Lewis, challenged me to examine what it means to be a sociologist and encouraged me to publish the results of this study. My mentor and good friend, Suzanne Model, continually worked with me to improve my writing skills and has been very supportive of my work as my career has unfolded. The integrity they show in their work continues to inspire my own.

In addition, a special thanks is due to the following people for their encouragement and helpful comments in writing this book: Sam Cotton, Susan Ferguson, Elizabeth King, Julie Lam, Melissa Latimer, Carson Mencken, Suzanne Slater, Brenda Stiers, Heather Stiers-Dorn, Tom Stiers, and Georgia Willis. From the beginning, they all affirmed the importance of publishing a book on lesbian and gay ceremonies.

I would like to thank Martha Schwaab, who provided me with excellent editorial comments on chapters 1–3. I truly enjoyed the afternoons we spent together discussing grammar and punctuation. I also appreciated the wonderful secretarial support I received on this project from Barbara Day, Thora Dumont, Judy Fountain, and Cathy

Lewis. During 1992-1995, the Sociology Department at Smith College supported this project by providing me with office space and other resources necessary to complete my interviews.

I received invaluable support for this book from the following people at St. Martin's Press, Michael Flamini (senior editor), Alan Bradshaw (production manager), Donna Cherry (assistant production editor), Debbie Manette (copy editor), and Lisa Rivero (indexer). From our first meeting in Washington, D.C. at the American Sociological Society Meetings in August 1995, Michael Flamini provided both a great deal of encouragement and numerous suggestions on making the manuscript accessible to both a academic and general audience. Debbie and Donna also deserve many thanks for their patience in copy editing the final manuscript.

For cooking me dinners on the many long nights it took to finish this book, for helping me finish the final editing, for helping me mother our puppy Tosca, and for literally seeing me through "in sickness and in health," I would like to thank Silvana Solano.

PREFACE TO THE PAPERBACK EDITION

Our Common Humanity

Two years ago when I wrote the original preface for *From This Day Forward*, I was confident Hawaii was going to become the first state in our country to legalize same-sex marriages. The signs seemed clear. In May 1993, the Hawaii Supreme Court ruled that denying same-sex couples the right to marry was discriminatory. In their decision, the court asserted that unless the state of Hawaii could provide a "compelling state interest" against same-sex marriages, lesbian and gay couples should have the right to marry legally. In the fall of 1996, a Hawaii Circuit Court judge heard the state's case and ruled on December 6 that the state had no such "compelling interest." Subsequently, lesbian and gay couples won the legal right to marry in Hawaii, but only for a day. On December 7, the judge stayed the ruling and gave the state the right to appeal. By February 1998, it seemed only a matter of time before the Hawaii Supreme Court would formally legalize same-sex marriages.

The ten year legal battle for same-sex marriage rights in Hawaii is now over. The three same-sex couples who originally applied for marriage licenses in December 1990 will not be able to marry their partners in Hawaii. The Hawaii Supreme Court dismissed their case on December 10, 1999. The court stated the case was no longer relevant because of a constitutional amendment passed by Hawaii voters in November 1998, which gave the legislature the authority to define marriage as a right reserved for heterosexual couples.

Despite its defeat, the Hawaii case has fundamentally shaken our society's perception of the institution of marriage by challenging the core belief that a marriage only can take place between a woman and a man. Although thirty states now have passed laws banning same-sex marriages, other states have begun to recognize that lesbian and gay relationships should be granted the same legal rights and benefits as heterosexual couples. Like a phoenix rising from the ashes, the fight to legalize same-sex marriages continues on many fronts.

Today, there remains a great deal to celebrate. On December 20, 1999, the Vermont Supreme Court ruled that the state had to guarantee the same benefits and protections to lesbian and gay couples that it did to husbands and wives. The court left it to the Vermont legislature to decide whether to legalize same-sex marriages or adopt a comprehensive domestic partnership bill. The legislature is expected to make their decision by April 2000. Whether the state allows lesbian and gay couples to register as domestic partners or grants them the right to marry, soon Vermont will provide same-sex couples the most far-reaching "marriage" benefits in the country. Over the past two years, other similar victories have occurred around the world, including a new domestic partnership law in France, a ruling by Canada's Supreme Court that Ontario's legal system must recognize same-sex couples, and a ruling by Namibia's high court that same-sex and heterosexual couples have the same rights. In addition, Denmark, Greenland, Iceland, Norway, Sweden, Hungary, and the Netherlands all continue to grant same-sex couples the right to marry.

The ruling by the Vermont Supreme Court is inspiring. The Court stated that to "extend equal rights to lesbian and gay couples who seek nothing more, nor less, than legal protection and security for their avowed commitment to an intimate and lasting relationship is simply, when all is said and done, a recognition of our common humanity" (Goldberg, 1999, p.1). "A recognition of our common humanity"—this simple phrase strikes at the heart of the struggle not only to legalize same-sex marriages but to grant lesbians, gay men, and bisexuals equal rights in all areas of the law. Every year, women and men who identify as lesbian, gay, bisexual, or transgendered are fired from their jobs, beaten or murdered because they are not considered human beings. Matthew Shepherd, Brandon Teena, and Jamie Ray Tolbert are only a few of the recent people known to be brutally killed because of their sexual identity.

Today, there also remains a great deal to condemn. On March 7, 2000 California voters will voice their opinion on Proposition 22. If passed, the ballot measure will ban the legalization of same-sex marriages in California and give further credence to conservative initiatives in other states. As Melissa Ethridge recently commented in *The Advocate*, "We're moving ahead—we're on TV, in movies, our lives are being portrayed with realism, and then, oops, a bunch of people vote on something that says you have no rights" (Kort, 2000, p. 35).

The legalization of same-sex marriages and the passage of domestic partnership laws both are steps toward the acceptance of our common humanity, whether heterosexual, bisexual, gay, lesbian, or transgendered. All of us must keep working to insure that conservative initiatives, such as Proposition 22, fail, and to guarantee that more legislatures "do the right thing" by recognizing the equality of all couples, regardless of sexual identity. Only our collective effort will ensure equality for all in the new millennium.

Gretchen A. Stiers
Washington, D.C.
February 25, 2000

PREFACE

October 11, 1987: When I attended the second National March on Washington for Lesbian and Gay Rights in 1987, I was new to political activism and Queer politics. As I marched along with three close college friends and our partners, I marveled at the hundreds of thousands of people taking a stand for their rights as lesbians and gay men, as human beings. I was a "baby dyke" at the time. Only a few years had passed since I had "come out" as a lesbian to myself, my friends, and my parents. For me, that March on Washington was a catalyst to become more involved in lesbian and gay politics.

As a student at DePauw University, a small liberal arts college in Indiana, I had been fully absorbed with interpersonal issues around being a lesbian and coming out. The campus during the early 1980s was extremely homophobic; each year a number of students were expelled from their fraternities and sororities for being gay or lesbian. I was terrified other students in my dorm or in my classes would ridicule or attack me if they found out I was a lesbian. Luckily, I had a small group of very supportive friends, including a number of faculty members, who encouraged me to be myself and to embrace my sexual identity. Activism on campus, however, was limited. In four years, the only organized protest that occurred on campus involved students' inability to drink or eat in the library.

To DePauw's credit, with the college's support I was able to attend a number of national women's studies conferences in the Midwest as well as a large antinuclear weapons conference at Riverside Church in New York City. These conferences literally saved my life. They allowed me to meet not only other feminist women but students like myself who were struggling with their sexual identities. The women and men I met gave me the reassurance I needed that being a lesbian was not "abnormal." At the time, it felt like just being lesbian, gay, or bisexual was extremely radical and in itself a political statement.

After college graduation, I made two decisions that substantively altered the course of my life. The first was to attend graduate school in sociology at the University of Massachusetts in Amherst. Based on a number of wonderful sociology courses I had taken as an undergraduate student, I chose to pursue a Ph.D. where I could study issues of inequality. In graduate school I worked for a number of years as a research assistant on the National Health Care for the Homeless project funded by the Robert Wood Johnson Foundation. As I heard more news stories in the gay press about HIV/AIDS in the mid-1980s, I decided to write my master's thesis on the prevalence of AIDS among the homeless population. By examining this disease, I wanted to combine my graduate work with issues that were important to me as a lesbian. In graduate school, my approach to sociology quickly became based on feminist principles, including the view that "science" can be objective but never free from the values that propel us to engage in research in the first place. Later on my views as a feminist and as a lesbian influenced me to begin the research this book is based on.

The second decision I made was to come out to my parents over the Memorial Day weekend after I graduated from college. Despite having some initially rough moments that first year, my parents and my sister have become my largest supporters. As I often now joke with friends, we all moved through "the stages" of coming out together if not always in unison. In the mid-1980s, my parents lamented the fact that I would never get married or have children. I thought they were correct because I mistakenly believed that lesbians and gay men could not have ceremonies or children. Today my parents and my sister and her husband tease me about making wedding plans and starting a family! Now in my mid-thirties, I suddenly am faced with asking if these are things I want for myself. Do I want to be a "married lesbian with children"? As I discuss later in the book, although many lesbians and gay men do not believe that we should be striving for this kind of "mainstream" acceptance, others adamantly argue that the legal right to marry and parenting rights are essential to full equality.

The 1987 March on Washington opened my eyes to the larger political issues facing the lesbian and gay civil rights movement: discrimination in housing and the workplace, overturning state sodomy

PREFACE XV

laws, violence against lesbians and gay men, parenting and adoption rights, marriage rights, and the newly emerging AIDS epidemic. I shouted "shame" as we marched passed the Bush White House, chanted "We're here, we're queer, get used to it" as we went by a small group of counter-protesters from the Christian Coalition, and later wept when we stood silently at the first public showing of the AIDS Memorial Quilt on the Capitol Mall. Although I heard there was going to be a "pro-gay marriage" protest at the IRS building the day before the actual march, at the time I scoffed at the idea that same-sex marriage was an important political issue. As a young feminist and new gay activist, I believed discrimination, AIDS, and hate crimes were more important problems than the right to marry. I left Washington, D.C., that October idealistic and full of faith that, united together, lesbians and gay men could overcome the prejudice and discrimination that stood in their path to full equality.

April 25, 1993: Five years later when I went to the third National March on Washington for Lesbian, Gay, Bisexual Rights and Liberation in 1993, I was a veteran of national political demonstrations. I had been to Washington for the 1987 march, many pro-choice marches, the 1991 peace march protesting the Gulf War, and numerous showings of the AIDS quilt. I also had been politically active in Massachusetts, where I protested issues ranging from nuclear power plants, to violence against women, to the State's antigay foster care policy (which was later overturned), to promoting the passage of a statewide antidiscrimination in housing and employment law (which was passed in 1989). I had volunteered for years as an AIDS buddy. I had been arrested on the Amherst town common for "disturbing the peace" during an anti–Gulf War rally. I went to ACT UP demonstrations in Boston.[1] Every year I went to our local as well as statewide lesbian and gay pride march (all renamed in the early 1990s to reflect the diversity of lesbian, gay, bisexual, and transgendered lives). I even played softball in the "lesbian league" in Northampton on two wonderful teams: the "Resisters" and the "Hot Flashes"!

All of this, however, did not prepare me for the emotional experience I had while attending the 1993 march. Bill Clinton had recently been sworn in as president, and collective hopes were high that he finally would lift the ban on lesbians and gay men serving in the military. At last it seemed that the United States had a president who would help to end discrimination against gays not only in the military but in the country as a whole. The 1993 march was both a celebration of this hope and a recognition that many serious problems still affected lesbians, gays, bisexuals, and transgendered women and men, including HIV/AIDS, breast cancer, violence, discrimination in housing and employment, and a lack of parenting and marriage rights.

For the second time in five years, protesters gathered in front of the IRS building the day before the actual march to stage a mass protest against the inability of same-sex couples to marry. This time I eagerly went to the protest. As I stood watching the thousands of couples who came to celebrate their commitments to their partners and to demand the right to marry, I renewed a decision I had made to write my doctoral dissertation on the issue of lesbian and gay marriage. Although I had done several preliminary interviews with lesbians and gay men about their attitudes toward same-sex marriage, witnessing the love and commitment shown by the couples at the mass commitment ceremony reassured me that this type of research was extremely important.

I had first become aware of the debate over whether legalizing same-sex marriages was politically important while participating in a graduate course on gender at the University of Massachusetts—Amherst during the fall of 1990. One day a lively debate took place over whether lesbians and gay men "should" use the word "family" to describe their intimate relationships, have commitment or wedding ceremonies, or advocate legalizing same-sex marriages. During the debate, many lesbian students argued that lesbian and gay couples should be included in the institutions of marriage and family. Furthermore, they supported the legalization of same-sex marriages. In contrast, most of the heterosexual women criticized the institution of marriage because they believed it limited women's family and work choices. They also argued that new terminologies and practices needed to be developed around kinship and so-called fictive kin relationships.[2]

I was surprised that the lesbians in the class argued for legalizing same-sex marriages. As both an undergraduate and a graduate student, my worldview and sociological perspective had been shaped by feminism. Therefore, I wrongly assumed that most lesbians would oppose legalizing same-sex marriages on feminist grounds since many feminists have argued that the institution of marriage is oppressive to women. Although the debate was not (nor could be) resolved conclusively, I left the class that semester curious about the contemporary attitudes and behaviors of lesbians and gay men toward marriage and family life. I wanted to find out what they themselves thought about love, commitment, and the issue of marriage. After attending the IRS protest in 1993, I found myself ready to begin examining the issue of same-sex marriage seriously.

Between the summers of 1993 and 1994, I conducted ninety face-to-face interviews with lesbians and gay men about their relationships and their perspectives on the marriage debate. All respondents in the study lived in the state of Massachusetts. Although their views cannot be generalized to all gay people, they do reflect the divergent perspectives gay men and lesbians have about relationships, love, commitment, having ceremonies, and the right to marry. This book is the result of that research. While it is based on the attitudes and experiences of the people I interviewed, it ultimately reflects my personal interpretation of their lives. Appendix I, at the end of the book, provides detailed information about the research methods applied in this study.

Although the research originally was conducted for a doctoral dissertation, this book aims at a wide audience. It attempts to take a highly charged social and political issue and put faces and names behind the debates over same-sex ceremonies and same-sex marriages. Family scholars, lesbians and gay men, and general readers alike will find this work informative and interesting. For people involved in religious organizations that are struggling over these same concerns, the book can provide a starting point for in-depth discussions of these issues.

Today I am extremely excited about the legal events that have been taking place in Hawaii since 1993. This year Hawaii should become the first state in the country to legalize same-sex marriages. While not the primary concern for many gays, the legalization of same-sex marriages in Hawaii will set a historical precedent that ultimately will further full equality for all lesbians and gay men in the country. The history of civil rights legislation (for African Americans, people with disabilities, elderly people, women, and gays) suggests that the road to equality is slow and full of obstacles. The Hawaii case already has generated a significant public backlash against same-sex marriages. Recently these homophobic attitudes culminated in the passage of the Defense of Marriage Act (DOMA) by Congress in 1996. DOMA now gives each state the right to deny lesbians and gay men the legal right to marry and to disregard same-sex marriages performed in other states. Since 1996, twenty-seven states have passed these types of anti–same-sex marriage laws (Lambda, 1998).

Although I began this research skeptical regarding the need to advocate the legalization of same-sex marriages, my experience interviewing respondents about their own positions persuaded me that the right to marry *must* be part of a national lesbian, gay, and bisexual political agenda. It should not be the "only" issue, but it should be one of the concerns fought for as we enter the twenty-first century. In 1967 the Supreme Court ruled in *Loving v. Virginia* that marriage is a fundamental right of all citizens in the United States. The time has come for lesbians, gay men, and bisexuals to be awarded the same rights, including the right to marry, guaranteed all individuals in this country.

A Note on Terminology

Before proceeding, a discussion about some of the terms used in this book is necessary. In recent years there has been a great deal of discussion within lesbian and gay literature over the limited nature of the terms "gay" and "homosexual" (Weston, 1991). In this study, I primarily use the separate terms "lesbian" and "gay" in order to distinguish the unique experiences of lesbians and gay men. Where the term "gay" is used, it refers to both women and men.

Similarly, there has been a debate over use the phrase "lesbian and gay community." According to political activist and author Cindy

Patton (1985), it does not differentiate between the experiences of women and men, African Americans, Asians, Latinos, and Whites, or middle-class and working-class individuals. In order to begin to address these problems, I chose to use the phrase "lesbian and gay communit*ies*" throughout this study. The plural form of the term "community" signifies that lesbians and gay men often do not participate in the same networks or organizations or even live in the same geographic areas.

In addition, I interchangeably use the expressions "same-sex," "commitment," and "union" ceremony to refer to the rituals lesbians and gay men are creating to celebrate their relationships. Although these are not the only names used to refer to these ceremonies, they are neutral phrases that do not carry either political or religious connotations. Since many lesbians and gay men abhor the word "wedding," I use the term only when respondents specifically used it.

Over the past fifteen years, there also has been an ongoing debate among lesbian and gay scholars over use of the phrases "sexual identity" and "sexual orientation." In large part, this debate has stemmed from a larger controversy over whether homosexuality is innate (thus an "orientation") or chosen (thus an "identity"). Indeed, these two perspectives now are referred to as "essentialism" and "social constructionism" (S. Epstein, 1987; Foucault, 1978; Halperin, 1990). Although I think that there may be some "truth" to both perspectives (for example, homosexuals may be born gay but we each choose how to live our own lives), my view on this issue originally was shaped by Adrienne Rich's classic essay "Compulsory Heterosexuality and Lesbian Existence" (1986). Like Rich, my experience has led me to believe that there is a "continuum" of women-identified experience (some sexual, some not) in all women's lives. Only some women, however, choose to identify themselves as "lesbians." Since my theoretical perspective is closer to social constructionism than essentialism, I use the phrase "sexual identity" to refer to people's identification of themselves as "lesbian," "gay," or "bisexual."[3]

In order to protect respondents' confidentiality, I constructed pseudonyms to refer to all individuals in this study. Although a few lesbians and gay men told me they were comfortable having their real names used, I uniformly changed first and last names as well as other identifying pieces of information about each respondent. Since many of the people I interviewed had disclosed their sexual identities to family, friends, and coworkers in different degrees, it was important to guard each individual's privacy.

Gretchen Stiers
Morgantown, West Virginia
February 12, 1998

Lesbian and Gay Relationships

Our Love Is Here to Stay

Lesbian and Gay Relationships in the 1990s

Ron and Erick, I now pronounce you partnered.
—Minister to gay characters Ron and Erick on the television show *Northern Exposure*, May 2, 1994

Nothing makes God happier than when two people—any two people—come together in love.
—Minister to lesbian characters Carol and Susan on the television show *Friends*, January 19, 1996

DURING THE LATE 1980S AND THROUGHOUT THE 1990S, representations of lesbians, gay men, and bisexuals on weekly television programs began to increase (D. Dunlap, 1996a; Maupin, 1994; O'Connor, 1994). Regular lesbian, gay, and bisexual characters were featured on nighttime programs *Ellen*, *Roseanne*, *Northern Exposure*, and *Sisters* and now appear on a number of series, including sitcoms *Friends* and *Mad About You;* nighttime soap *Melrose Place;* and MTV's docudrama *The Real World*. Daytime talk shows such as *Oprah* and *Sally Jessy Raphael* frequently invite gay men and lesbians to talk about everything: sexuality, AIDS, parenting, wedding ceremonies, and legalizing same-sex marriages. Magazine news shows, such as *20/20* and *Dateline,* also periodically run segments on the lives of lesbians and gay men.

Prior to *Ellen*'s "coming out" episode in 1997, three of the more candid television programs to air with gay themes were CBS's 1994 *Northern Exposure* show on the wedding between gay characters Ron and Erick, ABC's 1995 *Roseanne* episode on the marriage of Leon and Scott, and NBC's 1996 *Friends* show on the union of Carol and Susan. Although based on fictional characters, these three shows were groundbreaking because for the first time they openly portrayed and discussed on television why lesbian and gay couples might choose to have a same-sex wedding or union ceremony. Indeed, all three programs highlighted the same answers: love and commitment. For example, in a play on the cliché that brides and grooms have doubts right before they marry, the *Roseanne* episode featured a segment where Roseanne persuades Leon to come out of the bathroom for the wedding ceremony by reminding him that he really is in love and committed to his partner, Scott.

According to Steve Warner, CBS senior vice president of program planning, addressing gay themes on television "is an accurate reflection of what's going on in society" (Lovece, 1994, p. 20). If Warner's pronouncement is correct, what does the increased representation of not only lesbian and gay characters but same-sex weddings in mainstream programs signify? A growing tolerance or even acceptance of lesbians and gay men? An increasing trend among same-sex couples to have weddings and commitment ceremonies? An expansion of the definitions of marriage and family in American society?

Taken alone, these weddings may not seem all that important: just three programs shown on television amidst the thousands broadcast every month. Weddings, however, are cultural symbols that evoke strong emotional reactions. In addition to explaining why lesbians and gay men might want to have ceremonies, all three shows presented the varied emotional reactions of each couple's family and friends. For example, in the *Northern Exposure* episode, the emotions of the show's characters ran from the total approval shown by Ron's mother to the initial disgust and later acceptance displayed by Erick and Ron's friend and nemesis,

Maurice. Mimicking real life, the mixed reactions of family and friends stemmed from each individual's different religious and social beliefs about the meaning of marriage.

Although marriage in the United States is legally defined by federal and state statutes, it is an institution that continues to be socially circumscribed by Judeo-Christian religious beliefs. In this country, 85 percent of all weddings still are performed by a minister, priest, or rabbi (Whyte, 1990). As religious rites of passage into adulthood, weddings traditionally mark the beginning of a heterosexual couple's new family, which consists of blood relatives and, often later on, children. Until the recent past, however, most religious organizations denounced homosexuality as a sin and did not sanction the unions of gay or lesbian couples. Not surprisingly, the issue of legitimizing same-sex marriages stirs up strong religious beliefs because it questions both the social and religious conception that marriage is a union between a man and a woman and that its main purpose is procreation.

Three important cultural changes currently taking place in the United States, however, are beginning to alter (albeit slowly) social and religious mores that historically have excluded lesbians and gay men from the institutions of marriage and family. Lesbian and gay culture and politics have shifted toward validating long-term relationships through commitment and union ceremonies; social and religious definitions of marriage and family have moved toward recognizing lesbian and gay relationships; and the legal system has shifted toward granting "marriage" and "family" rights to lesbian and gay couples.

In an attempt to understand the origins and character of the current changes taking place in the institution of marriage, this book specifically addresses the following questions: How do lesbians and gay men understand love, commitment, and marriage when few models (except heterosexual marriage) exist for them to follow? Why are some and not others choosing to have commitment or union ceremonies? What do lesbians and gay men want out of marriage: acceptance? economic benefits? legal rights? And last, why are some also advocating the legal right to marry?

This study situates lesbians' and gay men's attitudes and practices toward marriage within the larger discourse on family taking place in the

United States today. Although many conservatives argue that same-sex relationships are undermining "the family" (Bauer, 1994), many lesbians and gay men advocate so-called family values, such as love, commitment, and monogamy in their own relationships. Instead of rejecting the institutions of marriage and family as some did in earlier decades, in the 1990s many gays are attempting to gain entry into and change these same institutions. This is not to say that all same-sex couples want to have commitment ceremonies or to get married legally. These issues remain highly contested topics in most lesbian and gay communities.

The diverse partnership and family arrangements that lesbians and gay men create, however, are an integral part of the transformation of the structure and meaning of marriage and family in the late twentieth century. Indeed, the movement to legalize same-sex marriages and to have commitment ceremonies is one part of this larger social process. Although lesbian and gay ceremonies push the boundaries of what marriage means in our society, at the same time the very notion of having a commitment ritual is bound within an established cultural tradition. Thus, my central argument is that same-sex ceremonies and marriages should be conceptualized both as acts of resistance to traditional marriage and wedding norms and as acts of accommodation to these same standards. As the late poet Audre Lorde (1984) once wrote, "the master's tools can never dismantle the master's house" (p. 112). In the case of same-sex ceremonies and legalized marriages, however, they can be used to shake things up. What is still to be seen in the twenty-first century is the degree to which social, legal, and religious conceptions of marriage continue to expand to include lesbians and gay men.

The Current Political Debate

The idea that lesbians and gay men should have the social, religious, and legal right to marry has provoked intense political debates over the last few years. Public arguments over this issue have stemmed in large part from the 1993 Hawaii State Supreme Court ruling in the case *Baehr v. Lewin*. In May 1991 three same-gendered couples filed suit against the state of Hawaii because they believed that its prohibition against same-sex marriages violated their right to privacy and to equal protection under the Hawaii constitution. In ruling on this case, the Hawaii Supreme Court stated that denying same-sex couples the right to marry did violate the equal-protection clause of the state constitution. The discrimination, however, was based not on a right to privacy but on the plaintiffs' gender: a "suspect category" in legal terminology. In writing the court's majority opinion, Justice Steven Levinson argued that "'marriage is a basic civil right,' and that Hawaii's law 'denies same-sex couples access to marital status and its concomitant rights and benefits'" (Herscher, 1995, p. 1). As a case of gender discrimination, the state's marriage law was subject to the "strict scrutiny" test. This legal procedure placed the burden on the state of Hawaii to justify a "compelling state interest" in prohibiting same-sex marriages.

In December 1996 a Hawaii Circuit Court Judge ruled in *Baehr v. Miike* that the State failed to demonstrate such an interest. The state's main argument centered on the contention that children raised in families with two biological (i.e., heterosexual) parents were better off psychologically than those in lesbian and gay families. Subsequently, the state argued it was in its interest to uphold a marriage structure that supported procreation between heterosexual partners. Lawyers for the plaintiffs, however, effectively argued that quality of care, not the parents' gender, was the most important element in helping a child develop successfully. At present, the court's decision has been stayed pending the outcome of the state's appeal back to the State Supreme Court. By the end of 1998, Hawaii could be the first state to legalize same-sex marriages in the United States.

For both conservative and liberal political organizations, the 1993 and 1996 Hawaii Supreme Court rulings indicate a significant shift in marriage norms in the United States. For conservative groups, such as the Family Research Council, the rulings represent an attack on the institution of marriage and a threat to family values. According to Robert Knight (1998), director of cultural studies at the council, "Gay marriage is an oxymoron, an ideological invention designed to appropriate the moral capital of marriage and family toward the goal of government-enforced acceptance of homosexuality" (p. 4). In many of its writings, the Family Research Council argues that same-sex marriages should not be legalized because doing so would endorse homosexuality, threaten religious freedom, undermine heterosexual marriages, and, therefore, threaten the fabric of society.

For liberal groups, such as the Human Rights Campaign, the Hawaii rulings symbolize a real victory in the fight for lesbian and gay civil rights. As the Campaign's Marriage Booklet (1997) states, "making a commitment to a lifelong relationship is a fundamental human need that should not be denied to anyone. Marriage is a basic human right" (p. 2). To the Human Rights Campaign, the legalization of same-sex marriages would give lesbian and gay couples protection from discrimination and the basic right to marry another person regardless of gender. In its writings, the Campaign argues that giving same-sex couples the legal right to marry would strengthen rather than weaken the institution of marriage because it would support all couples who wanted to make that type of commitment. Groups on both sides of the political spectrum have used the Hawaii case as a bellwether for their particular agenda on marriage, although for very different reasons: on the conservative side, to lament the disintegration of the "traditional" nuclear family; and on the liberal side, to advocate for the inclusion of lesbians and gay men in the legal rights, responsibilities, and benefits of marriage.

This same debate entered the congressional arena in 1996, where a heated struggle took place over the passage of the Defense of Marriage Act: a piece of legislation designed both to deny federal recognition of same-sex marriages and to allow states to ignore, in the case of same-sex marriages, Article 4 of the Constitution, which states that "full faith and credit shall be given in each state to the public acts, records, and judicial proceedings of every other state." According to Representative Bob Barr (R-Georgia), who introduced the bill (H.R. 3396) in the House, the act was "a defense against 'homosexual extremists' who were trying to 'sow seeds of confusion' by insisting that states and the Federal government honor their unions" (Schmitt, 1996, p. 15). Similarly, Senator Don Nickles (R-Oklahoma), who introduced the Senate version of the bill (S. 1740), commented that it was not "mean spirited" but about defining "common knowledge"—that marriage is "the legal union between one man and one woman" (Lochhead, 1996, p. A3). Those supporting the act argued that the legalization of same-sex marriages would weaken the institution of marriage by explicitly separating procreation from marriage and by legitimating homosexual relationships.

Many Democrats, such as Representative Barney Frank (D-Massachusetts), counterargued that legalizing same-sex unions would not undermine or demean heterosexual marriages. According to Frank, the bill was "not about the defense of marriage" but was "an offense to gay men and lesbians" because it sought to deny them the status and benefits given to married, heterosexual couples (Schmitt, 1996, p. 15). Frank argued passionately that the House bill was only a political ploy and that heterosexual marriages would not be threatened by lesbian and gay unions. Despite ardent opposition, however, both the House and Senate bills passed by large majorities. In September 1996 President Clinton signed the Defense of Marriage Act into law.

The passage of the Defense of Marriage Act raises an important question: Why are so many people threatened by the idea of legalizing same-sex marriages? Few liberals or conservatives would argue that no changes have occurred in the social, religious, or legal definitions of marriage in the United States over the last 200 years. For example, between 1864 and 1886, after the emancipation of slaves, many states altered their definitions of who could marry legally and passed laws acknowledging the new legality of "ex-slave marriages" (Gutman, 1976). It was not until 1967 that the U.S. Supreme Court ruled in *Loving v. Virginia* that state antimiscegenation statutes, many of which specifically prohibited Black-White marriages, were unconstitutional. Although this legal ruling was not popular among the "public," the Supreme Court acted, in this case, as an arbiter of social change. As Justice Warren's ruling for the majority stated, "The freedom to marry has long been recognized as one of the vital personal rights essential to the orderly pursuit of happiness by free men. . . . To deny this fundamental freedom on so unsupportable a basis as the racial qualifications embodied in these statutes, classifications so directly subversive of the principle of equality at the heart of the Fourteenth Amendment, is surely to deprive all the State's citizens of liberty without due process of law" (A. Sullivan, 1997, p. 90).

Today, the same-sex marriage debate has reopened the question of "What is marriage?" Instead of challenging social prejudices about race, the Hawaii case has brought up questions about both the gendered structure and the purpose of marriage. Although not specifically acknowledged in every state's marriage law, historically, marriage has been conceptualized as a union between a woman and a man who came together to bear children. Yet over the last thirty-five years, childbearing has become increasingly separated from the institution of marriage, leaving the gender distinction as marriage's only obvious defining feature. Thus, opponents of same-sex marriages are afraid that without the male/female contract, the institution of marriage will no longer exist as it has in the past.

To a certain degree, this fear is justified. According to Professor of Law Nan Hunter (1991), "what is most unsettling to the status quo about the legalization of lesbian and gay marriage is its potential to expose and denaturalize the historical construction of gender at the heart of marriage" (p. 18). In the United States, the court system established the legal concept that marriage is an authority/dependence relationship based on biological male/female differences. In challenging the gender distinction in marriage law, same-sex marriages contest the linkage of power/subordination with the categories "husband" and "wife." Indeed, the legalization of same-sex marriages would give lesbians and gay men not only the legal right to marry but also the potential to change the power hierarchy within heterosexual relationships.

On the other hand, the legalization of same-sex marriages will not change other fundamental aspects of the institution. Beyond any changes in power differentials between "husbands" and "wives," marriage will remain a legal contract that confirms rights and responsibilities to the partners involved. Marriages still will receive special protections and legal benefits. They will continue be valued as the starting point for creating families and raising children and they will remain both private and economic arrangements. In fact, the legalization of same-sex marriages would serve to strengthen the institution of marriage by further legitimating long-term, committed lesbian and gay relationships.

Just as the Supreme Court acted as an agent of social change in eliminating racial discrimination from marriage laws, the courts should take the lead in redefining marriage to include same-sex couples. Lesbian and gay couples deserve to have the "freedom to marry" guaranteed by the principle of equality in the Fourteenth Amendment. Although giving these couples the legal right to marry will fundamentally change the gendered assumptions implicit in marriage laws and customs, same-sex marriages will not undermine the primacy of marriage as a central institution in our society. The legalization of same-sex marriages, however, will be yet another step forward in the ongoing transformation of family life in the United States.

Shifting Family and Marriage Norms

Historically, the condition of "the family" has been a controversial social and political issue in the United States. As historian Linda Gordon (1988) notes, "for over 150 years, there have been [numerous] periods of fear that 'the family'—meaning a popular image of what families were supposed to be like, by no means a correct recollection of any 'traditional' family—was in decline" (p. 3). Today many social critics cite changes in sexual attitudes and divorce laws, the availability of contraceptives and abortions, the increasing number of female-headed families, the growing number of women with young children in the labor force, as well as the increased visibility of lesbian and gay relationships as evidence that the institution of family is in crisis. For at least fifty years, a central debate within the field of family sociology has been whether modifications in the structures and functions of "the family" constitute its decline and decay or merely represent a redefinition of that institution (Bane, 1976; Bellah et al., 1985; Berger and Berger, 1984; Goode, 1971; Lasch, 1977; Parsons and Bales, 1955; Scanzoni, 1982; B. Wilson, 1980; Zaretski, 1976).

For many people, the terms "family" and "marriage" are synonymous with the phrase "the nuclear family," that is, a household arrangement based on marriage and consisting of a wage-earning husband, a wife who keeps house, and their biological children. Currently, however, households containing married couples with children represent only 26 percent of all households in the United States (*Statistical Abstracts,* 1997a). Many different types of households coexist today, including extended, adoptive, one-parent, remarried, cohabiting, and lesbian and gay. Thus, what constitutes a family clearly has changed and been redefined over time.

These diverse family arrangements form what sociologist Judith Stacey (1990) describes as "postmodern families," in which traditional family patterns are transformed and new types emerge. In the past, many people believed that lesbians and gay men could not have or raise children because having a family "required" two people of the opposite gender. Today, however, lesbians and gay men are forming families both with and without children. For some couples, forming a family also includes having a commitment or wedding ceremony. These ceremonies are part of postmodern family life because they both use and contest traditional notions of marriage. Instead of symbolizing a decline in the meaning of family and marriage, they represent the desire of many lesbian and gay couples to celebrate and mark their relationships using a fairly conventional and therefore understandable format.

In the United States, lesbians and gay men have become active participants in the movement to transform the "traditional" boundaries of family life. Over the last forty years, however, not all gays have embraced the notion of having commitment or wedding ceremonies or advocated the legal right to marry. In the 1980s and 1990s, a number of historical processes brought many to the place of embracing the marriage issue. These processes included shifts in lesbian and gay politics and legal tactics as well as in religious, social, and legal views toward same-sex marriages.

Shifts in Lesbian and Gay Politics

Until recently many lesbians and gay men considered the terms "family" and "marriage" to be the antithesis of gay identity (Hocquenghem, 1978). In the 1970s lesbian feminists and gay liberationists joined other social movement activists in challenging society's conceptions of sexuality, marriage, and family. In particular, these activists rejected the belief that heterosexual relationships and marriage were the only proper sites for sexuality (D'Emilio and Freedman, 1988). In fact, some argued that the nuclear family itself had to be abolished in order for lesbians and gay men to gain complete equality in society. As writer and political scientist Dennis Altman (1979) commented: "By and large it seems true that as long as the concept of the nuclear family remains the central reference point of social organization, the homosexual will necessarily be excluded from society. . . . The subordination of homosexuals rests on the fact that the [nuclear family] requires the sublimation of homosexuality and the definition of masculinity and femininity in purely heterosexual terms" (pp. 43-44).

To many lesbian feminists and gay liberationists, the act of having a "marriage" ceremony went against the principles of freedom they were fighting for. As one gay man wrote in 1970, "Homosexual marriages submitting to the guidelines of so-called conventional rites must be classed as reactionary. . . . [It] isn't relevant to gay liberation when we start imitating meaningless, bad habits of our oppressors. . . . That isn't *our* liberation. That *isn't* the freedom we want" (Hall quoted in Hunter, 1991, p. 12).

Outside of lesbian feminist and gay liberation circles, however, there were many gay people who did want to "marry" their partners. As the following quote from another gay activist in 1970 suggests, the marriage issue actually had adherents on both sides. "Another Cause-with-a-capital-C that keeps coming up every so often is the Right of Homosexuals to Marry—to Marry each other, that is. For some reason, lesbians seem to be more prone to this one than the gay boys; but they aren't immune. . . . [M]ost modern women are trying to *escape* the legal and other restrictions of marriage, so it is funny to see these 'enlightened' lesbians trying to get into them" (Dennison quoted in Friedman, 1987/1988, p. 142-143).

Although there is no way to estimate how many lesbians and gay couples may have had weddings, the *Advocate* (a nationally syndicated gay newspaper) suggested that a "gay marriage boom" was taking place in the early 1970s (Sherman, p. 7). Ironically, this "boom" was triggered by the lesbian feminist and gay liberation movements. In the 1970s both movements advocated publicly acknowledging one's homosexual identity as a way to challenge public stereotypes of lesbians and gay men. As more and more people came out about their sexual identities, many began to claim they should have the same social and legal right to marry as heterosexual couples. Instead of conceptualizing gay identity and politics in opposition to mainstream institutions, these lesbians and gay men began to claim inclusion in the institutions of marriage and family. During this period, however, celebrations of their relationships were largely personal affairs, at most fairly private rituals that took place within lesbian and gay circles.

Research conducted for this book suggests that quite a few couples had same-sex ceremonies during the 1960s and 1970s. Approximately one-fourth of the people interviewed knew of couples who had a same-sex ceremony before the early 1980s. According to one respondent, Brian Rickerby, the first gay wedding he attended was in 1968 in Colorado.

> I was a senior in high school and two gay men decided to buy a house together. They were going to promise each other not to sleep with anybody else and they felt like they wanted to do something more than just pretend to play house. So they had a huge potluck picnic. They got married. They were saying in front of all these people "This is it, we are married," and there was a big argument about who was the "wife." It was a way for them to get the community to recognize that "We're buying a house, we're moving in together, we're getting our finances mixed up together somehow, and the rest of you leave us alone!" It was very informal. They were both in drag. I was seventeen then.

During the 1960s and 1970s, it was not unusual for gay men to dress in drag for their ceremonies (Sherman, 1992). For some gay men, dressing in drag has been an avenue for subverting traditional masculine gender roles. The first gay ceremony Ken Brown attended was in New York City in the early 1970s. As Ken recalled, the ceremony he attended took place

> at the Church of the Beloved Joseph on Twentieth Street. . . . I mean, it was a bizarre kind of a church but one of the things they instituted

right away were "Services of Holy Union." And two of my friends, Lenney and Dougie, were married, were unioned, whatever the hell, at the Church of the Beloved Joseph. I went. It was very straight. It was basic with a lot of incense and hoopla. You might have thought you were in a sort of Catholic ceremony where the Pope had allowed you to improvise certain parts of it. Altar, vows, ring exchanges, absolution, flower girl, some boys dressed up in drag. It was absolutely awful. It was tacky but at the time it was wonderful. That was the only one I went to there. A few people were doing that at that time. That was 1971 or 1972.

Lesbian couples also were having ceremonies during this period. Some took on butch/femme roles in their ceremonies. Lori Morrison recalled first stumbling into a lesbian wedding at her aunt's apartment in 1972. As she commented:

> I have an aunt who's a lesbian who sent away for a minister's certificate or whatever they get when they become ministers. She used to marry lesbians. Totally in gowns and with bridesmaids and the whole routine. I once came home, I was living in my grandmother's house, in the midst of one of these marriages, and I didn't get it. I didn't realize that everybody in the ceremony was a woman because it was 1972. They were pretty hard looking, you know. They were all Black. The bride looked like a bride and the groom looked like a groom. They were totally butched and femmed out. So I couldn't tell that the butches were really women and not men. So somewhere in the middle of it, I was looking at them and they looked a little peculiar. There was something odd about them, and then I realized that the groom was a woman. Then I realized that all women wearing tuxedos were women. I just said, "Oh my God!" This is interesting, there's a marriage going on in my grandmother's house. I mean, I knew that my aunt was a lesbian and that she had a lover but . . .

Not all lesbian ceremonies in the 1970s, however, mimicked gender differences by insisting on butch/femme roles. At the time, some lesbians began to center their ceremonies around goddess rituals rather than traditional wedding ceremonies. As Sally Pearce recalled, the first ceremony she knew about was in

> oh, probably, 1974. I got invited to it. Friends of mine. That was so long ago. That's almost twenty years ago. . . . They were close but recent friends and I went. It was howling at the moon. It was a very woman, goddesses, moon, spiritual, kind of a ceremony. Since I'm not really orientated toward that I was kind of amused. It was in a barn and there was a lot of holding hands and circles. There were other people who were doing ceremonies too. It wasn't uncommon at the time.

Indeed, since the early 1970s, the women's spirituality movement has emphasized the importance of rituals for women (Starhawk, 1982). According to editor Becky Butler (1990), many lesbians have drawn from this movement in order to create ceremonies for their relationships.

Seeking the Legal Right to Marry in the 1970s

During the 1970s some lesbians and gay men also began to advocate the legal right to marry. The advent of the gay liberation and lesbian feminist movements coupled with an increased emphasis on minority rights within the law may have influenced a few people to advocate the legalization of same-sex marriages and to seek marriage licenses. In the United States, laws concerning who could marry had remained largely unchanged until the mid-1960s. By the early 1970s, however, the civil rights and women's movements not only affected public perceptions of Blacks and women but altered the law's perception of the rights these groups deserved as well.

According to Hunter (1991), "the invocation of rights claims is one of the most powerful weapons available to a movement seeking justice for the excluded and disempowered" (p. 27). During the 1960s and 1970s, the legal system both reacted to these rights claims and further established basic rights for many minorities, including the right to marry. As was previously mentioned, in 1967 the U.S. Supreme Court ruled in *Loving v. Virginia* that marriage was an essential right of all citizens, thereby striking down all remaining state statutes barring interracial marriages.

Lesbians and gay men attempted to use this precedent to seek their own rights claims. In 1970 the first marriage designed to challenge state marriage laws was performed by the Reverend Troy Perry in Los Angeles. On June 12, 1970, the Reverend Perry married Neva Joy Heckman and Judith Ann Belew. According to authors Del Martin and Phyllis Lyon (1991), the founders of the Daughters of Bilitis,[1] this ceremony was different from previous covenant services because it was "conducted under a provision of California Law that allows a common-law liaison to be formalized by a religious ceremony" (p. 100). In these cases, a couple does not need to obtain a marriage license from a city or town hall. Later on, however, the court reconsidered the case and found the marriage was illegal because the California statute specifically stated that a marriage must take place between a woman and a man.

Around that time the issue of legalizing same-sex marriages also was discussed in a number of national and local newspapers. The *San Francisco Chronicle,* for example, ran a series of editorials on the right of homosexuals to marry. As one 1970 editorial concluded: "Members of the heterosexual majority derive great security, pride, and social acceptance from this 'rendering public' of an honest, social commitment in the eyes of 'God and Man.' It would seem only in keeping with the times that consideration be given to allowing the homosexual minority the same rights to this sense of fulfillment" (quoted in Martin and Lyon, 1991, p. 101).

A number of gay and lesbian couples sought court-ordered marriage licenses. In 1971 two Black lesbians in Wisconsin "filed a class action suit against the Milwaukee County Clerk for refusing to issue them a marriage license" (Butler, 1990, p. 36). Three other cases that occurred in the 1970s were *Baker v. Nelson* in Minnesota, *Jones v. Hallahan* in Kentucky, and *Singer v. Hara* in Washington State. It is clear from legal accounts concerning these cases that the couples seeking marriage licenses believed they were engaging in a radical political act to change the consciousness of society. According to Michael McConnell, a plaintiff in the *Baker v. Nelson* case: "We want to cause a re-examination and re-evaluation of the institution of marriage. We feel we can be the catalyst for that. Our getting married would be a political act with political implications. I sincerely believe that my love for Jack [Baker] is as valid and as deep as any heterosexual love, and I think that it should be recognized—I demand that it be recognized!—by the state and by society!" (Friedman, 1987/1988, p. 143).

In all of these cases, however, the courts interpreted state marriage statutes as implying that marriage could only be a relationship between partners of the opposite sex. Each of the three courts denied the couples's applications for marriage licenses on the grounds that social and religious customs dictate that the function of marriage is reproduction. In *Singer v. Hara*, the Washington Appellate Court directly stated that it was constitutional to deny lesbian and gay couples the right to marry because they could not reproduce.[2]

By the mid-1970s, however, the issue of legitimizing and legalizing same-sex marriages virtually was gone from most discussions of gay politics, except for the support accorded holy unions by the Metropolitan Community Church. By the late 1970s and early 1980s, interest in legalizing same-sex marriages declined for a number of reasons. It may have been related to the public's growing acceptance of nontraditional sex roles, remaining single, not having children, premarital sex, and cohabitation. The feminist movement, with its perception that marriage was restrictive and unnecessary, also may have influenced lesbians' attitudes toward marriage.

At the time, lesbian feminists and gay liberationists focused on what they considered to be more pressing issues, such as violence directed toward gay men and lesbians and the antigay campaigns of Anita Bryant in Florida and John Briggs in California (Adam, 1987). Although most were not actively involved in lesbian feminist or gay liberation organizations, many lesbians and gay men were influenced by the political atmosphere that these movements created (D'Emilio, 1989). Those same-sex ceremonies that occurred remained fairly private and largely invisible outside of lesbian and gay circles until the mid-1980s when the issue was brought back into the public eye during the 1987 National March on Washington for Lesbian and Gay Rights.

Shifts in Religious, Social,
and Legal Views toward Same-Sex Marriages

By the late 1980s, same-sex ceremonies had taken on a more public and visible format. Within lesbian and gay communities, their increased visibility was related in part to the publicity generated by "The Wedding" that took place in front of the Internal Revenue Service the day before the 1987 March on Washington. According to Frank Zerilli, confidential assistant to the Reverend Troy Perry (founder and moderator of the Universal Fellowship of Metropolitan Community Churches), this wedding ceremony was both a political protest and a serious commitment service.

Planned by the leaders of Couples, INC. of Los Angeles, Walter Wheeler and J. Carey Junkin, the ceremony allowed lesbian and gay couples both to celebrate their relationships and to protest their exclusion from the benefits heterosexual couples receive when they get married. These benefits include access to annuity and pension plans, protections in housing rights, Social Security and veterans' benefits, custody and visitation rights after a divorce, and access to employment benefits, such as medical insurance (Sherman, 1992). As news of the wedding spread after the march, lesbians and gay men began to once again publicly debate the issues of having weddings and legalizing same-sex marriage. In fact, the success of "The Wedding" at the 1987 march led the Reverend Perry to organize a second ceremony/protest in front of the Internal Revenue Service building prior to the 1993 March on Washington for Lesbian, Gay, and Bisexual Rights and Liberation.[3]

Although each couple has personal reasons for their decision to have a ceremony, a number of significant changes in society also facilitated a renewed interest in same-sex marriages and commitment ceremonies toward the late 1980s and early 1990s. While many factors may have expedited this reconceptualization of marriage, six stand out as most significant. These are shifts in religious reviews on same-sex marriages, the domestic partnership movement, the increased numbers of lesbians and gay men having or adopting children, the Thompson-Kowalski guardianship case, the HIV/AIDS epidemic, and the general shift to a more conservative political climate in the United States as a whole.

Religious Views

In part, the visibility of same-sex ceremonies increased as mainstream religious organizations began to debate whether to sanction same-sex unions. Although John Boswell's (1994) book *Same-Sex Unions in Premodern Europe* argues that religious rituals for same-sex marriages may date as far back as the Middle Ages, not until the 1970s did modern churches begin to debate the question of whether they should sanction same-sex ceremonies. Lesbians and gay men who wanted to have ceremonies initially found support from the Universal Fellowship of Metropolitan Community Churches.[4] This church was founded in 1968 by the Reverend Troy Perry as an organization to minister to lesbians and gay men and was "the first religious group to include union ceremonies for gays and lesbians in its bylaws" (Sherman, 1992, p. 5). During his first four years as pastor, the Reverend Perry conducted approximately 250 "services of holy union" (Butler, 1990, p. 40).

Other religious organizations did not begin to recognize the importance of supporting such unions until the 1980s. While most still deny lesbians and gay men the right to celebrate their relationships, some Methodist, Episcopal, United Church of Christ, and Quaker churches now allow ceremonies to take place within their sanctuaries. In addition, a few reformed synagogues also have voted to recognize same-sex unions. While these changes are laudatory, they unfortunately remain based on the "goodwill" of each separate congregation. Only the Unitarian Universalist Society has voted as an entire organization to recognize and validate same-sex ceremonies.

Domestic Partnership Legislation

During the 1980s some lesbians and gay men began to argue that the legal rights and economic benefits associated with marriage should not be limited to individuals who married. They further claimed that the definition of family should not be dependent on the formation of a legal marriage. In its place, they began to propose domestic partnership legislation. This movement originally began in 1982 when San Francisco Supervisor Harry Britt "introduced a city ordinance to allow unmarried city employees to include their partners on the city's health plan" (Horn, 1991, p. 10). Although the ordinance was not made into law until 1989, it raised the idea of granting "domestic partners" the legal rights associated with marriage.

The phrase "domestic partnership" refers to a household partnership or interdependent relationship of adults (over the age of eighteen) who are financially and emotionally interdependent (Lambda, 1990). Domestic partnership legislation centers on granting economic benefits (such as employer-provided health benefits) and legal rights (such as hospital visitation) to unmarried heterosexual and homosexual couples. By 1994, 150 cities had passed domestic partnership laws, and the idea of gaining the economic rights associated with legal marriage was well known to many lesbians and gay men.[5]

Parenting Rights

In addition to domestic partnership legislation, lesbians and gay men became concerned not only about their rights as adults but also their right to be parents. As many began to have or adopt children, they increasingly became concerned about their legal rights as parents and their partners' rights as coparents. For example, while many employers provide health insurance for a spouse's children if a couple is married, they do not cover the children of unmarried partners. Thus some lesbians and gay men began to seek the economic and legal benefits associated with marriage through the courts, through domestic partnership legislation, and by seeking the legal right to marry.

As courts and legislatures dealt with issues concerning the legal rights of unmarried partners, lesbians' and gay men's rights began to expand in the area of family law. During the 1970s and 1980s courts began to incorporate individuals who lived together but were not married, including (but not limited to) lesbian and gay couples, into existing laws. In some cases, the legal system used existing contract laws to settle cases.[6] In other cases, however, courts have expanded the functional definition of family to include unmarried heterosexual and lesbian and gay couples.[7]

The Thompson-Kowalski Guardianship Case

During the 1980s media publicity over the long battle Karen Thompson waged to gain visitation and guardianship rights to see her disabled partner, Sharon Kowalski, also underscored the need for lesbian and gay couples to gain the legal protections related to marriage, such as the right to visit and make health decisions for a hospitalized or institutionalized partner. After Sharon's car was struck by a drunken driver in November 1983, she suffered a serious brain stem injury that left her severely disabled and unable to care for herself. Although Karen fought to become Sharon's caregiver, in April 1984 the Minnesota state court made Sharon's father her legal guardian. Not satisfied with this outcome and barred from seeing Sharon by her parents, Karen waged a seven-year custody battle to reverse the court's decision. In 1991 the Minnesota state court finally granted Karen guardianship rights after the court ruled that Sharon's parents were not caring for her in the best possible manner.[8]

The HIV/AIDS Epidemic

In the 1980s and 1990s the HIV/AIDS epidemic also altered the priorities and political concerns of many gay men and lesbians. The epidemic highlighted the legal importance of gaining access to the economic benefits associated with marriage, especially hospital visitation rights and coverage by a partner's health insurance policies. Indeed, these two areas became one of the first concerns of many AIDS organizations (Kessler et al, 1988). From the very beginning of the epidemic, stories circulated in the gay and lesbian press about gay men routinely being denied visitation rights to see their partners who were hospitalized due to AIDS.

Shift toward Conservative Political Climate

Lesbians' and gay men's growing concern over gaining the benefits accorded married heterosexual couples in part reflects a larger shift in American politics toward the right. Since the late 1970s there has been a deepening conservative trend in the formation of public policy and in the influence of the new religious right over governmental practices (Harper and Leicht, 1984; Moore and Whitt, 1992). In fact, this more general conservative trend has influenced individuals' political attitudes. Instead of seeking "justice" for all the oppressed, many people have adopted a "market view" of social inequality (Seddon, 1990). This view emphasizes changing who gets access to certain legal rights instead of altering the laws those rights are based on. Seeking the legal right to marry is not a revolutionary political act. It is an act that attempts to give lesbian and gay couples access to the benefits of marriage, which may change the gendered "definition" of marriage without radically changing other aspects of the institution.

Lesbians and gay men, however, can change the conventions and traditions that surround wedding ceremonies. They can and do create ceremonies that entail new meanings and symbols. As Butler (1990) notes, many are discussing what new concepts of marriage and family might mean. When two women discuss having a union ceremony: "The first question . . . [is], What does the ceremony mean? It's an astounding question, really, and one that is especially vital in the creation of new forms and new traditions. . . . What does it mean for two people to create a life together?" (Butler, 1990, p. viii). What does it mean? The following chapters examine how the lesbians and gay men interviewed for this book answered that question. (Please see Appendix I for an in-depth discussion of the fieldwork and methods used in the study.)

Conclusion

In November 1989 Patrick Gill and Craig Dean made national head-lines after filing a million-dollar lawsuit against the District of Columbia for denying their application for a marriage license. Standing in front of the District Courthouse and in front of television cameras, Dean commented: "We want the right to have a relationship in the legal sense. We have been together for 4 ½ years. At this time in our relationship and at the ages we are in our lives, we want to get married. If we were a heterosexual couple, we would definitely be granted a marriage license.

It is only fair that we seek the same rights as everyone else."[9] Although Gill's and Dean's attempt to marry legally could be considered an anomaly, their actions are part of a growing effort to legalize same-sex marriages in the United States.

Over the past twenty-five years, enormous changes have taken place in the legal rights granted to lesbians, gay men, and bisexuals in the United States. Although lesbian and gay marriages are not yet legal in Hawaii or any other state, the ruling by Hawaii's State Supreme Court signifies the "coming of age" of the issue of legalizing them. As *New York Times* reporter Jane Gross (1994) wrote:

> [Hawaii] . . . could become the first to legalize marriage between people of the same sex or at least to offer marital benefits for gay couples who register as domestic partners. Whether by sanctioning gay marriage . . . or by passing America's first statewide domestic partnership act, Hawaii would lead the way in this fundamental redefinition of family, which some see as a sweeping expansion of civil rights and others see as an erosion of traditional values. (p. A1)

As the following chapters suggest, some lesbians and gay men are attempting to claim and redefine these "traditional family values." Instead of rejecting the ideals of commitment, monogamy, and marriage, many are questioning what these sentiments mean in the context of same-sex relationships. The chapters are divided into three sections. In part I, chapters 2 and 3 examine lesbians' and gay men's attitudes and practices toward love, commitment, and the idea of "being married." In part II, chapters 4, 5, and 6 focus specifically on commitment and union ceremonies. In part III, chapter 7 discusses lesbians' and gay men's attitudes toward the legalization of same-sex marriages and domestic partnership legislation and ends with conclusions about the future of lesbian and gay marriage rights.

CHAPTER TWO

As Long as I Have a Heart

On the Meaning of Love in Lesbian and Gay Relationships

Communication is absolutely the most important thing, and honesty. Being able to talk about your feelings and express them, share them. Being able to state what you need and want from the other person and being able to compromise.

—Paula Hughes

We have to trust each other and be completely honest with each other even if it is something that we are feeling embarrassed or ashamed of or angry about. Enjoy doing the same things together. Share similar but not identical views of the world. Have a satisfying sexual relationship.

—Christopher Avery

AS THESE EPIGRAPHS SUGGEST, lesbians and gay men value communication, honesty, trust, and sexuality in their love relationships. Contrary to the myths that homosexual couples are "less in love" than heterosexual couples or are not even capable of developing lasting love relationships, many are deeply in love with their same-sex partners (Testa, Kinder, and Ironson, 1987). For lesbians and gay men, love is an essential aspect of serious relationships. Similarly, love has become the central principle behind heterosexual marriage and "living together" as well. Thus any discussion of lesbians' and gay men's view toward relationships would be incomplete without a discussion of their views toward love.

In order to examine lesbians' and gay men's beliefs about love, this chapter addresses the following questions: To what extent do lesbians and gay men adhere to modern conceptions of love? Are there significant differences in how lesbians and gay men view love? And finally, how do their views about love reinforce the controversial view that same-sex marriages should be legalized? Although marriage has not been a legal option for same-sex couples, the historical development of modern conceptions of love for lesbians and gay men as well as heterosexuals is intertwined with the development of modern ideals about marriage.

Modern Conceptions of Love and Marriage

Prior to the early 1800s, love was not a critical aspect of marriage in the United States. In the colonies, marriages among White European immigrants were "regarded as a social obligation and an economic necessity" (Mintz and Kellogg, 1988, p. 56). All individuals were expected to marry and participate in family life, and very few men or women remained unmarried.

In colonial society, legal marriage was based on the Christian belief that "marriage was a sacrament, a holy union between a man and a woman, a commitment to join together for life" (Weitzman, 1985, p. 1). For families with property, marriages primarily were economic relationships. Fathers arranged their children's marriages to form property alliances with other affluent families and to ensure their children's economic success. For less affluent social groups, however, love as well as economic considerations influenced marriage choices. Nevertheless, for all classes, marriage was predicated on financial obligations (Degler, 1980; D'Emilio and Freedman, 1988; Gerstel and Gross, 1989).

During the colonial period, procreation was intimately connected to married life. As historians John D'Emilio and Estelle Freedman

(1988) noted, "reproduction and production went hand in hand, for family survival in an agricultural economy depended on the labor of children, both in the fields and in the household" (p. 16). Protestant churches also reinforced reproductive sexual activity. According to their teachings, the only proper form of sexual expression took place within marriage and led to reproduction. Sexual acts that took place outside marriage and those within marriage that did not lead to reproduction were classified as "sins." Often churches disciplined individuals caught in nonprocreative behaviors through fines and other punishments.

By the end of the eighteenth century, however, industrialization and urbanization had begun to significantly alter White middle-class family life and subsequently marriage practices. This was a "pivotal period in the transformation of the family. From the 'family economy' character- izing Colonial America, industrial capitalism gradually fractured job site and household into separate spheres" (Gerstel and Gross, 1989, p. 91). During this time the "democratic family," based on a new doctrine of gender relationships, emerged among the White middle-class (Mintz and Kellogg, 1988). This ideology, called the "cult of domesticity" or the doctrine of "separate spheres," emphasized the interdependent but separate roles of women and men in the household. Women were viewed as moral guardians: Their proper role was to care for the family and its emotional needs and to help tame their husband's "animallike" sexuality. In contrast, a man's role was to support his family through participation in the wage labor force (Gerstel and Gross, 1989; Welter, 1983). Thus the "ideal" modern family consisted of a husband who earned a "family wage" (enough to support his family), a wife who cared for the emotional needs of her family, and their children.[1]

In contrast to the colonial period, an ideology also developed that cast love, not economic and family considerations, as the basis of family ties. As industrialization created employment opportunities outside of owning land and farming, individual choice began to inform both sexual and marriage partners. Over time the power of families over their daughters' and sons' marriages decreased. Increasingly, women and men were expected to choose their marriage partners on the basis of mutual attraction and feelings of love. In fact, "love as the basis for marrying was the purest form of individualism; it subordinated all familial, social, or group considerations to personal preference" (Degler, 1980, p. 14).

By the early 1900s the nature of marriage had changed from an institution that dictated social and economic obligations to a ritual premised on the ideal of love and personal choice. As modern, industrialized life continued to alter family patterns, a newer, modern conception of companionate marriage developed. The phrase "companionate marriage" was first used by judge Ben Lindsay and co-author Wainright Evans in their book, *Revolt of Modern Youth*, which was published in 1925 (Mintz and Kellogg, 1988, p. 115). Lindsay and Evans argued that marriages should not be based on social pressures or religious conceptions of duty but on mutual affection, sexual attraction, and equal rights. Thus the goal of modern, companionate marriage was not financial security but emotional and sexual fulfillment.

In the 1960s and 1970s marriage norms shifted even further as many feminists, lesbians, and gay men radically critiqued the institution of marriage and, in many cases, called for its eradication. To these groups, marriage, even the newer companionate ideal, was oppressive to women and to lesbians and gay men. The new model of companionate marriage was full of contradictions. Although spouses expected verbal and sexual intimacy to be part of marriage, wives and husbands remained unequal. Despite the rhetoric of equality, men still retained a great deal of economic, legal, and sexual power over their wives, and women remained responsible for the emotional needs of their husbands (Cancian, 1987). Thus the cultural notion of marrying for romantic love obscured the reality that marriage remained an economic contract: Women provided men with emotional and sexual services in return for financial support.

During the last thirty years, however, marriage has continued to be idealized within popular culture as an institution grounded in both the companionate ideal and the concept of romantic love. As public acceptance of contraception, sex outside of marriage, and cohabitation has increased, love, not procreation, has become the cornerstone of contemporary relationships: dating, married, or living together. Cultural conceptions also have impacted the attitudes of lesbian and gay men toward romantic love and relationships. Although some reject the

companionate ideal, many others embrace it, reflecting society's contemporary emphasis on affection, communication, and personal growth
within relationships.

What Makes a Good Love Relationship?

The seventy lesbians and gay men in this study who were currently in a
significant relationship were asked questions about their attitudes
toward love, commitment, and the idea of being married. Specifically,
they were asked the following open-ended question: "What qualities do
you think make a good love relationship?" In discussing their views on
love, these respondents mentioned over fourteen different qualities that
they believed were important in a good love relationship. Five characteristics, however, were mentioned most often: communication, honesty,
physical attraction, trust, and sharing similar interests.[2] (See table 2.1 for
a list of the ten most frequently mentioned attributes.) Ironically, these
same traits also were associated with conflict. The modern emphasis
within relationships on values such as communication and honesty
create high expectations, which can lead the way to conflict and
disappointment. As their accounts suggest, overall these lesbians and gay
men held relationship values very similar to those of heterosexuals.

Communication

The majority of the lesbians and gay men interviewed discussed the
importance of communication in their intimate relationships. As Riccardo Hernandez stated: "If there is not communication, there will never
be understanding. Communication is very, very important. To express
what you feel, sit down and talk things out, share things together, be
there for one another, feel close." In their answers, most respondents
prioritized communication: sharing one's feelings, talking about issues,
and trying to understand their partner's point of view. Thus communication was connected to emotional intimacy.

Although both lesbians and gay men valued emotional expression
in their love relationships, some of these same respondents also discussed

TABLE 2.1

QUALITIES IMPORTANT
IN A LOVE RELATIONSHIP

	MEN	WOMEN	TOTAL
QUALITIES	%	%	%
Communication	63	69	66
Honesty	57	43	50
Physical Attraction	54	37	47
Trust	31	57	44*
Similar Interests	34	40	37
Compromise	26	34	30
Respect	14	37	26*
Be Caring/loving	23	29	26
Have Fun	23	20	21
Independence	23	17	20
	N=35	N=35	N=70

*Percent differences between men and women significant at $p < .05$

the struggles they encountered over communication. According to
Martha Price: "I wish she would share more of herself with me. I'm not
sure I always know what she is thinking. Maybe I shouldn't. She'll say a
lot about other people and other things but not about herself."

Conrad Gardner also mentioned difficulties he was encountering in
his current relationship. Although he stated that communication was
the "primary" quality important to him in a relationship, he lamented
that he and his partner were having problems discussing their different
career and relationship goals. He believed the problem was that they
"communicated in some kind of shorthand and sometimes didn't
communicate very well at all.'

Many of the problems lesbians and gay men discussed about
communication were related to individual differences in relational

standards, which are personal ideals that people use to judge the effectiveness of discussions (Montgomery, 1988). Often they are hard to qualify because they are produced in personal interactions and unique in every relationship. Thus each individual in a relationship brings her or his own ideals (which may change over time) about what communication means and how much discussion should take place. Communication problems escalate in relationships where individuals have different views or standards about the amount of factual and emotional information that should be disclosed (Cleek and Pearson, 1985; Fitzpatrick, 1988; Kurdek, 1991). While communication is an important aspect of lesbian and gay relationships, it is a skill that entails struggle and work.

Honesty

Most respondents also mentioned honesty as an important quality in a love relationship. For many, honesty and communication were essentially the same. As Brian Davies stated, honesty is the "ability to communicate anger or confusion in a relationship." Honesty entailed sharing one's feelings, being sincere, remaining open, and being straightforward. Most respondents believed that honesty was an important aspect of communication and equated honesty with "being truthful" about feelings. According to Francis Divine, honesty was the most important quality in a gay relationship. As he remarked, "Honesty is most important—always saying what is really on your mind. No hidden agendas." A number of lesbians and gay men, however, also mentioned that being truthful was not always easy. As Andrea Gorchov remarked:

> All of these things are kind of abstract, like take honesty. It's really a good idea and really important. But you know damn well that if you are honest with yourself, you are not always honest. It's not that you are lying. It's that you are not facing what you are feeling.

Although most studies on gay and lesbian relationships have not examined the importance or meaning of honesty, a few studies have noted the importance people place on honesty in relationships. In her study on partnership priorities, sociologist Mary Laner (1977) noted that heterosexual and homosexual women and men ranked honesty as the most important trait in a relationship.[3] In addition, sociologist Francesca Cancian (1987) has indicated that her heterosexual respondents mentioned honesty the fourth most frequently when she asked them to state the qualities they believed were important in a love relationship.[4] Thus communication and honesty seem to be highly valued qualities in both heterosexual and homosexual relationships.

Physical Attraction

In contrast to the stereotype that lesbians are more interested in verbal than sexual intimacy, many lesbians as well as gay men emphasized the importance of physical attraction in their relationships.[5] According to Cathy Newman, one of the most important qualities in a love relationship was "an initial sexual attraction. I've had to will myself to love certain people whom I was not attracted to, and it doesn't work. Sex is really important." Or as Barry Mullins replied, "Good in the sack!"

Some respondents, however, remarked that although they thought sexual attraction was important, they were not sure whether they valued it more than other aspects of a relationship. As Conrad Gardner replied: "I think sexual attractiveness fits in there somewhere too but I'm not sure where. I'm not sure it is as important as some of the other things, like communication and having similar interests."

In the past, studies that concentrated on gay men's sexual practices may have overemphasized the relative importance of sexuality within gay relationships (Bell and Weinberg, 1978). Research done with a broader focus has suggested that while gay men do value sexuality, they also value other relationship qualities. In a study by psychologists Letitia Anne Peplau and Susan Cochran (1981), gay men listed "sexual compatibility" as being the third most important item after "being able to talk about my most intimate feelings" and "having our own careers" (p. 6).

The importance lesbians place on physical attraction may be the result of "the recent trend towards viewing sex as a way for men and women to mutually express intimacy . . ." (Cancian, 1987, p. 77). The increased availability of contraceptives and changes in sexual norms have given all women greater freedom to express their sexuality and to focus on sexual satisfaction (D'Emilio and Freedman, 1988). In addition, normative changes have occurred within the lesbian community that altered the value lesbians place on sex. While sex was downplayed by some lesbian groups (such as the Radicalesbians) in the 1970s, today lesbian sexuality is celebrated in many diverse outlets: From lesbian magazines that focus on sexuality *(On Our Backs)*, to lesbian sex manuals (Joanne Loulan's *Lesbian Sex*), to performances that highlight the diversity of lesbians' and bisexual women's erotic experiences (Annie Sprinkle's "Post Porn Modernist").[6]

Along with discussing the importance of physical attraction, however, some lesbians and gay men also discussed the difficulties they had in maintaining sexual energy and passion in their relationships. As Leslie Walker commented: "Maintaining some kind of sexual energy. The more I talk to people the more I get the sense that the longer you are in a relationship, the harder it is to maintain the sexual energy. And I think we are struggling with that, too." Many researchers have noted that the nature of love and expressions of love change over time in intimate relationships (Reedy, Birren, and Schaie, 1981; Swenson, Eskew, and Kohlepp, 1981). In particular, numerous scholars have reported that sexual activity and desire decline in long-term lesbian and gay relationships (Blumstein and Schwartz, 1983; Johnson, 1990).[7] Just as with communication and honesty, the very qualities of physical attractiveness lesbians and gay men desired created an expectation that could not always be met.

Despite recognizing difficulties in maintaining sexual energy, many lesbians and gay men emphasized the importance of physical attraction. The equal emphasis they placed on sexual attraction, however, contradicts the results discussed in studies of heterosexual couples where men emphasized physical attractiveness more than women (Peplau and Gordon, 1985). The interviews for this book suggest that, in the arena of sexual appeal, lesbians may emphasize different relationship values than heterosexual women.

Trust

The lesbians and gay men interviewed distinguished between honesty and trust. In contrast to honesty in which a person's truthfulness was emphasized, trust was related to a person's dependability. While an honest person was someone who told the truth, a trustworthy person was someone who could be relied on. According to Samuel Phillips:

> I would say the sense of being able to trust someone. Now people would say, "How do you manifest trust?" I think trust can be manifested in ways that you can see and in terms of saying that you are going to do something and you do it. It speaks of their commitment to doing things too. That's a plus for a lot.

Many authors have noted that trust is fundamental for a relationship to develop successfully (Hatfield, 1988; Hendrick and Hendrick, 1992; Holmes and Rempel, 1989). As psychologists Clyde Hendrick and Susan Hendrick (1992) have noted, trust requires a reciprocity that is fostered by self-disclosure, intimate conversations, and the buildup of consistent behaviors. They argue that "trust development is a 'process' involving increasing security and reassurance of a partner's intention" (p. 167).

Given that trust is something that develops, it is not surprising that many lesbians and gay men discussed trust as a trait that developed over time. As Barry Mullins commented:

> It has taken us awhile to work out issues of communication and trust. It gets nicer and better every year because we end up trusting each other more because you know more about each other. When you go through problems and good times you just feel more comfortable with each other and you trust each other more.

Although sexual passion may decrease over the course of a relationship, trust increases the longer a couple spends time together.

Share Similar Interests

In addition to communication, honesty, sexual attraction, and trust, a number of lesbians and gay men discussed the importance of sharing similar interests with their partners. To Brenda Wood, it was important to have "mutual leisure interests. To share things. Things that you like together. Reading, camping, theater, whatever."

Previous research on gay and heterosexual couples has implied that men and women, regardless of sexual orientation, value having similar interests and sharing activities with their partners. In sociologists Philip Blumstein and Pepper Schwartz's (1983) study, 42 percent of the lesbians, 31 percent of the gay men, 41 percent of the heterosexual women, and 32 percent of the heterosexual men replied that having the same interests as an ideal partner was extremely important. In addition, psychologists Susan Cochran and Letitia Anne Peplau (1985) noted that in their study, heterosexual women and men equally valued sharing activities with their partners and spending time together.

Many of the respondents who mentioned sharing interests, however, stressed that this did not mean giving up one's autonomy. According to Lori Morrison:

> Being comfortable doing nothing. Sitting around with one person reading and the other knitting and having that be okay. Being comfortable with having a partner who may have very different interests than you. You each have your separate interests but you have your "comings together" around the relationship. You also can enjoy doing similar things together.

As Lori's remarks suggest, she did not view herself as being exclusively "autonomous from" or "dependent on" her partner. Indeed, this conception of love was similar to Cancian's (1987) notion of interdependence, where individuals share similar interests with their partners but also want to maintain a strong autonomous self.

Overall, the lesbians and gay men in the study valued many of the same qualities in love relationships, including communication, honesty, physical attraction, trust, and sharing similar interests. Studies on heterosexual women and men also have noted that both sexes value affection, companionship, communication, and personal development in their intimate relationships (Hendrick and Hendrick, 1992). A number of significant gender differences, however, did occur in the responses of lesbians and gay men in this study.

Gender Differences in Conceptions of Love

Although many of the characteristics lesbians and gay men mentioned were very similar, the frequency that respondents mentioned the importance of trust and respect as part of a love relationship was related to gender. Lesbians were more likely than gay men to state that they valued trust and respect in their relationships. (See table 2.1.) On the other hand, both sexes were equally likely to discuss the importance of communication, honesty, physical attraction, and sharing activities together.

Trust and Respect

As mentioned earlier, lesbians and gay men defined trust as being able to have faith in their partners' actions and to be able to depend on them. As Julia Gomez remarked:

> Trust is very important. I'm talking about somebody who's willing to make an effort, somebody who's willing to work at keeping the relationship going and working out the kinks in the relationship. It is related to commitment in that sense but it requires effort. There is a lot of effort involved so you have to have some kind of trust and commitment to do it.

Lesbians, however, may value trust in their relationships more than gay men because of their experiences as women in our society. As many feminists have argued, women often are in a subordinate position to men in all types of relationships, including those between friends, lovers, and coworkers (Lorber, 1994). Women also are more likely than men to have been sexually abused or battered by a partner (McBride and Emerson, 1989). Indeed, many women may emphasize the importance of trust because they have experienced being placed in a weaker, less powerful position in relation to men at some point in their lives. This subordination may increase the value women place on trust even when they are involved in same-sex relationships.

In addition to trust, lesbians also were more likely than gay men to state that respect was an important aspect of a love relationship.

According to Melanie Obermeier, respect developed along with trust: "In the beginning, the spark, the attraction is there. Then eventually you have a mutual respect for each other and then you trust them." Jackie Miller also commented that respect was crucial in a relationship. "I think we have a great deal of respect. I think she has a lot of respect for me and I have respect for her. We respect each other's wishes."

For most of the lesbians in the study, respect meant having a reciprocal consideration for one another's needs and honoring each other's feelings. Many mentioned the importance of respecting each other's differences. As Anna Blumberg commented, respect was related to having autonomy within a relationship.

> In the way that we treat each other, I feel that we really respect each other. We have continued to have our own interests, to do things separately, and to develop interests together. I think that respect is related to trust. Trust that you can stand alone as well as stand as a couple.

For Anna, the notion of respect focused on personal autonomy. Her comments imply that she and her partner wanted to maintain their independence. Thus for her and for many other lesbians, the term "respect" was a symbol of this autonomy.

In addition to autonomy, however, four respondents mentioned that respect included accepting and supporting their religious beliefs, their parenting styles, or their class backgrounds. As Deborah Lieberman remarked:

> It is important that people I am involved with respect my involvement with my family. Also, I am Jewish and it is critical for me that they respect that. Not only respect it, but also want to be a part of it in their own way. Not ask me to convert, but to respect my beliefs.

Toni Abbott also stated that respect had to do with acceptance.

> Class issues. There has got to be respect. And I mean being classist is one way of being disrespectful and intolerant. That really has to be in place. I can't stand that. And respect for me as a parent.

Understanding that I define my parenting and the other person is not the parent. I want support but that is all.

These respondents' remarks also are related to their conceptions of "interdependence." They want their relationships to be based on mutual understandings of how they differ from their partners.

Although lesbians emphasized respect more than gay men, both groups had a similar definition of what the term meant. Respect is an aspect of love that occurs between equals. Their views stand in direct contrast to psychologist Zick Rubin (1973), who defined respect as "liking that is based on another person's admirable characteristics or actions" (p. 27) and is "directed toward persons of higher status" (p. 41). The meaning lesbians and gay men in this book ascribed to respect fit more closely with psychologist Erich Fromm's (1956) definition in his book *The Art of Loving*. According to Fromm, respect "denotes, in accordance with the root of the word (*respicere* = to look at), the ability to see a person as he is, to be aware of his unique individuality" (p. 28).

Although only a small percentage of respondents specifically mentioned "independence" as important an quality in a love relationship, the emphasis lesbians placed on respect suggests that they highly value "autonomy." For many, respect meant being able to have freedom within their relationships to have their own interests. The importance these women placed on autonomy corresponds with previous studies on heterosexual and homosexual relationships that have noted that women are more likely than men to state they value independence within romantic relationships (Cochran and Peplau, 1985; Peplau and Cochran, 1981; Peplau, Cochran, Rook, and Padesky, 1978). As Cochran and Peplau (1985) noted, however, this may be a "false" gender difference, in that women may state that they endorse "egalitarian autonomy" values, such as having their own career and separate interests, more than men because men may consider autonomy to be a given in their relationships.

Communication

Although there was not a significant gender difference in the degree respondents mentioned the importance of communication, it is essential to ask if "the sexes interpret values . . . in similar ways?" (Peplau and Gordon, 1985, p. 262). While most of the gay men in the study considered communication to include in-depth conversations about their feelings, some emphasized that communicating meant talking about what was going on in their lives. They highlighted the sharing of information between partners rather than the sharing of emotions.[8]

According to Hendrick and Hendrick (1992), communication has a "content or informational component" as well as "an affective or emotional one" (p. 172). As Mike Reilly stated, "Communication is important. Physical attraction is a part of it but what attracts me is the person's intellect. I love to talk." When discussing his current relationship, Mike further mentioned that "talking about stuff that's going on" was important to him. As he explained, "If I have had a bad day, I feel I am able to vent that with Carl. We've done tremendous amounts of talking and we know a lot about each other on many subjects." Thus some men may interpret the term "communication" to mean sharing information rather than sharing emotions.

There was not a significant gender difference, however, in how lesbians and gay men discussed the meaning of the term "communication." For the majority of respondents, communication meant sharing one's intimate feelings. In contrast to researchers who have argued that men have difficulties being intimate (Rubin, 1983), the accounts of the gay men in this study suggest that at least some men value the expression of feelings within intimate relationships.

Gay men, however, may differ from heterosexual men in how they define communication in their love relationships. Gay men have to negotiate the parameters of how and when to express their feelings because gender does not automatically decide who will be assigned to facilitate communication in their relationships. They cannot rely automatically on a woman to perform the "emotional work" in a relationship as heterosexual men often do (Fishman, 1978; Tannen, 1990). In addition, gay men may value being emotional more than heterosexual men because they may place less of an emphasis on withholding their feelings as being part of their "masculine" self-image. Although traditional gender ideologies posit that being "a man" means concealing one's feelings and being "a woman" means expressing emotions, gay men may develop their self-identities in opposition to this dichotomy.

Love and Definitions of Marriage

Today love remains a central tenant of marriage in the United States. Ideal conceptions of marriage continue to reflect both the older "democratic" as well as the newer "companionate" models discussed at the beginning of this chapter. Scholars, however, hotly dispute what else beyond love defines contemporary marriages. In the 1990s the issue of legalizing same-sex marriages has catapulted the debate over what marriage means back into the public arena.

According to the editors at *Commonweal,* a liberal Catholic magazine, the "rationale for marriage as a social institution cannot rest on the goods of companionship alone" (1987, p. 55). They argue that love must include biological, relational, and procreative dimensions. Marriage is a procreative bond that ties sexual attraction to love and love to children. Clearly, the implication behind this viewpoint is that lesbians and gay men cannot be included in any definition of marriage since they cannot "biologically" have children together.

This perspective is shared by Robert Knight of the Family Research Council, a conservative organization founded to "protect" families. Quoting *Webster's International Dictionary,* Knight maintains that marriage is an institution "whereby men and women are joined in a special kind of social and legal dependence for the purpose of founding and maintaining a family" (1997, p. 114). Marriage a priori is an institution that is defined as being between one man and one woman. If this fundamental aspect of marriage is changed, the relationship is no longer a marriage. Thus the perspective that a marriage can only exist between a husband and a wife whose focus is to bear and raise children is shared by many liberals as well as conservatives.

This conceptualization of marriage directly stems from the "democratic" view of marriage popular in the 1800s, where the purpose of marriage was to provide a sheltered place for the rearing and socialization of children, a place where men would be domesticated, and a place where women and men would become reliable caregivers. Women were to act as moral agents who tamed men and controlled their sexuality. Recently even some gay scholars have reiterated these same archaic sentiments about the functions of marriage.

According to author Jonathan Rauch (1996), modern, secular marriage includes love but is not defined solely by love. As a social and legal institution, the purpose of marriage is to tame men's sexual impulses, to instill responsibility in both women and men, and to provide a place for caring for children. Despite his conservative approach, however, Rauch argues that same-sex marriage should be legalized because the institution would help curb gay men's sexual impulses and would create a bond of obligation between partners. In addition law professor William Eskridge (1996) has argued that marriage would civilize both gay and heterosexual men. He contends that legalizing same-sex marriage is important because it would create more interpersonal commitment, lessen gay male promiscuity, and lead toward the further inclusion of lesbians and gay men in mainstream society.

Despite their source (liberal or conservative, heterosexual or gay), there are two major problems with arguments that either discredit same-sex marriages because lesbians and gay men supposedly cannot have children or praise them for their "power" to tame men's sexual impulses. First, both types of arguments are based on a historical ideal of "the family." Reducing the functions of marriage today to the model espoused for White, middle-class families during the nineteenth century disregards the realities of family life both then and now. The "democratic" model of marriage was an ideal based on essentialist notions of human nature. Since women biologically could bear children, they were responsible for their care. Since men biologically were oversexed, they needed a women's moral guidance to keep them from being promiscuous.

Although biology certainly plays a role in shaping individuals' lives, it does not determine human destiny. Gender roles and expectations are created by the societies in which people live. Monogamy is a value individuals hold and is not maintained or forsaken because people are married. In addition, women as well as men have illicit affairs. Therefore, it is erroneous to argue that same-sex marriages should be legalized in order to keep men in monogamous relationships.

Second, it is just as inaccurate to renounce same-sex marriages on the basis that lesbians and gay men cannot have children. Many lesbians and gay men do have children, through previous heterosexual marriages, adoption, or artificial insemination. In addition, children are no longer the basis of many heterosexual marriages. Heterosexual women and men are not asked whether they plan to have children before they are granted a marriage license. Many heterosexual couples choose not to have children or find out they cannot do so after they are married.

In contrast, Andrew Sullivan (1996), senior editor at *The New Republic,* makes a better argument for justifying the legalization of same-sex marriages in his book *Virtually Normal.* Although his position is based on conservative principles, he insists that lesbians and gay men should be given the right to marry because, at its heart, marriage is an emotional and economic contract.

> The center of the public contract is an emotional, financial, and psychological bond between two people; in this respect, heterosexuals and homosexuals are identical. The heterosexuality of marriage is intrinsic only if it is understood to be intrinsically procreative; but that definition has long been abandoned in Western society. No civil marriage license is granted on the condition that the couple bear children; and the marriage is no less legal and no less defensible if it remains childless. In the contemporary West, marriage has become a way in which the state recognizes an emotional commitment by two people to each other for life. (p. 126)

To Sullivan, marriage is an anchor that promotes stable families by nurturing the values of love, commitment, and monogamy.

While the need to tame men's (and allegedly women's) sexual impulses is debatable, Sullivan correctly asserts that any two people who make an emotional commitment to each other should have the legal right to marry. As this book suggests, many lesbians and gay men value not only love in their relationships but emotional intimacy as well. Thus the institution of marriage should be redefined legally to reflect the realities of today's relationships, whether they are between a same-sex or heterosexual couple.

Conclusion

Throughout history, many writers have attempted to define love, from Plato, who depicted "eros" as the journey toward finding one's complementary other half, to Freud, who described love as the result of either expressed or repressed sexual impulses. For other authors, love has entailed pleasure in the company of another person, a strong emotional affinity between adults that includes sex and tenderness, and attachment, caring, and intimacy (Goode, 1959; May, 1953; Rubin, 1973; Santas, 1988). As psychologist Rollo May (1975) noted, "no word is used with more meanings than this term" (p. 114). Although there were some differences in responses between women and men interviewed for this book, overall similar qualities were mentioned regarding love relationships. Therefore, among these respondents neither gender nor sexual orientation produced a "uniquely" male/female or lesbian/gay style of love.

The lesbians and gay men interviewed certainly mentioned aspects of intimacy, passion, and, to a lesser degree, commitment as important qualities in a love relationship. For these people, intimacy consists of communication, honesty, trust, the ability to compromise, respect, caring, and having fun. Indeed, the term "intimacy" refers to having a profound knowledge or understanding of a person. The word stems from the Latin *intimus,* which means "inner" or "inmost" (*Oxford Latin Dictionary,* 1982). Although many researchers have argued that intimacy is more important to women than to men (L. Rubin, 1983), both lesbians and gay men discussed intimacy as an important part of love relationships.

In fact, love consists of intimacy, passion, and commitment. Although only a small percentage of lesbians and gay men explicitly mentioned commitment as an important aspect of a love relationship, subsequent questions during the interview process touched on the high value they placed on commitment. Commitment is different from love. Love implies "positive feelings" about an individual, while commitment refers to people's intention to continue a relationship. While love can be measured by levels of attachment, intimacy, and caring, commitment should be evaluated by the "expectation" that a relationship will last and by the types of investments made in relationships (Kelley, 1983; Lund, 1985; Rosenblatt, 1977). Thus commitment is discussed separately from love in chapter 3.

CHAPTER THREE

The Power of Two

On the Meaning of Commitment and Marriage in Lesbian and Gay Relationships

I show my commitment in the things that I do, and that runs the gamut from doing the food shopping to doing the cooking to getting tickets for a play. I picture being together forever and a day. I see no end to the relationship, barring death. We are two Black men who show it is possible to make it in a long-term relationship.

> —Samuel Phillips on his thirteen-year monogamous relationship with Terry Maxwell

SAMUEL PHILLIPS'S WORDS ABOUT HIS COMMITMENT to Terry Maxwell are striking for two main reasons. First, they are remarkable because Samuel's and Terry's relationship contests stereotypical images of gay men. In the past, gay men often were portrayed as self-centered, promiscuous, and unable to make a commitment to a partner (Humphries, 1970). Second, as a couple who have spent thirteen years together, Samuel and Terry also challenge the prevailing opinion that both heterosexual and gay relationships are inevitably doomed to failure in this age of high divorce rates. Since 1965 the divorce rate in the United States has more than doubled, and currently the median duration of marriages is lower than eight years (Norton and Morman, 1987; *Statistical Abstracts,* 1997b).

The media often portrays marriages, family relationships, and committed love as being in serious trouble. The "crisis" in the family and the "decline" of commitment are common themes in newspapers, magazines, and television news programs (Raspberry, 1997). Recently these concerns were prominently featured in the Republican Party's "Contract with America" (Berke, 1995; Toner, 1995).

Reports about the deterioration of the family raise the question as to the extent these worries actually characterize the condition of family life in the United States today. In order to explore this issue, this chapter examines one type of family, that among lesbians and gay men who are in partnered relationships. Specifically, the chapter addresses the following questions: First, what do lesbians and gay men who are involved in relationships think about commitment and marriage in their lives? Second, to what extent are their views on commitment and marriage homogenous? And finally, what can lesbians' and gay men's views about commitment and marriage tell us about the larger public debate concerning the legalization of same-sex marriages?

Sociological Literature on Commitment and Marriage

Over the past twenty-five years, public policy discussions about the state of "the family" have begun to include concerns about the rights of so-called alternative families: families that do not fit the nuclear mold of husband, wife, and 1.84 children (*Current Population Reports,* 1998; Radsken, 1998). Although domestic partnership legislation and other acts to offer so-called family rights to single parents, siblings, and gays have become part of the larger political landscape in this country, very few sociological studies have examined lesbians' and gay men's beliefs specifically about commitment or marriage. Social researchers interested in the concept of commitment theoretically have modeled the commitment of individuals or organizations;[1] examined the factors associated with marital commitment;[2] or debated the importance of commitment in heterosexual relationships.[3]

In the first tradition, scholars such as Elizabeth Kanter and Howard Becker examined notions of commitment and how they "bind personality systems" to a broad range of institutions, from organizations to family relationships. In his examination of commitments to social organizations, Becker (1960) developed the concept of "side bets" to explore the types of mechanisms that produce commitment. As he noted, commitments can be achieved by "staking something of value, something originally unrelated to one's present line of action, on being consistent in one's present behavior" (p. 36). For example, an individual's concern for his or her children could be considered a "side bet" that would make it difficult for him or her to divorce as spouse. Similarly, Kanter (1968) researched the "commitment mechanisms" related to long-lasting utopian communities. In order to be enduring, she argued that successful social organizations had to utilize strategies that could demonstrate both the benefits of continuing and the costs of leaving to their participants. For example, members' investments of time and money operated to reinforce personal commitment.

In another tradition, researchers have studied marital commitment. A number of scholars have focused on going beyond Becker's definition of commitment as a wager on the future to identifying the actual determinants of commitment within heterosexual marriages.[4] These researchers suggest that the degree of commitment is related not only to "future orientation" but to relationship satisfaction, investment of resources, availability of alternative partners, amount of caring, strategies for conflict resolution, and expectations about gender roles. Thus, according to this literature, a number of interrelated factors influence marital commitment.

In addition, a few quantitative studies have examined satisfaction and commitment in gay and heterosexual relationships.[5] Using an investment model approach, psychologists Duffy and Rusbult (1985-86) examined the determinants of satisfaction and commitment within heterosexual and homosexual relationships. Rusbult's investment model predicted that commitment increases with high relationship satisfaction, with the investment of resources in a relationship, and with a small pool of alternative partners.

Finally, other scholars have focused on explaining the decline of marital commitment. As sociologist Jessie Bernard first suggested, changes in gender roles have undermined the traditional belief that permanence is a fundamental feature of marital commitment (Scanzoni and Arnett, 1987). In her book *The Future of Marriage,* Bernard (1982) noted that the definition of "commitment" as entailing permanence has deep roots in the Judeo-Christian religious tradition. In the United States, this tradition has emphasized both permanence and sexual exclusivity as the foundations of marriage. It has shaped both legal conceptions of marriage and cultural attitudes toward commitment.

In contrast, newer norms and values have developed that drastically differ from more conventional notions of commitment. According to Bernard (1982), these newer values emphasize that "the risks of growth include the risks of growing apart" (p. 89). Similarly, Bellah and coauthors (1985) have noted that these newer values stress individual autonomy over family responsibilities. They argue that this change has occurred in the contemporary movement to replace obligation in intimate relationships with self-actualization and personal development. This perspective counsels each man and woman to "find and assert his or her true self because this self is the only source of genuine relationships to other people" (p. 98).

The degree to which heterosexuals have abandoned obligation for autonomy has been hotly debated in the family literature. None of the three traditions just discussed, however, examines the qualitative or subjective meanings of commitment or marriage. Thus little is known about what lesbians and gay men (or heterosexual women and men) mean when they use terms like "commitment" and "marriage."

Following Scanzoni and Arnett (1987), in this book commitment is defined as "the degree of willingness to work toward continued and future maintenance of one's close relationship" (p. 137). As Rosenblatt (1977) notes, "willingness" can be conceptualized as arising from personal devotion to one's partner and from external pressures, such as the expectations of others and society toward a couple. Although lesbians and gay men cannot legally marry, societal norms and values shape their beliefs and expectations surrounding long-term relationships. Thus the following section specifically examines the degree to which the respondents in this study value commitment in their relationships.

Meanings of Commitment

As mentioned in chapter 1, seventy of the ninety gay men and lesbians in this study were in a primary relationship with a same-sex partner. Of these seventy respondents, 33 percent had been in their current relationship two years or less, 30 percent three to seven years, and 37 percent eight years or more. (See table AII.13 on page 203.) The following discussion is based on these respondents' own accounts of what commitment meant to them. During their interviews they were asked specifically: "What does it mean to you to be committed to your partner?"

Overall, these lesbians and gay men discussed commitment in many different ways: from having the same interests to sharing financial responsibilities. As it turned out, conceptually their responses fell into two broad theoretical categories: beliefs and investments. As Becker (1960) has noted, it is important to define what qualities actually make up the term "commitment."

Beliefs

Overall, lesbians' and gay men's views of commitment focused on a number of similar beliefs. For example, they were equally likely to consider commitment to entail a sense of permanence and working on personal growth. (See table 3.1.) The majority of respondents mentioned permanence as an important aspect of commitment.

As is clear from the table, in contrast to the common perception that gay male relationships do not last, 77 percent of lesbians and 73 percent of gay men believed that commitment entailed spending the rest of their lives with their partners. Luke Fontaine, for example, stated that commitment meant being together for life and "not being separated until one of us goes down into the ground in a casket." As Patrick Flemming replied:

TABLE 3.1

MEANINGS OF COMMITMENT

	MEN	WOMEN	TOTAL
MEANINGS	%	%	%
1. BELIEFS			
Permanence	73	77	76
Working on problems	36	49	43*
Personal growth	36	31	34
Exclusivity/monogamy	10	32	21*
2. INVESTMENTS			
Buying a house	20	20	20
Living together	14	17	14
Raising children	9	17	13*
	N=35	N=35	N=70

*Percent difference between men and women significant at $p < .05$

I am committed for life. We don't talk about it so much any more. It is assumed. Lately, we have talked about where we are going to be buried together. I would consider any change in our commitment to be very serious. It would be like getting a divorce.

Several lesbians and gay men mentioned being buried together; one woman even discussed being buried with her "in-laws."

In addition, many respondents discussed commitment as entailing emotional growth for themselves and for their partners. They highlighted the importance of growing as individuals within their relationships. According to Pamela Gatland: "Commitment means that we continue to grow separately as individuals and together as a couple. My intention is to remain in the relationship and to attempt to work out extreme differences between us." Luke Fontaine also stressed the importance of personal growth as being part of a committed relationship, of "being willing to accommodate any changes that he might want to make for his own personal growth and him being willing to do the same for me." In contrast to the image created in the media and by many social researchers that individuals have abandoned long-term commitments for a focus on individualism, these lesbians and gay men did not consider commitment and personal growth to be mutually exclusive.

Investments

In addition to beliefs, lesbians and gay men also talked about commitment in terms of financial investments, such as making joint purchases or living together. Investments are not about emotional characteristics but the financial and time contributions individuals make to maintain their relationships: They are a type of side bet. They are not directly related to personal commitment, but they do increase the stakes of changing that commitment.

Although they did not mention them as often as beliefs, both lesbians and gay men equally mentioned investments, such as buying a house. According to Matthew Richards, "Commitment means that you work to foster the relationship and help the other person in any way you can." When asked if commitment meant anything else to him, Matthew continued: "Well, we just bought a house together. A lot of what we are doing is working toward the future. In fact, we talk a lot about the future and what we will be doing. I mean we realize we are going to be living together until the day we die."

Gender Differences in Beliefs and Investments

Specific gender differences did exist in how lesbians and gay men spoke about commitment. Lesbians were more likely than gay men to mention the importance of working through difficult issues, monogamy, and having children as important aspects of commitment. (See table 3.1.) For example, 49 percent of lesbians compared to 36 percent of gay men discussed their expectations that working out problems was a part of making a commitment. According to Lisa Chang, "The relationship is

something I want to see continue. If hard things happen, then a lot of
the commitment means dealing with it and trying to resolve it."

Gender differences in certain aspects of commitment may be due to
discrepancies in how women and men are taught to adopt feminine and
masculine personalities and gender roles. As sociologist Nancy
Chodorow (1978) has argued, variations in male and female personality
traits result from contrasts in the relational dynamics between mothers
and young girls and boys in childhood. Through their relationships to
their mothers, girls are taught to internalize values related to expressive-
ness and connectedness and boys to reject emotions and embrace
independence. Thus lesbians (just like heterosexual women in other
research) may emphasize the importance of working on problems more
than gay men because as women they have been taught to value that
aspect of relationships.

Lesbians also were more likely than gay men to talk about the
importance of monogamy as part of their commitment to their partners.
While 32 percent of lesbians in relationships mentioned monogamy as
an important aspect of commitment, only 10 percent of the gay men
did. As Kathleen O'Brien joked: "Commitment is the realization that no
shiny toys[6] that come along are worth it. I've made the decision that
Valerie is the person I want to grow old with. That there is no one else
that is going to be important enough to give up what I have with her."

Gender differences in the importance of monogamy may, in part,
reflect gay men's gender socialization. Some scholars have argued that
men—heterosexual and homosexual—place a greater emphasis on
sexual activities than women (Gagnon and Simon, 1973). But it also
may reflect norms specific to the gay community that emphasize
sexuality. Research prior to the mid-1980s—before the HIV/AIDS
epidemic—noted the high number of gay men engaging in anonymous
forms of sexual activity (Bell and Weinberg, 1978; Humphreys, 1970).

Current research, however, has found that the HIV/AIDS epidemic
has changed gay men's attitudes toward coupled relationships, intimacy,
and sexuality (R. Berger, 1990 and Carl, 1986). Fear of contracting HIV
may be pushing more gay men to maintain longer-term relationships
than was true in the past. Indeed, the accounts of many of the men in
this study substantiate reports in the gay press suggesting that new

norms advocate more exclusivity and a renewed importance of being in a couple. In fact, when respondents for this book were asked in their interviews what type of agreement they had with their partners concerning sex outside their relationship, 92 percent of the lesbians and 81 percent of the gay men stated they had either agreed to be monogamous or assumed the relationship was monogamous.

Finally, 17 percent of the lesbians compared to only 9 percent of the gay men discussed having children as an important aspect of commitment. Again, as mentioned earlier, as women, lesbians may be socialized to focus on the creation of family more than men—heterosexual or homosexual. In addition, they are more likely than gay men to have custody of children conceived in a prior relationship. For Anna Blumberg, commitment meant "making a home and raising a family together." Similarly, Andrea Gorchov remarked: "We have both operated on the assumption that we are committed. Like we moved in together. We built our house together. We bought a car together. And we've raised my two kids together."

In summary, two major points emerged from respondents' discussions of commitment. First, lesbians and gay men talked about commitment in two different ways: as a set of beliefs and as financial investments. Second, substantive differences between their responses suggest that gender is an important characteristic in shaping beliefs about commitment.

Length of Commitment

Besides being asked about the meaning of commitment in their relationships, respondents were asked how long they felt they would be committed to their partners. The question was: "For what length of time do you think you will be committed to your partner? For life, for a long time, for a while, or only briefly." Overall, 86 percent of respondents commented that they were committed for life or for a long time, 10 percent for a while or a brief time, and 4 percent not at all. Since conceptions of commitment often included permanence, it is not surprising that most respondents stated they were committed to their

TABLE 3.2

LENGTH COMMITTED TO PARTNER

	MEN	WOMEN	TOTAL
LENGTH COMMITTED	%	%	%
Life/long time	80	91	86*
While/short time	11	9	10
Not at all	9	0	4
	N=35	N=35	N=70

*Percent differences between men and women significant at p <.05

partners "for life!" However, the length of time respondents stated they thought they would be committed to their partners varied by gender. More lesbians than gay men stated they were committed for life or for a long time. (See table 3.2.)

This gender difference, however, may be related to whether respondents lived together or not; living together was found to influence how long people stated they would be committed to one another. (See table AII.14 on page 204.) Ninety-six percent of respondents who lived with their partners, compared to 60 percent of those who did not, stated that they were committed for life or a long time. Lesbians and gay men may emphasize living together as a major marker of commitment because historically they have been excluded from traditional events, such as engagement parties and wedding ceremonies (R. Berger, 1990). Overall, gay men may be more likely than lesbians to say they were committed only for a while or brief time because of a greater tendency among gay men to have partners or lovers they do not live with (Jay and Young, 1979).

The length of time respondents stated they would be committed varied by how long they had been together as a couple. Respondents were asked when they first started "dating" or seeing their partner and when they first considered themselves to be a couple, that is, in a more serious relationship. Not surprisingly, 98 percent of respondents who had been in their current relationship four years or more, compared to 67 percent of those in a relationship for fewer than four years, were committed for life or a long time. In general, commitment to a partner may be strengthened as a couple interacts more routinely with one another. Psychologist Paul Rosenblatt (1977) suggests that "the more a couple [heterosexual or homosexual] has acquired interlocking patterns of living, the more committed the two spouses will be to their relationship" (p. 82). Increased interaction, however, could stem either from living with a partner or from spending more time with him or her. Thus it is not surprising that the majority of gay men and lesbians who had been in their relationships for a longer time and lived with their partners were more committed than those who were involved for a shorter period.

Only three respondents in significant relationships stated they were not at all committed to their partners. These respondents were all gay men who did not live with their partners and who specified different reasons for their lack of commitment. For example, Michael O'Neill stated that he thought that he and his partner were not compatible because they came from different class backgrounds. He felt he was more rational and that his working-class partner more emotional. Harry Martin, however, felt that his primary commitment was to his grown children and not to his lover.

Although gay men were more likely than lesbians to make shorter commitments, it is important to note that the majority of both lesbians and gay men thought of their current relationships as permanent and commitment in general as long term. This finding may be attributed to the fact that these respondents were in relationships that they considered to be "significant" and not "affairs," regardless of how long they had been together as couples. In addition, the relationship between commitment and permanence may be due to the number of respondents who had or were planning a commitment ceremony of some type. Having a ceremony or ritual "helps to define the relationship as one of high commitment" (Rosenblatt, 1977, p. 81). Therefore, it is not surprising that 100 percent of the lesbians and gay men who had or were planning to have a ceremony considered commitment as being for life.

Among those who had not had a ceremony, however, the previously mentioned gender differences in length of commitment were accentuated. Ninety-one percent of lesbians but only 70 percent of gay men in this group considered their current relationships to be for life or a long time. Again, this contrast may be attributable to gender differences in how women and men are socialized, or to norms specific to lesbian and gay communities. Despite their differences, the majority of persons interviewed clearly valued maintaining their long-term intimate relationships.

Strikingly, many lesbians' and gay men's conceptions of commitment were similar to modern notions of marriage that emphasize personal growth in addition to working on maintaining a long-term relationship. Indeed, many married heterosexual couples are torn between viewing love as an expression of inner freedom and as a set of obligations that transcend immediate feelings (Bellah et al., 1985). Similarly, some respondents mentioned the importance of commitment as well as personal growth in their relationships. Others, however, emphasized aspects of commitment more reminiscent of traditional images of marriage that highlight permanence and obligation. The extent that respondents emphasized the importance of conventional values in their relationships raises an important question. Do lesbians and gay men think of their relationships as marriages? The next section examines the extent to which respondents think of themselves as "being married" to their partners.

Being Married

In addition to their views on commitment, respondents were asked: "Do you think of yourself as being married? Do not restrict this to a legal marriage or one involving a ceremony." If they did, they were asked what "being married" meant to them. Approximately half of the lesbians and gay men said that they thought of themselves as married to their partners. (See table 3.3.) Similar to notions of commitment, meanings of marriage focused on permanence, working on issues, and emotional bonding. Lesbians and gay men who used the term "marriage" to refer to their relationships did not differentiate between marriage and commitment: For them they were identical concepts. Indeed, the majority of respondents who used the term "marriage" stated that it was a long-term

TABLE 3.3

THINK OF SELF AS BEING MARRIED

	MEN	WOMEN	TOTAL
THINKS SELF MARRIED	%	%	%
Yes	57	51	54
No	43	49	46
	N=35	N=35	N=70

commitment and included working on problems. According to Andrea Gorchov:

Being married means to me that I am in a committed, lifelong relationship. That my life is intertwined with Eleanor's. I don't mean in a sick way, like a codependent way. But I think about doing things with Eleanor. For example, we are going to plant trees this afternoon. We think about being here when we are old. I think about being old with Eleanor.

Many respondents also thought that marriage meant working through difficult issues. As Conrad Gardner stated, "It means working out problems. That you can't just walk away from them." Kathleen O'Brien replied:

Being married means building commitment. It also means that throughout the hard times—times when we might not feel as crazy about each other—I will love her enough to work through them instead of just walking away because it is too hard or too tedious or it isn't fireworks anymore.

Other lesbians and gay men mentioned that marriage consisted of love and emotional intimacy. According to Tom Douglass: "Being married means that I know in my mind, in my heart, that this person is whom I love and am emotionally attached to. The person I can share everything with and who I can be completely free with." A small number of respondents stated that they felt their relationship was more permanent and therefore more like a marriage because they had had a commitment ceremony or wedding. As Celeste Davis stated:

Having a ceremony made it different for us, for our families, for our kids. We stepped over a bridge because it changed the way we thought about our relationship. The experience of the ritual itself made us feel a level of permanence and safety that wasn't there before. Now my partner knows she can count on me to be there and that we can work together on our relationship. Now I think of myself as married.

Paula Hughes also remarked:

After we got married, a lot of people asked me, "Do you feel different?" And I said, "Yes." Because the ceremony made me feel different. It made me feel that we are married now. It's something written in stone. It is more permanent.

Rituals, such as weddings, help participants to indicate major life transitions (Roberts, 1988). Clearly for both Celeste and Paula, ceremonies served to create a more personal sense that their commitment would be enduring. Even though they are not legally sanctioned, same-sex ceremonies act to enhance new bonds as well as to verify long-standing commitments. As Patrick Flemming commented:

We had our commitment ceremony on our fifth anniversary and I guess that is when we said we were married. I think the ceremony solidified our commitment. Having our family and our friends witness us saying these things to each other made it more serious and deeper. It made it more of a social thing and less of a personal thing. But I also think that it deepened the personal commitment.

Just that Joel was willing to stand up in front of all the people that were important to him and say this is the person I choose to spend my life with.

Same-sex ceremonies can be both a personal marker of commitment and an avenue for social legitimation of a couple's relationship. (See chapters 4 to 6 for a detailed discussion of same-sex ceremonies.)

One-third of the lesbians and gay men who thought of themselves as married, however, qualified their initial responses. They also discussed the difficulty they had with the heterosexual connotations of the term. For Kristen Johnson, for example, the term "marriage" brought up a heterosexual image of a man and a wife. "But," she stated, "when you get rid of that image and just talk about commitment and love, we're extremely married." As Deborah Lieberman commented: "I guess I think of myself as married. But I have a hard time with that word because it is such a straight word. Too many heterosexual marriages are not happy and yet people stay together."

In fact, many of the respondents who had difficulty with the word "marriage" discussed the problem of coming up with a new vocabulary to describe commitment within gay and lesbian relationships. As Deborah further elaborated:

> Part of it is struggling with language and struggling with the straight world. I see myself using the term "married" more but I am still trying to think about language. It is too easy to use the terms of straight society, and I am not sure that the term marriage fits who I am. Who *we* are.

Similarly, Barry Mullins stated: "I might use the word 'marriage' sometimes but not very frequently. It is hard to separate a relationship from a marriage because marriage is so universal a term. But I can't think of another term that has the same meaning."

Thus, among respondents who thought of themselves as "being married," there was some skepticism over using the language of marriage to refer to relationships.

Marriage Does Not Fit
Lesbian and Gay Relationships

Almost half of the lesbians and gay men who were in a significant relationship, however, did not consider their relationships to be like a "marriage." These respondents stated that they had major problems with the institution of marriage and did not want to be a part of it. As Theresa Barry commented:

> I have been married before and I found it was not a positive experience because you had to play a certain role, like coming home and cooking. If I work, you can cook your own food. I am into equality. I look at this relationship very differently than when I was married to a man. What is unique about lesbian, gay, and bisexual relationships is that we can use other terms. We can commit ourselves without saying we are married.

Samuel Phillips also replied:

> I don't see us as being married. When I think of marriage, I think of it in a heterosexual context. I think of it as something where you are told that your relationship is okay. Of course we know that in this society, it is not okay for two men to be right for each other.

As these quotes suggest, most of the lesbians and gay men who did not perceive themselves as being married were, in fact, committed to their partners. However, they did not equate commitment with "feeling married." For various reasons, they did not want to use the term "marriage," with its mainstream connotations, to refer to their relationships.

Other lesbians and gay men did not use the term "marriage" to refer to their relationships because they had not been in their relationship long enough to be "that committed." These respondents did not object to the term "marriage"; rather, they avoided it because they did not have that "level" of commitment in their current relationship. As Theo Nelson replied: "I do feel there is a point where I still have to come to where I can say flat out that this is for life. I haven't said it yet, and that's why I don't feel married."

One lesbian and two gay men also stated that they did not think of themselves as married but they did consider themselves to be "engaged to be married." All three of these respondents said that they would use the term "marriage" in the future, after they had a ceremony. According to Riccardo Hernandez, "No, we are not married, but we want to get married in a church if it is possible. Right now we are engaged." Similarly, Lynn Ettelman stated, "I think of myself as being engaged. I'll be married when I live with her, and I want to have a ceremony before we move in together. How traditional!"

Yet not all respondents who had a ceremony considered themselves to be married. While all of the gay men who had a ceremony did consider themselves married, two lesbians did not. They both gave slightly different reasons for their rejection of the term "marriage." According to Beth Epstein:

> After we had our ceremony, people would refer to us as married, particularly our heterosexual friends. I'd get really upset with people and say don't use those words. To me, marriage implies that two people mesh into a new unit, a couple, and lose their identity or individuality. And that does not appeal to me at all. It was real clear to me when we were planning our ceremony that we each have our own separate paths in addition to our shared path.

Sarah Weinberg, however, had a different reason. "It has to do with being a feminist. I feel that the power relations of marriage doesn't describe us. That the heterosexual conception of marriage does not capture the mutual respect we have for each other." Thus, these respondents had diverse reasons for their decisions not to use the word "marriage."

Age Differences

Although no gender or race differences emerged in respondents' accounts about thinking of themselves as "being married" or not, age

TABLE 3.4

USE TERM "MARRIAGE" TO DESCRIBE
SAME-SEX RELATIONSHIP (BY AGE)

	18-39 YEARS	40-89 YEARS	TOTAL
USE TERM	%	%	%
Yes	69	32	54
No	31	68	46
	N=42	N=28	N=70

was an important variable. In general, the majority of lesbians and gay men who thought of themselves as "married" (even if they had trouble with the language of "marriage") were under age forty (see table 3.4) and had not been married previously in a heterosexual relationship. These lesbians and gay men may be more willing to use the term "marriage" to refer to their current relationships because they have not experienced what many older respondents referred to as the "confining" roles inherent in heterosexual marriage. They also may be more likely than older gays to accept the term because they "came out" in the era of gay civil rights. As anthropologist Kath Weston (1991) noted, "The meaning of coming out has shifted steadily over the years, gradually assuming its current dual sense of claiming a lesbian or gay identity for oneself and communicating that identity to others" (p. 44). Age, as it related to birth cohort—people born during a similar time period—distinguished which respondents thought of themselves as married.

Many lesbians and gay men in their twenties and thirties would have begun both to identify themselves as gay and to express this identity to others in the 1980s and 1990s. During this period, the lesbian and gay movement shifted its tactics away from rejecting and toward claiming inclusion in mainstream institutions. According to sociologist Barry Adam (1987), in the 1980s the gay and lesbian civil rights movement focused on gaining civil rights through legislative change, particularly "the introduction of sexual orientation into human rights codes" (p. 122). The overall goal of the movement to gain inclusion into institutions, such as marriage and the family, may have influenced some younger respondents to accept rather than reject the traditional terminology related to marriage.

Most of the thirty-two respondents who did not use the term "marriage" to refer to their relationships were over age forty: 65 percent of the lesbians and 53 percent of the gay men. For some of these people, past experiences in heterosexual marriages tainted their current views of marriage. Thirty-one percent of those interviewed had been previously married in a heterosexual relationship.

For others, however, their reluctance to use the term "marriage" was simply a political position. For these lesbians and gay men, rejection of the term "marriage" may have been related to the period in which they came out. During the 1960s and 1970s, both feminists and gay liberationists were challenging traditional sex roles. At this time, cultural radicals were "preoccupied with finding alternatives to the nuclear family" (Altman, 1979, p. 47). They were concerned with creating a new language for relationships and new ways of relating to sexual partners.

For lesbians and gay men in their forties and fifties at the time of the study, these sentiments may have helped shape their conceptions of gay relationships. Russell Porter, for example, said:

> One reason I like being gay is because there are no conventions about what a gay relationship is. I get to define the terms of our relationship on an ongoing basis and revise them. In a marriage you have thousands of people with notions of what a marriage is in their heads and they love to enforce it on you.

Similarly, other respondents stated that they did not like to use the term "marriage" because they did not believe they needed to have their relationships legitimized by legal or religious institutions. As Richard Hudson commented: "Marriage has negative connotations to me because it is connected with religion and the law. It also reflects a picture of a man and a woman and kids. I don't relate to any of that. None of my friends use that terminology for their relationships."

In addition, a number of lesbians and gay men aged sixty and over argued that the idea that gay relationships are the same as heterosexual marriages was anathema. According to Brenda Wood, "The word 'marriage' doesn't fit gay relationships. The description is heterosexual, that's all. It's not me. It's not my generation." This sentiment also was echoed by Harry Martin: "I was married and this relationship isn't the same thing. I don't think homosexuals should use the term because it kind of knocks marriage. In a marriage you make a commitment and stick to that. In a gay relationship, it isn't necessarily that way." In contrast to Brenda, who focused on the negative implications of marriage, Harry believed that gay men often had less committed relationships than those between women and men.

For these lesbians and gay men, rejection of the term also could be related to their coming-out processes. Many older respondents identified themselves as gay in the "pre-Stonewall" era. The beginning of a visible lesbian and gay movement in the United States often is attributed to a raid by police, and subsequent riot by gay patrons, at the Stonewall Inn in New York City on June 27, 1969. Prior to the Stonewall riot, homosexuals often hid their sexual identities because they feared prosecution by the law, and subsequently, being fired from their jobs (Weston, 1991). Some even married in heterosexual relationships because they felt they had no alternative for survival. In fact, all respondents aged sixty and over who rejected the term had been married previously in a heterosexual relationship. These respondents might have rejected the term "marriage" because to them it signified the roles and obligations inherent in traditional marriage relationships.

Feminist Beliefs

For both lesbians and gay men, whether they considered themselves to be married generally was associated with whether they called themselves feminists. (See table 3.5.) Respondents used the term "feminist" in different ways, from being for equal rights for all people to specifically stating they were against women's subordination. Among respondents who considered themselves feminists, 56 percent of the lesbians and 75 percent of the gay men considered themselves married. For those who did not think of themselves as feminists, however, only 47 percent of the

TABLE 3.5

USE TERM "MARRIAGE" TO DESCRIBE
SAME-SEX RELATIONSHIP (BY FEMINIST IDENTIFICATION)

	MALE	FEMALE	TOTAL
CONSIDER SELF A FEMINIST			
USE TERM	%	%	%
Yes	75	56	82
No	30	44	18
	N=20	N=18	N=38
DO NOT CONSIDER SELF A FEMINIST			
USE TERM	%	%	%
Yes	33	47	41
No	67	53	60
	N=15	N=17	N=32

lesbians and 33 percent of the gay men thought of themselves as married.

The high percentages of lesbians and gay men who considered themselves feminists and married, however, is startling. In the past, many feminists have been critical of the institution of marriage and the unequal sexual and property relationships it creates (Barrett and McIntosh, 1982). The large number of respondents who thought of themselves as feminist and used the term "marriage" could be due to the various connotations of the term "feminist." Over time the word has taken on a diverse set of meanings (Delmar, 1986). It is possible that lesbians and gay men who are accepting of the term "marriage" might think of feminism in terms of gaining civil rights for women within institutional structures, such as the family, marriage, and the law. Conversely, those who reject the term "marriage" may conceptualize feminism as a vehicle for fighting women's oppression outside of mainstream structures.

To summarize, lesbians' and gay men's attitudes toward "being married" were equally split between those who thought of themselves as married and those who did not. Interestingly, age as it relates to birth cohort and not gender distinguished those who used the term "marriage" and those who did not. For half of the lesbians and gay men in this study, "being married" was one feature of their commitment to their partners. Other respondents, however, stated they believed it was important *not* to use the language of marriage to signify their commitments.

Similarly, in her sample of over 400 lesbians and gay men across the country, Mary Mendola (1980) found that over half of her respondents were comfortable with using the term "marriage" to refer to their relationships. According to the *American Heritage Dictionary*, the verb "to marry" is defined as "entering into a close relationship, uniting or forming a union." Thus, as Mendola suggests, the term "marriage" can be applied legitimately to any "committed" relationship.

Conclusion

In contrast to media images that suggest that in society at large the ideals of marriage, commitment, and family are slipping, the majority of lesbians and gay men in this study continue to value these same principles. Respondents who were in primary relationships with a same-sex partner discussed commitment as entailing notions of love, personal growth, working through difficult problems, permanence, sexual exclusivity, and investments. However, "commitment mechanisms," or the processes through which commitment is created in a relationship, involve social influences as well as individual attitudes and behaviors.

For lesbians and gay men, social influences on commitment often are contradictory. On one hand, they face homophobic attitudes that undermine their ability to maintain long-term relationships. As social worker Dennis Daily (1977) notes, "gay persons have been coerced to view their relationships as transient, illegal, immoral, unnatural. Not only do large segments of the population hold these attitudes (i.e., homophobia) but gay persons themselves have been socialized to view their relationships in the same light" (p. 82). Thus many struggle with viewing their relationships as legitimate and long term in light of negative social views toward gay relationships.

On the other hand, lesbians and gay men are influenced by cultural ideals that stress commitment and marriage as important aspects of the adult life cycle (McGoldrick, 1988). Even though they are barred from marrying legally, lesbians and gay men do value intimate relationships. As this chapter suggests, the majority of respondents thought of their relationships as being like traditional marriages: permanent and sexually exclusive. In addition, about half stated that they considered themselves "married."

Gays and heterosexuals alike are affected by changing social norms. In fact, the value placed on marriage has changed significantly over the past thirty years. As social worker Monica McGoldrick (1988) notes:

> Men and women are having sex earlier but marrying later than ever before. An ever increasing proportion are living together before marriage, or even living together with several partners before deciding to marry. Marriage used to be the major marker of transition into the adult world. . . . [Now] it is the transition to parenthood that confronts couples more sharply with the problems of traditional sex roles. . . . (p. 210)

Many of the lesbians and gay men in the study were critical of the institution of marriage. About half stated they did not think of themselves as "married."

Lesbians and gay men also are affected by norms that specifically develop within gay communities. The lesbian and gay as well as the feminist movement has changed focus over the past thirty years from an emphasis on changing oppressive institutions to gaining civil liberties. Thus many gays may have developed or changed their attitudes toward commitment and marriage in the context of the movement's overall demand for acceptance and equal rights.

It is paradoxical that lesbians and gay men are using terms related to the institution of marriage at a time when marriage norms for heterosexuals are changing within society. Although there are no census data on lesbian and gay couples, this book suggests what many people might consider to be ironic: Despite the political and media images that suggest that the heterosexual community no longer adheres to the idea of "family values," they certainly exist among many of the lesbians and gay men interviewed for this book.

One of the largest changes in the lesbian and gay communities over the last ten years has been an increase in the visibility of couples having commitment or union ceremonies. Although same-sex ceremonies have a long tradition, not until the 1980s did they become more public and visible both in the gay and mainstream media. Rather than strictly imitating heterosexual weddings, these ceremonies seek to transform both the private and public meanings of commitment. The following chapter discusses both the character of same-sex ceremonies and the meaning of these rituals for individuals who choose to have them.

Lesbian and Gay Commitment Ceremonies

For Richer, For Poorer?

Same-Sex Ceremonies as Rites of Passage

I think we wanted to make that level of commitment to each other and we wanted to do it in a way that included friends and family. We really wanted a ritual for ourselves that would provide a marker in terms of where we were in our relationship. We both thought there was no reason that the ritual of marriage had to be an exclusively heterosexual privilege. There was no reason why lesbians couldn't also have their own rituals and ceremonies.

—Maria Siggia

I guess it's not for me. I don't think it makes your relationship more valid if you have a ceremony. It seems like jumping on the bandwagon in a way. Like I can do it too! I'm just as important or as good as you are and I can get a minister, etc. I am resistant to identifying in any way with that sort of lifestyle. I think that's why I rebel a little about joint checking accounts, savings, wills, and all that because it's similar to, reminds me of heterosexism in a way. I think it's their values, what the heterosexual community has said is important to do to make one's life valid and fulfilled.

—Richard Hudson

AS DISCUSSED IN CHAPTER 1, some historical evidence suggests that same-sex ceremonies are not a "new" phenomenon within lesbian and gay communities in the United States. In the past, many same-sex couples said vows, and even may have exchanged rings, to commemorate their unions. In most cases, these ceremonies took place in private without public witnesses or the support of biological family members.[1] Over the past twenty-five years, however, increasing numbers of lesbians and gay men have had "public" ceremonies: rituals in which families and friends are invited to witness the event. While these rituals focus on declaring a couple's love and commitment to each other, one of their central purposes is to garner support and validation for lesbian and gay relationships. Many same-sex ceremonies are rites of passage that not only "create family" but also "build community."

As the two epigraphs to this chapter suggest, not all lesbians and gay men choose to have ceremonies. Among the ninety people interviewed, thirty-two had or were planning to have a same-sex ceremony. Of the remaining fifty-eight individuals, twenty-eight commented that they might have a ceremony sometime in the future; thirty stated that they did not want to have a ceremony either with their current partner or in a future relationship.

In order to examine motivations for having or not having a same-sex ceremony, this chapter focuses on three questions: What reasons do lesbians and gay men state for having a commitment or union ceremony? What motivations do other lesbians and gay men have for considering having a ceremony? What reasons do some state for not wanting to have a ceremony?

The following two chapters further examine same-sex ceremonies. Chapter 5 examines the language used to refer to same-sex ceremonies. It shows how that language simultaneously involves resistance and co-optation of traditional marriage ideals. Chapter 6 explores the varied political meanings attached to same-sex ceremonies. It suggests that many of the specific rituals used in these ceremonies also can be viewed both as acts of resistance and acts of accommodation to "traditional" conceptions of marriage.

Same-Sex Ceremonies as Rites of Passage

According to anthropologist Terence Turner (1977), rites of passage are in essence a series of rituals that mark the transition from one social state to another. Although no one accepted definition of "ritual" exists within the anthropological literature, the term generally refers to acts that are conventional and repetitive celebrations or social demarcations of important events (Goody, 1977). Therefore, rites of passage involve sequences of customary and standardized behaviors that designate life-changing events, such as birth, marriage, and death.

As anthropologist Arnold van Gennep (1960) first noted, rites of passage consist of three primary stages: a period of separation, a time of transition, and a reintegration phase. Although the importance of each stage varies, traditional marriage rites generally contain all three phrases. The betrothal or engagement period serves as a transitional stage for a couple from their status as separate individuals (from distinct families) to the creation of a new relationship (with extended kinship ties to both blood families). Most important, the wedding ceremony itself ends this transitional stage and serves to incorporate the couple into its "new" family.

Even though norms have changed in the United States, marriage remains a significant rite of passage for many heterosexual women and men. It continues to be an important rite of passage for them in part because it signals adulthood, the merging of two distinct kinship networks, the intention to have children, and the formation of a new family unit (Roth, 1985). Traditional marriage rites typically (although not always) take place through a series of rituals: betrothal, engagement party, wedding shower, bachelor party, rehearsal dinner, wedding ceremony, reception, and honeymoon.

For lesbians and gay men, however, no corresponding rites of passage exist to signify important changes in their adult roles or family relationships. In part, this lack of rites and rituals has stemmed from society's long-standing condemnation of homosexuality. Lesbian and gay couples do not receive the same legitimation and support as heterosexual relationships. In sharp contrast to the approval bestowed upon married couples, parents and other relatives of lesbians and gays often invalidate homosexual relationships by acting as if these relationships do not exist, which renders them invisible, or by recognizing the relationships but considering them not genuine (Roth, 1985).

Many lesbians and gay men, however, are choosing to create their own rituals and ceremonies to mark their own significant life transitions. Although these ceremonies vary in their content and structure, they are rites of passage; that is, they involve rituals of separation, transition, and integration that demarcate a couple's "partnered" status. As the following section points out, however, respondents' motivations for having a ceremony are both similar to and different from the reasons heterosexuals have weddings.

Motivations for Having a Same-Sex Ceremony

As mentioned, thirty-two respondents either had a ceremony or were planning to have one within a year. Among these respondents, same-sex ceremonies fell into two distinct categories: celebrations of recent commitments and celebrations of existing commitments. Eighteen respondents had ceremonies to acknowledge "recent" commitments—relationships that had lasted less than five years. As will be discussed in more detail in chapter 5, most of these respondents used either the phrase "commitment ceremony" or "holy union" to refer to their ceremonies on their invitations. All of these ceremonies took place between six months and four years after the couples had first met. Although their current ages ranged from twenty to forty-four, most respondents were in their twenties or early thirties at the time of the ceremonies.

In addition, five respondents were planning ceremonies to celebrate "recent" commitments within the next year. These respondents had been with their partners for less than two years. Four respondents stated they were planning to have a "wedding," and one woman commented she was planning a "union ceremony." All five respondents were under the age of forty and had never been married legally.

In contrast, five lesbians and two gay men had ceremonies to celebrate their established, long-term relationships. While most of the lesbians called their ceremonies "anniversary celebrations," the gay men used the phrases "holy union" and an "exchange of vows." Regardless of their names, however, all of these ceremonies took place between ten and sixteen years after the couples first met.[2] Unlike the respondents celebrating newer commitments who were in their twenties and early thirties, these lesbians and gay men were in their thirties, forties, and fifties at the time they had their ceremonies.

Although they cannot marry legally, lesbians and gay men are aware of the purposes weddings serve in the larger community. Correspondingly, respondents who had or were planning a ceremony discussed two main reasons for their decisions: to show their commitment and love to each other and to receive public validation of their commitments from friends and family. Noticeably absent from their accounts, however, were the traditional functions of separating from their families of origin or having children.

According to Patrick Flemming, he and his partner decided to have a ceremony because "we loved each other. We felt committed to each other for our lives and we wanted to let people know that in a very ritualized, public way that they could participate in too." Kathleen O'Brien also commented on the importance of social affirmation.

> I thought that Valerie and I deserved to have some public recognition
> and support of our commitment. That I deserved the right to hear
> myself say that I believe we have what it took and that I was willing
> to commit to that publicly. That our relationship deserved that
> intangible level of support and recognition.

Similarly, Randall Harris stated, "At the time we started planning to do it we had not yet been living together quite a year but we knew we wanted to make a commitment in a public way with some friends and family there."

In particular, respondents who had "anniversary celebrations" emphasized the need for more "public" support of gay and lesbian relationships. In their accounts, they often used the term "public" to refer to support from friends and family as well as from the larger gay and lesbian community. As Beth Epstein commented, she and her partner wanted to celebrate their twelfth anniversary because we really were feeling the need for public support. We had moved to this area just a few years before. We were really still establishing roots here and felt like we just needed some support. We also just really wanted to be able to express publicly to each other our commitment to the relationship, which had undergone some changes once we moved.

Indeed, many respondents stated that it was important to create support since lesbians and gay men have few avenues for gaining social recognition for their relationships. As Melanie Obermeier remarked:

I think people should have more ritual in their lives. There's not enough. Especially in gay relationships. You get a lot more support if your partner is straight even if you're not religious. You get a lot more ceremonies that give you landmarks and things to remember back to. You don't get those when you are gay. You have to make your own.

For a small minority of respondents, religious recognition and support also were important factors in why they had a ceremony. For Kathleen O'Brien and her partner Valerie, it was extremely important to have their "commitment ceremony" in a Unitarian church because of their religious convictions. As Kathleen explained:

We had been attending services at the Unitarian church for probably about six months when we realized that the Unitarian Society as a religious institution, not just as a church in Lesbianville,[3] recognized the union of gay and lesbian people as legitimate as straight people. Then we knew that is where we wanted to have our ceremony because we both had a very strong religious upbringing and the power of the symbol of the church was very important to us.

Similarly, Celeste Davis stated that she and her partner, Grace, had their "holy union" in a Unitarian church because of their religious beliefs. According to Celeste, "We were going to the Unitarian church and were familiar with their dogma. Their perspective reflected our beliefs about religion and having a ceremony."

All five of the respondents who referred to their ceremonies as "holy unions" commented that making a public statement included making a commitment before God. Although Luke Fontaine and his partner, Ben, did not have their "holy union" ceremony in a church, they had strong religious convictions. As Luke recalled:

> I wanted to make my commitment to Ben public and I wanted him to make his to me public. I think that making a commitment to each other before God and before witnesses is a very important step in making your relationship work. It's not so easy to walk away from something when you've made a public promise that you'll be together till death do us part.

For these respondents, same-sex ceremonies included religious recognition and support from their religious communities.

Different Motivations from Heterosexual Weddings

Similar to heterosexual weddings, same-sex ceremonies can help lesbian and gay couples integrate into kinship and community networks. For many such couples, however, the functions a ceremony performs often diverge from the heterosexual model. While same-sex ceremonies serve many of the same purposes as traditional heterosexual weddings, they differ in five important respects.

First, lesbian and gay unions do not necessarily begin the process of separating individuals from their families of origin. Since most individuals experience some level of rejection when they come out and identify as gay, typically they already have gone through a process of separation from their families. For this same reason, many same-sex ceremonies are not organized by blood family members and take place outside the traditional context of kin relations. Indeed, as will be discussed in more detail later, a primary purpose of many same-sex ceremonies is to create "chosen" families that include close friends.[4]

Second, although many heterosexual couples marry in order to gain public recognition of their relationships, public support has an additional significance for lesbians and gay men. For many respondents, the desire for such support from friends and family not only stemmed from wanting affirmation as a "couple" but also acceptance as a "lesbian" or "gay" couple. As Barbara Mercer remarked, "I think having a ceremony is important to show the rest of the world because it can give more validity to the fact that these are real relationships just like straight folks have." Unless heterosexual couples are of mixed races, ethnicities, or religions, they do not automatically face the same level of social rejection as lesbian and gay couples.

The support many same-sex couples who have ceremonies receive not only affirms the couple's relationship but also can be compensation for the lack of acceptance they often feel from biological family members and "the world at large." As Maria Siggia remarked:

> It was important to have that support of friends and family in terms of the kind of isolation that goes along with being part of a subculture or oppressed minority group. It seemed to us that it was very important to have some way to balance out all of the negativeness about being gay or lesbian. That it's really important to affirm our relationship and to ask people to actively support us and help out since the culture doesn't allow for that.

Other respondents also elaborated on the importance of rituals as an avenue for reinforcing the dyadic ties of lesbians and gay men. According to Melanie Obermeier:

> It's a really hard thing to do to have a relationship, and you need all the help you can get. If you're a heterosexual you get incredible support from the community to stay together even when people shouldn't. There is almost a pressure to stay together. And in the gay community there's none. There's none of the baby showers, wedding gifts, anniversaries. None of the "You buy silver on your tenth anniversary and Hallmark cards to my lovely wife" kind of thing. We get nothing, absolutely nothing. I think these types of rituals help maintain relationships.

Third, many respondents discussed how their ceremonies made an important statement to other lesbian and gay couples. This sentiment was articulated especially by couples whose ceremonies celebrated anniversaries. As Margaret Dubek explained:

> We just felt really good about the fact that we were still together after ten years. There aren't too many role models in the community that are able to do that. We wanted to celebrate it for ourselves and invite our friends to help us. I think it is good for our community and our friends to know that there are some successful relationships. That we can survive all the difficulties our society puts on us. We should celebrate that.

Kristen Johnson also remarked that it was important for other couples to have long-term, lesbian relationships as role models.

> The tenth is a milestone and I think that comes from tradition. Even within this community, I think it was important for us and for our friends that a tenth could be celebrated even in the midst of other long-term relationships breaking up. It was a moment of celebration.

One of the most important purposes of having a same-sex ceremony is the creation of recognition for a relationship within lesbian and gay communities. In the past, couples in long-term, monogamous relationships often received little support from other lesbians and gay men. As sociologists Philip Blumstein and Pepper Schwartz (1983) commented in their study *American Couples:* "There is a general fear in both gay and lesbian circles that relationships are unlikely to last. Long-lasting relationships are seen as quite special. They are unexpected, and therefore newly formed couples are not treated as though they will remain together for fifty years. . . . When a couple is not treated as [sacred], the less likely the partners will see themselves that way" (p. 322).

Similarly, many respondents in this study thought that long-term relationships did not receive enough support from other lesbians and gay men. To quote Melanie Obermeier again: "Sometimes the gay community doesn't take its own relationships seriously enough and that's part of the reason we have a hard time maintaining relationships. Because even as a community we don't take ourselves seriously and recognize our own relationships."

Even today there remains a perception among many lesbians and gay men that same-sex couples do not remain together for very long. As auhors Berger (1982) and Johnson (1990) have noted, however, many lesbians and gay men do have long-term relationships that last over ten years. Berger (1982) suggests that one reason older lesbian and gay couples seem invisible is that they do not share the same social circles as younger gays and, therefore, remain hidden to them.

Fourth, lesbian and gay ceremonies often are not celebrations of "new" commitments; that is, they may take place at any time during a couple's relationship. For example, Kristen Johnson and her partner decided to have a "tenth-anniversary celebration" instead of a commit-ment ceremony. According to Kristen:

> We feel very married and have felt very married right from the year one. Because of our insecurities around our sexuality for the first three or four years we were together, we never had a service. Now we don't think it is really appropriate or necessary to have a commitment ceremony since we have that commitment and have since the year one.

Similarly, Beth Epstein remarked:

> We called it a "recommitment celebration." We felt that we couldn't just call it a "commitment celebration." Obviously we had already made some level of commitment to be together for twelve years. Recommitment. Like on this day we publicly recommit to each other. That somehow really captured it for both of us.

Although heterosexual couples may live together without being married, and thus face a similar decision about publicly acknowledging their commitment, nothing prevents them from marrying. Heterosexual couples have a choice whether to marry legally; lesbians and gay men do not and, in addition, often face prejudice, which can prevent them from having a commitment ceremony.

Married heterosexual couples may decide to "renew" their vows on a significant anniversary. For such couples, wedding anniversaries are occasions to celebrate the date of their marriages. Since lesbians and gay men do not have the same kind of "formal" date to mark the length of their relationships, often they observe many different relationship anniversaries, including when they first met, had sex, moved in together, or decided to make a commitment. These anniversaries have added significance because they help to validate relationships in a society that discounts them. As a further way to gauge the legitimacy of their relationships, lesbian and gay couples may decide to have some type of ceremony when they reach a significant anniversary. In these instances, the length of the relationship becomes a substitute for conventional forms of societal recognition that heterosexual couples receive (Slater and Mencher, 1991).

A few respondents stated that their ceremonies were political acts with political consequences. As Patrick Flemming shouted, "We were saying that we were gay and we were proud. So there!" Similarly, Tom Douglass replied, "I have to admit part of what we were doing was a protest. To say, 'The church says no; the state says no; we say yes!'"

Lesbians' and gay men's political motivations for having a ceremony centered not only on validating gay relationships but affirming gay identity. Ever since politician and gay activist Harvey Milk's admonishments to "come out" in the mid-1970s, being publicly open about one's sexual identity has been considered a political act within lesbian and gay culture.[5] When asked to discuss her reasons for having a ceremony, Melanie Obermeier commented on the importance of taking a stand about one's sexual identity.

> If we don't do it for ourselves, who's going to do it for us? We're not going to hear anybody in the "het" community saying "hey, you guys, you should all be having ceremonies and celebrations." They're not going to do it for us. If we aren't out for ourselves, they won't be out for us.

Similarly, Esther Gould remarked:

In fact, I think same-sex ceremonies are more legitimate than "weddings." I think they are much braver thing to do. It's so easy to be heterosexual and get married. It's hard not to, in fact. I think it's a brave and really sort of profoundly creative thing for lesbians to create a ritual like that.

Given lesbians' and gay men's inability to marry legally, it was surprising that so few respondents specifically mentioned political motivations for having a commitment or union ceremony. In contrast to the political slogan of the 1970s "the personal is political," most of these respondents did not stress a connection between their personal motivations and larger social change within society. In fact, some specifically commented that their ceremonies were "not political events." Their reasons for having a ceremony focused more on personal aspects of commitment than on social change.

Like heterosexuals, lesbians and gay men clearly have ceremonies because they love their partners and want to acknowledge that bond publicly. Indeed, like heterosexual weddings, lesbian and gay ceremonies serve to integrate a couple into larger kinship and community networks. At their core same-sex ceremonies are rites of integration as well as rites of passage; their two primary objectives are the creation of family and the building of community. As the next section discusses, these "family" and "community" networks are very different in form from those generated for heterosexual couples.

Creating Family

In contrast to traditional marriage ideals, lesbian and gay commitment and union ceremonies do not focus on either procreation or the joining of two biological families into a new kinship unit. Instead, they emphasize the creation of what Weston (1991) has defined as "families we choose." Since many lesbians and gay men are ostracized from their biological families, same-sex ceremonies can help construct who comprises "family" for them. While chosen families may include biological family members, they are comprised predominately of partners, friends, ex-lovers, and children. Therefore, same-sex ceremonies are about family but not in the traditional sense of the word. Instead, they help denote the boundaries of a couple's "chosen" family. As Margaret Dubek remarked, "Marriage in its best sense is about two people who are committed to each other for life and who want to make a family!"

Three different avenues for creating family emerged from the accounts of the thirty-two lesbians and gay men who had or were planning a ceremony. Same-sex ceremonies assisted some couples in making a statement to their friends, to their family, and even to themselves that they now were part of a couple that constituted a family. According to Luke Fontaine, he and his partner, Ben, felt like more of a family after they had their "holy union" ceremony: "My sense of us changed. We went from being a couple who was living together to being a couple who is married, in my own definition. We are a family now." Luke interpreted the term "family" to mean the pairing of two adults. He and Ben were planning to adopt children, but Luke believed they did not have to have children to be a family.

Maria Siggia also commented on how same-sex ceremonies help define a couple as being a family. Maria recalled that she and her partner, Linda, decided to have a "commitment ceremony" because:

> We needed to make a statement about what we were doing with this relationship and where this relationship was going. I don't think we could think of how else to make that statement. It was a way of saying this is somebody who is very important to me. This is the person I want to spend the rest of my life with, so I want you to welcome this person into our group of family and friends. Weddings and marriage, I think that is what they are about. You meet each other's families and friends and there is something about that. Oh, these two are a couple now. That recognition of being a family.

According to Maria, the ceremony itself also changed how she and Linda viewed their relationship. They felt "somehow more officially a couple" and "more of a family." Similar to Luke and Ben, Maria and Linda did not have children but were thinking of having a child in the future. Like Luke, Maria believed that a couple could be a family with or without children.

For some lesbians and gay men, having a ceremony also highlighted and affirmed the boundaries of their chosen family. According to Kristen Johnson, she and her partner, Evelyn, wanted to celebrate their tenth anniversary with their family, which consisted of their closest friends. As Kristen explained:

> It was important for us to celebrate with our friends. We considered every one of the people who were there family. That one way or another, they are part of the community we are in. We consider them extremely important, and I don't think we'd hesitate to call on any one of them if we needed to. We'd consider about twelve people immediate family, who we have more daily contact with, but we consider them all family.

Although Kristen merged the concepts of family and community, she clearly distinguished between immediate family and individuals whom she thought of as family because they were part of her larger community of friends. To Kristen, immediate family consisted of friends whom you could call on in a crisis and with whom you shared a mutual commitment, friendship, understanding, and love.

Similarly, Patrick Flemming remarked that the friends and relatives who were at his "commitment ceremony" comprised his family. Patrick and his partner, Joel, even had a section in their ceremony where they discussed whom they thought of as family. As Patrick commented, the "closing thoughts" were "mostly about the fact that the people who were there were our family." Similar to Kristen, Patrick's notion of family included close friends who

> you know they have to be at your funeral. That's a joke, but I think you know that they will be there for you. And that if they are not, then something is really wrong. Like if you are sick or something, your family should take care of you or make sure that things are taken care of for you somehow.

For some respondents, the creation of family was a modern form of insurance against sickness and other crises. In part, their motivation for "creating family" was to ensure that they would have someone to count on if they could not rely on their biological relatives.

Many lesbians and gay men also discussed the traditional family roles that their closest friends had in both planning and carrying out their ceremonies. According to Tom Douglass, friends helped organize his wedding ceremony. As Tom recalled, the idea of having a "wedding" snowballed over time as friends took over various aspects of its organization.

> John and I often joke about the fact that we were registered at the local coffee shop called the Blue Moose. But that's how it got away from us. When I say got away from us, I meant the whole idea kind of snowballed. Our friends took it over and said we are going to do this.

When asked for an example, Tom continued:

> At one point I remember Margie, a friend of ours, said to us, "So and so asked me what they could get for you. I told them I didn't know." And we looked at each other and said, "We don't know either. We don't know what people are planning to get for us." She said, "Tell you what, why don't I take that over." Now she was working at the Blue Moose, so we told people we were registered at the Blue Moose. If they needed to find out, call the Blue Moose and ask for Margie. That fit right into our kind of fun-loving lifestyle.

Similarly, Esther Gould remarked about the jobs her friends took on in organizing for her "simcha" (meaning "happy event" in Hebrew) and tenth-anniversary celebration:

> In fact, our friends gave us "the wedding" to the extent that anybody gives a wedding. My closest friend at that time, I sort of teased her and called her the mother of the bride because she planned all the food and did all the ceremony preparation. . . . Ya know, when you get married your mother does all this stuff traditionally. . . . We also had our closest women friends hold the chuppah for us, which is a part of a Jewish wedding. It is the canopy the couple stands under.

For both Esther and Tom, friends played an integral part in their ceremonies.

Almost all of these lesbians and gay men asked chosen family members to be a part of their ceremonies. Anna Blumberg and her partner, Carol, asked their closest friends, whom they considered to be family, to participate in their "wedding." "The people that were in the ceremony were my 'family.' They're the people that I'm really, that we both feel like these are the people we go to when we have a problem, they will share responsibility with us and the success of this merger with us."

Who respondents included in their "family" varied enormously. For some, family primarily included their close friends. For others, it extended to their families of origin. For example, Anna and Carol asked Carol's parents to participate in the ceremony. According to Anna, Carol's parents were part of her family.

> Since I got together with Carol and met her family, I think about how my definition of family has changed because this is her family of origin and I feel very much that they are my family too. I understand how families can choose members and how families can blend together. . . . In our wedding, Carol's mother read a passage from the Old Testament, the one about love that everyone always reads, and then Carol's father got up and read the Sheva Brachot, which are the seven blessings.

Only a few respondents had their parents, their "in-laws," or other biological family members actually participate in their ceremonies.

Overall, only four out of the twenty-seven lesbians and gay men who had ceremonies did not invite any of their own or their partner's blood relatives to their ceremonies. Fifty-two percent of respondents, however, did not invite their parents to their ceremonies. In large part, this was because they had not disclosed their sexual identity to them or because they felt rejected by them for being gay or lesbian.

For example, Teresa Dufour and her partner, Jesse, originally wanted to have a large, public ceremony that included their biological relatives as well as friends. They decided, however, to have a more "private" commitment ceremony with their two closest friends because Teresa had not told her father she was a lesbian. As Teresa recalled:

> We originally wanted it to be a public ceremony but it ended up being a more private one. I was raised Catholic, so I knew that weddings were a public sign of this private bond, this bond that "God has joined." In my conception, a ceremony is an outward symbol to others but also a symbol to ourselves, "Yes, here we are and we're committed and I love you forever." So, it was for ourselves as well as a public sign even though we didn't have a public ceremony. . . . I'm really sorry that we had to miss out on that because I am not out to my dad.

Indeed, these respondents made specific choices about which biological relatives to invite to their ceremonies based on whom they were "out" to and whom they thought would be comfortable coming to the event. As Tom Douglass recounted:

> I was still coming out to my mother. I thought that it would have been such as traumatic thing for her at that point, as we were in this coming-out process. I took on the responsibility of not asking her specifically so not to put her into what I considered an uncomfortable situation.

Beth Epstein also did not invite her parents because she thought they would be ill at ease. When asked why she did not invite her parents, Beth replied:

> Because I wanted it to be a complete day of celebration. I did not want to have to be emotionally responsible for anybody else but myself. I knew if my parents came I would be worrying that they might be uncomfortable and that I would have to go over and make sure they were doing okay. The other piece was that I would have to worry whether my father was having too much to drink and making a scene, and I was not wanting to have to be aware of that on that day.

In contrast, Esther Gould affirmed her choice to invite her parents even though she felt that they had not been supportive enough of her relationships in the past. As Esther commented:

> It was important to me for our families to see our lives. To see that we had this very wonderful community of friends and colleagues that were able to love us and accept us and feel comfortable with our lesbian family in a way that I don't think either one of our biological families could have believed. I mean, they certainly had no experience with it before our ceremony.

Parents who attended their daughter's or son's ceremony had both negative and positive responses to the event. According to Patrick Flemming, his mother had mixed feelings about his "commitment ceremony." As Patrick recalled:

> I think she had fun and I think she was ashamed. I think it was a mix. I think a lot of her feelings about my being gay were there. At one point one of the parishioners came and asked what was going on inside the hall. My mother wouldn't tell her. My mother tried to put the woman off, and she couldn't say to her that it's a "commitment ceremony." My son is gay. I couldn't say I felt that my mother was proud. I don't know that was a day on which my mother felt proud of me. She never told me that.

Other lesbians and gay men recalled that members of their and their partner's families behaved in different ways. As Kathleen O'Brien recalled, both her mother and her brother were supportive of her having a ceremony. Kathleen thought her mother was "uncharacteristically supportive." In fact before the ceremony her mother had said that, "My daughter only gets married once. Of course I'm going to be there." Her partner's sister's husband, however, was not sympathetic. According to Kathleen:

> Both of Valerie's sisters were invited and both came. One sister brought her husband who is very open about the fact that he loves

the two of us but he thinks that it's immoral. We told him, "Frank, this is what is happening, and we would love for you to be there. But if you can't be there, then please don't come." But he came and he sat in the back row, because another close friend of the family told him [he] better not make a scene. "Sit in the back row if you don't think you can take it." And he left at the beginning of the ceremony. Before we even started, he was at [a local ice cream store]. But he stayed for the party afterward and made nice little homophobic comments. He was a drag.

Changes in Family Members' Definitions of Family

For a small minority of respondents, however, having a ceremony altered the meaning of family for some of their biological relatives. In particular, attending a same-sex ceremony changed how some parents understood their daughter's or son's sexual identity as well as the nature of their relationship. Although most lesbian and gay couples do not "consciously" decide to have a ceremony for this reason, the ceremony itself may change how they are accepted by and included in their biological families. When asked to elaborate on why she and her partner, Susan, did not involve any of their blood relatives in their ceremony, Esther Gould replied that the majority of them did not initially understand or accept their relationship. "We didn't have our families involved in the ceremony at all because we felt they were not very supportive, oh, except my sister and her children. My sister Ruth and her children were involved in the ceremony. But other than that, friends participated in the ceremony."

Although Esther and Susan were "out" about their sexual identity to their respective families and invited them to their simcha, they did not feel comfortable having them participate in the actual ceremony. Afterward, however, Esther and Susan were surprised at the extent the ceremony changed their relationships to each other's biological relatives. As Esther reflected, "I didn't anticipate how much it would feel like an event that had to do with making a family." Esther further elaborated on what she meant by "making a family."

A friend of mine said she thought Susan and I would feel a lot more committed, more powerfully about each other after the ceremony. And I said to her no, that's not right because I think we had made some type of powerful commitment before that. But it did something in terms of our families. To them it made a real difference about how they understood our relationship. And it changed my relationship to Susan's family and mine to hers. So in that way it felt like a traditional wedding.

In particular, the ceremony dramatically altered how Esther's mother thought of Susan.

My mother didn't get how important the ceremony was until it happened. But she came. After the ceremony and at the party that followed it, she went up to Susan and held her. There are a million photographs of this long period in which she cried and held Susan and said to her, "I didn't understand before, I understand now." She said to Susan that she's glad that I chose her to be with. That if she had a choice of my being with a man or with Susan, that she was glad I chose Susan. She was just completely transformed by the ceremony. For Susan, it really did mean some new level of acceptance by my family, especially my mother.

Patrick Flemming and his partner, Joel, also found that their "commitment ceremony" altered the degree to which their biological families accepted their relationship. According to Patrick:

I think that it was very important for our families and our friends to validate our relationship and celebrate it in a kind of organized ceremony. It made us a couple in their eyes. I think that it change some of our friendships and our relationships with our families to a certain extent.

When he elaborated on how it changed their family relationships, Patrick explained:

For some of the family members, it was very hard to even go to this thing. For instance, Joel's father. He talked about this during the ceremony. He said that just seeing how many people love Joel and that Joel was surrounded by all this love really impressed him. That if I loved Joel as much as I seemed to, then that was good. That made him happy. So seeing that, it really was a watershed in my relationship with Mr. Shulman, because before that he had resented me. It was a very emotional speech. It was a very important time for him. Of all of our family members, he was the one who had the biggest breakthrough at the ceremony.

In a similar fashion, Anna Blumberg recalled how her wedding altered her godmother's relationship to her and her partner, Carol.

My aunts and cousins seemed to enjoy it. They stayed through the meal and they took pictures. My godmother, I think, was very moved. Since then we have corresponded. She has written inviting us to come visit, that Carol is always welcome, and that she's part of the family.

Thus for some parents, siblings, and other extended family members, the act of attending a same-sex ceremony was a transformative event that changed their level of acceptance of the gay or lesbian couple having the ritual.

Clearly, same-sex ceremonies often demarcate the boundaries of a lesbian or gay couple's chosen family. Primarily, these ceremonies build family by declaring that a couple constitutes a family and by indicating what invited guests comprise a couple's chosen family. For a number of the lesbians and gay men who had ceremonies, the "creation" of family also meant a reconnection with their families of origin.

For others, having a ceremony was not a rite of passage that dramatically altered their relationships with their blood relatives. This was most clear for those who had not come out to their families. For example, when Nancy Greenwood and her partner, Cindy, planned their "commitment ceremony," they had not discussed their sexual identities with their families. As Nancy explained:

At the time, we weren't out to most of our family members, so it wasn't appropriate to invite them. It didn't fulfill the rite-of-passage stuff for us because they didn't even know it was happening. I really think that what it was about was a declaration to the people who, at that time, were our closest friends, and to one another, that we were now really a couple and intended to stay that way.

Although their commitment ceremony did not serve to integrate Nancy and Cindy into their biological families, it did announce to their friends that they were a couple. As such, the ceremony helped to integrate them into their larger community of heterosexual and gay friends.

At that point all of our friends were connected to graduate school and mostly they were straight. They were feeling kind of confused about our relationship. So, in part we did it to sort of help out our friends understand what we were about.

Thus, instead of creating family, this ceremony served to connect Nancy and Cindy to their community. While same-sex ceremonies help some individuals reconnect with what is conventionally thought of as "family," they assist others in replacing their biological relatives with "chosen family" members. In either case, same-sex ceremonies also create community.

Building Community and Communitas

The *Oxford American Dictionary* defines the term "community" in three ways: "as a body of people living in one place, a group with common interests or origins, and a fellowship that is alike in some way." Same-sex ceremonies can integrate lesbians and gay men into "community" in all three of these meanings. They may facilitate a couple's integration into a geographical community, into a community of friends with whom they share similar interests, or into the larger fellowship of "married" couples. Many lesbians and gay men discussed how having a ceremony both built and strengthened their sense of being part of a community. According to Maria Siggia, ceremonies are important not only "for the two people but also because they are a shared community event."

According to Randall Harris, community support was a main reason he and his partner, Lenny, wanted to have a "holy union" ceremony. During their ceremony, the two men made a commitment not only to each other but to their community of friends as well. As Randall explained: "It was a commitment between the two of us that meant we'd try harder to make it work. Also, it was a commitment with our community. With all our friends. And it just wasn't gay people who were at the holy union, there were a lot of straight people there too." When asked why it was important to make a "commitment" with his community, Randall replied:

> Even the minister talked about this during the ceremony. It is important to have your relationship confirmed or affirmed by your community. That's one of the reason's why people do big weddings. They invite all their friends. They do it in front of everybody. They're saying it in front of everybody that they are making a commitment, so all these people know. The minister went on to say that it is the responsibility of the community to support the relationship and recognize it.

In the context of their ceremony, Randall and Lenny defined "community" as consisting of their gay and heterosexual friends. Randall stated that he did not consider his friends to be part of his family; his family consisted of his biological relatives. Instead, his friends were his "community."

In addition to building and supporting a community as a group, same-sex ceremonies can help establish a kind of "communitas" between a couple and their friends who attend the event. The term "communitas" refers to "an expression of sociability . . . that stresses equality and comradeship" (V. Turner, 1974, p. 232). Communitas is a spontaneous existential fellowship, not a physical community, and develops as individuals relate to one another during a ritual.

Two distinct types of communitas emerged from the accounts of the lesbians and gay men who had ceremonies. First, a sense of communitas developed as gay, lesbian, and heterosexual friends and family pledged to support and assist a couple in maintaining their relationship. For most respondents who had a ceremony, affirming this community support was crucial. Ben Fletcher felt that having this type of support was important for maintaining gay relationships.

> If you have a ceremony, you should have a support group there who are witnesses. People that know you are committed to one another for life. Then if there are any problems, there is a support group there saying that we want to do what we can to help continue this relationship.

For many respondents, the building of community was a form of modern emotional insurance. They wanted to be situated in a community that they could rely on for emotional support. Thus a sense of communitas developed out of the pledge of support lesbian, gay, bisexual, and straight family and friends gave them during their ceremonies.

A second meaning of communitas also appeared in respondents' descriptions of their ceremonies. For some lesbians and gay men, having a ceremony was an explicit way to claim inclusion in the larger institution of marriage. These respondents specifically included language, symbols, and rituals from traditional, heterosexual wedding ceremonies as a way to stress how similar their ceremonies were to heterosexual weddings. As social worker Elizabeth Sullivan (1991) has noted, traditional wedding symbols have a historical significance; their use in a same-sex ceremony can provide that ceremony with meaning that "transcends the participants and includes the larger [heterosexual] community" (p. 19). Thus ceremonies can position lesbian and gay couples into a larger communitas or fellowship of married, heterosexual couples whose membership is based on their common experience of "getting married."

A number of respondents discussed that they wanted heterosexual women and men to understand that their ceremonies were analogous to having a heterosexual wedding. As Barbara Mercier commented:

> When we were planning our "commitment ceremony," there were two other women where I worked at the time that were engaged and

were getting married. One of them got married in September. A
woman that worked for me got married in October, the same fall.
They were all talking and flashing their diamonds around and
talking about this and that. It was like I was really conscious of
wanting to make sure that they understood that this was the same
thing. I talked about it at work. They gave me a little party. A
wedding shower.

Similarly, Maria Siggia commented that she and her partner had a
"commitment ceremony" in part to join the larger community of
married, heterosexual couples.

Lesbian relationships can be long term. Two women can make it
work. It doesn't have to be about changing partners every few
years. It doesn't have to exclude taking one's place in the larger
community as a couple, the larger heterosexual community as a
couple.

Although most respondents did not state explicitly that they wanted
to be a part of the larger heterosexual community, their ceremonies often
served to integrate them into it. According to Tom Douglass, his partner
John's employers not only understood what it meant to "get married"
but decided to provide health insurance to Tom as John's spouse after
their "wedding." As Tom recounted:

John's employers are wonderful, wonderful people. They not only
came to the wedding but they supplied the flowers. They decorated
our apartment with flowers from their own flower garden. They
understood the seriousness of our commitment to each other. . . .
They understand it is real. It is strong. It is life long. They are
obviously intelligent people. If they recognized in any way, shape, or
form that this was some kind of frivolous thing, they would not have
gone for it. So when their business was able to afford health insurance
for John, I was included in that because I am in this lifelong,
committed relationship. That's that whole thing about community
support for a newly formed family.

Indeed, the willingness of John's employers' to define Tom as John's "spouse" clearly was predicated on their understanding of Tom and John as a "married" couple who constituted a family.

Even lesbians and gay men who explicitly did not want to be a part of this larger communitas found that heterosexual friends classified them as "married" anyway. According to Beth Epstein:

> There were some of our heterosexual friends who wouldn't stop calling our "recommitment ceremony" a "wedding," especially these friends of ours who came from New York City. We were at their wedding. They were like "We have to come to your wedding." I said, "It is not a wedding." But they insisted, "Oh, come on, it's a wedding" because that's the only way they could see it.

As these accounts suggest, same-sex ceremonies, like heterosexual weddings, are rites of passage that integrate a couple into larger community networks and, in two primary ways, create a sense of communitas. Communitas can be generated out of the support generated for a couple's relationship by the people in their community and also by the recognition they may receive as a "married couple" from heterosexual friends and family members. Thus same-sex ceremonies not only create family but build community as well.

Reasons for Having a Ceremony in the Future

In addition to respondents who had or were planning a ceremony, thirty-three lesbians and gay men in the study stated they might have a same-sex ceremony sometime in the future. These respondents discussed a number of different reasons why they would consider having a ceremony. Only one lesbian, however, said that she would have a ceremony in order to help establish legal recognition for her relationship. According to Cathy Newman:

> I'm thinking about having one, and registering [the relationship] in New Haven and Springfield, because I'm really worried about this

two-state thing. My family lives in Connecticut, and when you cross state lines from Massachusetts to Connecticut it's harder to make decisions for somebody. I want a paper in both states that says we're a couple. If we do have a ceremony, I think I would like us to do something small, just to exchange rings or something and not have anyone else present. That would be just to establish legal connectedness.

For Cathy, having a ceremony was not important as a rite of passage but it could help establish her legal rights. The majority of respondents, however, had more personal reasons for considering having a ceremony.

Most thought that lesbian and gay relationships would benefit from more recognition and validation from family and friends. They believed that ceremonies were an important rite of passage for same-sex couples. For example, Deborah Lieberman stated she would consider having a ceremony if her partner came out to her relatives so they could be invited. As Deborah remarked:

> I have started to realize how important that some recognition or ritual is. Partially it's hearing people do it, and then also trying to do some rituals for myself. Like when my ex-partner and I were together, I think I started realizing how hard it was when we weren't being recognized. Like when we bought a house and moved in together, my mom gave us some presents. But it wasn't like when a straight couple gets married and they move into a house. . . . There wasn't more of a community sense of acceptance. I started realizing what a toll that took. That it is important to make public or formalize our relationships.

Deborah stated that she might have a ceremony in order to gain the public recognition and support given married heterosexual couples.

For Brian Davies, the reason to have a ceremony centered on the importance of ritual in strengthening a couple's dyadic bonds. He replied:

> My partner and I have talked about it but we have nothing planned. We just thought we might do something. . . . For some reason the

enactment of something strengthens the bond or the reality of whatever you are celebrating. It has a tremendously powerful effect to do that. Partly because it is witnessed by so many people. It helps you change into what you are going to be from what you used to be. In terms of the relationship with the other person and also just effective in your own personal terms. You're going to be something different.

Lori Morrison underscored the importance of having a "public" ritual. She said that she would not have a ceremony until she could be more open about her sexual identity to her family, friends, and coworkers: "I will not have a ceremony until I'm out a lot more than I am now. I think it would be a waste. Nobody would come. Ideally it would be nice to be out to everybody, have it be accepted, and then have a ceremony."

In addition, eleven respondents stated that they would consider having a ceremony if they were in a committed, long-term relationship. According to Mike Reilly:

We haven't gotten that far yet or talked about it. I would imagine that if we'd been in a relationship that long where the subject would come up then more than likely it would come to that. If the relationship were that long and we were seriously talking about it. Yes, we probably would.

Harold Zaleski also said that he might have a ceremony if he was in a serious relationship:

Being committed would mean being monogamous. In a marriage ceremony, you commit yourself in sickness and in health. . . . I think if I were to live with someone and have a monogamous, sexual relationship, I'd like to have a ceremony just for my friends and family. To show them I had made a commitment to be together.

Two lesbians and one gay man stated that they would consider having a celebration or ritual for their tenth or twelfth anniversaries. As Colleen Ivy remarked, "Probably at what we define as our tenth anniversary. We want to have a big party but we haven't really talked about what kind of ceremony yet." As Samuel Phillips also remarked, "We have talked about that as we approach our twelfth year this July, having some friends over and sharing food with them."

Overall, these respondents discussed two main reasons for why they might consider having a ceremony in the future. For some individuals, having a ceremony was a way to generate support and recognition for their relationships from family and friends. Others stated that a ceremony might strengthen their commitment to their relationship. Their motivations for having a ceremony were very similar to those articulated by respondents who had or were planning one.

Reasons for Not Having a Ceremony

Twenty-five out of the ninety lesbians and gay men interviewed insisted that they did not want to have a ceremony either now or in the future. These people articulated four reasons for their decisions. First, the majority stated that they did not need "public" validation for their relationships from family, friends, or state and religious authorities. Richard Hudson stated, "No, I don't think it is important to publicly validate my relationship with my partner." Similarly, Emily Atkinson commented:

> Personally, I'm not that into ceremonies. I see part of the reason for having that kind of ritual as bringing all the people who are important to you together to recognize your relationship. I feel that in terms of my friends, my friends recognize our relationship so I really wouldn't see a purpose for having some kind of ritual for them to recognize it. I also think your family is an important part of that. I just don't think most of my family or my partner's would come to something like that because they live so far away.

Second, a number of respondents strongly stated that they did not think that having a ritual would help keep a relationship together. According to Andrea Gorchov:

I think they can be just as dumb as those for heterosexual couples. . . . I'm not into it. To publicly say that you are committed for the future doesn't make a lot of sense to me. I guess if people want to do it, it's okay. I like to celebrate what I've done and not talk about what I am going to do. I know lots of couples that have broken up. They have these commitment ceremonies and then the next year they are dividing the silverware.

Ray Young articulated the same sentiment:

I'm not big on ceremonies to begin with. I question whether someone thinks this sort of symbolic action is going to make their relationship more long lasting or stable. My experience has been exactly the opposite. Personally, it doesn't mean shit. I come from a generation that has been thoroughly divorced! If this relationship is going to stay together, then any ceremony or symbolic action isn't going to have any impact on it at all. It's either going to continue to happen or it's not going to continue to happen.

Third, other lesbians and gay men discussed how being married previously in a heterosexual relationship and later divorced had affected their attitudes toward same-sex ceremonies. For Cheryl Foley, her experiences made her want to separate her finances as well as her sense of self from her partner. As she reflected:

Well, I'm still going through a messy divorce [from my ex-husband]. I don't think I would want to put myself through a "marriage or marriagelike ceremony" or to commit myself that way. . . . I guess it's sort of like what's mine is yours and yours is mine and I'm still in the process of disentangling myself from that kind of situation once already. I lost everything. I finally have my house back, but when I buy things now I say right to myself this is mine. I guess that's tacky but I've had to rebuild everything. I guess I want to keep myself more a separate entity for the time being anyway.

Finally, one gay man stated that he did not want to have a ceremony because he felt that lesbians and gay men should work to change the privileges associated with being married. According to Conrad Gardner:

> Maybe it's just my aversion to using the term "wedding." I like the idea of fighting for the same kind of privileges that people that are married have in this society. So I guess I am more interested in attaining those or figuring out ways that everyone, regardless if they are straight living in an unmarried situation or gay living in an unmarried situation, can have access to those same kind of privileges.

Clearly, the majority of these respondents believed that they did not need a rite of passage to mark or validate their commitments. They did not need anyone, including family, friends, or the legal system, to legitimize their relationships. Similar to those who had or might consider having a ceremony, however, these respondents' accounts did not stress overt political motivations. Instead, they focused on more individual and personal reasons.

Differences in the motivations lesbians and gay men articulated for having, considering, or rejecting same-sex ceremonies, however, raise an important issue. What social characteristics distinguish these three categories of respondents? The following two sections examine how these three groups varied by age and previous heterosexual marital status.

Age Differences

Although most respondents either had or would consider having a same-sex ceremony, attitudes varied by age and birth cohort. As mentioned in chapter 3, the phrase "birth cohort" refers to a group of individuals born during a similar time period. Forty-two percent of lesbians and gay men under the age of forty had or were planning a ceremony compared to only 29 percent of respondents age forty and over. (See table 4.1.) As discussed earlier in this chapter, the younger respondents may have more positive attitudes toward same-sex ceremonies because they belong to a

TABLE 4.1

HAD OR WOULD CONSIDER HAVING
A SAME-SEX CEREMONY (BY AGE)

	18-39 YEARS	40-89 YEARS	TOTAL
CEREMONY	%	%	%
Had	42	29	36
Consider	33	29	31
No	25	42	33
	N=48	N=42	N=90

birth cohort that came out during the era of the lesbian and gay rights movement.

Most of these lesbians and gay men viewed same-sex ceremonies as an important avenue for the recognition of gay relationships in the larger society as well as for gaining support from friends and family. In addition, individuals under forty may be more entrenched in the language and politics of gay rights than those over forty. Instead of seeking to alter mainstream institutions, such as marriage, the gay and lesbian rights movement of the 1980s and early 1990s focused on attaining equal rights for gays within these same institutions. In contrast, people who discovered their homosexuality prior to or during the 1970s may hold negative attitudes toward the institution of marriage because of their personal experiences as well as being in a birth cohort that was influenced by the lesbian feminist and gay liberation movements. As was discussed in chapter 1, both the lesbian feminist and the gay liberation movements of the 1970s advocated abolishing, not emulating, traditional marriage and family forms.

Previous Heterosexual Marital Status

In addition to age differences, respondents' attitudes about having or not having a same-sex ceremony varied by their previous heterosexual marital

TABLE 4.2

HAD OR WOULD CONSIDER HAVING
A SAME-SEX CEREMONY (BY PREVIOUS MARITAL STATUS)

	PREVIOUSLY IN HETEROSEXUAL MARRIAGE	NEVER MARRIED	TOTAL
CEREMONY	%	%	%
Had	19	41	36
Consider	18	37	31
No	53	22	33
	N=27	N=63	N=90

status. More respondents who had not been previously married than those who had been married had or planned to have a commitment ceremony. (See table 4.2.) Not surprisingly, individuals who have been married previously in heterosexual relationships were more adverse to using the same format in their same-sex relationships. Since most respondents who had been married previously were forty or older, their attitudes may have been influenced by both their personal experiences with the institution of marriage and their generational cohort. Today younger lesbians and gay men experience less pressure from family and friends to marry heterosexually than was true in the past (R. Berger, 1982). Indeed, many older respondents commented that their families expected them to marry and that there were few options in the 1950s, 1960s, and 1970s for carrying out long-term lesbian and gay relationships.

Conclusion

At their heart, same-sex ceremonies help to create family and community through socially recognized rites of passage. Ceremonies may be particularly important for lesbians and gay men because their relationships remain stigmatized in North American society. In contrast to heterosexual couples whose wedding ceremonies most often serve to integrate them into preexisting kinship and community networks, lesbian and gay couples may use commitment ceremonies to establish and create their own families and communities.

For approximately one-third of the respondents in this book, however, commitment ceremonies were a problematic mechanism for obtaining social integration. These lesbians and gay men did not think having a ceremony would generate more support or respect for their relationships. Instead, they discussed personal, and in a few cases political, motivations for why they did not want to have commitment ceremonies.

In contrast, most lesbians and gay men stated that they either had or would consider having a same-sex ceremony. Indeed, many felt that ceremonies provided a context in which to mark significant passages in their relationships. Anna Blumberg commented, "I feel rituals are important and that they have a real place in my life. While I haven't had many, I feel it's real important to mark passages." Thus, rituals help individuals identify their experiences in a meaningful manner (Roberts, 1988).

Although the thirty-two respondents who had or were planning a commitment ceremony did not mention many political motivations, later they discussed in more detail political and personal reasons for why they incorporated certain rituals and symbols into their ceremonies. The structure of each commitment ceremony varied. While some followed a more traditional "wedding" format, others incorporated rituals and symbols from many other traditions. The next two chapters further examine these respondents' personal and political motivations for naming and creating their commitment ceremonies.

CHAPTER FIVE

Going to the Chapel and I'm Going to Get _____?

Same-Sex Ceremonies and the Politics of Naming

We called ours a "commitment ceremony." We wrote the whole thing and wanted to make it our own. We were doing something new. It was different and new. I guess that is the best way to say it. We created it and we didn't want to use the old word. "Wedding" carries a lot of baggage.

—Patrick Flemming

"Commitment ceremony" sounds like you're checking into the local institution. It's too clinical. We used "wedding" as we were planning ours. The term embraced everything we wanted to include. I had some conversations with feminists who felt we shouldn't use the word "marriage" because it meant property and ownership and patriarchy and all that. But anyone who was at our ceremony would know it wasn't about all that. It meant union to us.

—Anna Blumberg

BY THE END OF THE 1980S, more and more lesbian and gay couples had begun to announce publicly to friends, family, and the larger society that they were having celebrations of commitment, union ceremonies, commitment ceremonies, and weddings. As sociologist Judith Stacey (1996) has noted, these couples can now "proudly announce their weddings and anniversaries, not only in the gay press, which now includes specialized magazines for gay and lesbian couples, like *Partners Magazine,* but even in such mainstream, Midwestern newspapers as the *Minneapolis Star Tribune*" (p. 118). These ceremonies were qualitatively different from those that had preceded them. Not only were they noticeable to all people outside a couple's intimate circle of friends and family, but often they were held in accepting churches, synagogues, or temples. Although it is not possible to quantify to the degree to which the number of lesbians and gay men having same-sex ceremonies has risen over the last two decades, the visibility of their unions has greatly increased.

In order to examine the reasons some couples have for taking this public step in their relationship, this and the following chapter examine the experiences of the thirty-two lesbians and gay men studied who had or were planning to have a ceremony. This chapter focuses on the language the respondents used to name their ceremonies. Unlike most heterosexual couples, who do not have to question use of the word "wedding," often lesbian and gay couples are concerned with the political implications of the words they choose. Thus respondents were asked what terms they used to refer to their ceremonies. Should they use traditional words, or create new terms to refer to their ceremonies? Does use of the term "wedding" constitute an act of resistance or accommodation? As was discussed in chapter 4, same-sex ceremonies are important rites of passage for lesbians and gay men who choose to have them.

Are Same-Sex Ceremonies Acts of Accommodation or Acts of Resistance?

During the last ten years, lesbian and gay scholars have debated whether same-sex ceremonies and the subsequent movement to legalize same-sex "marriages" act to help assimilate gay couples into the mainstream or to break down conventional meanings of marriage (Ettlebrick, 1989; Stoddard, 1989). Although analyzing same-sex ceremonies as rites of passage implies that they are inherently assimilationist, such ceremonies include both "strategies of accommodation" as well as "strategies of resistance." According to anthropologist Louise Lamphere (1987), strategies of accommodation are activities that help individuals endure oppressive experiences and situations in their daily lives. These strategies, however, often coexist with strategies of resistance that help undermine the coercive practices and institutions the individuals must adapt to.

In her work on immigrant women, Lamphere argues that women who work in the labor force are "active strategists" who utilize accommodative coping strategies in order to survive their specific work situations. In addition, women also use resistance strategies to undermine the authority of management and the control supervisors have over their lives. Thus women do not "passively" accept their working conditions but actively manage their work situations.

In a similar vein, anthropologist Ellen Lewin (1994) described the strategies of resistance and accommodation lesbians use to "manage" motherhood and their dual identities as lesbians and mothers. Lesbians who choose to be mothers face the opposing cultural beliefs that women "naturally" are good mothers and that homosexuality is "unnatural." Lesbians are categorized by default as "unfit" mothers. Motherhood, however, permits "lesbians to be more like other women" while at the same time it empowers them to refute "the equation of homosexuality with unnaturalness . . . allowing the lesbian mother to resist gendered constructions of sexuality" (E. Lewin, pp. 348-349).

In creating and having same-sex ceremonies, lesbians and gay men also actively participate in both reinforcing and subverting traditional ideals about gender, sexuality, and marriage. They may utilize accommodation strategies in order to gain the status and recognition accorded married, heterosexual couples. Simultaneously they may use resistance strategies that question the "abnormality" of homosexuality and the hegemony of traditional gender relations within marriage. Although some lesbians and gay men frame their ceremonies in the context of traditional marriage norms, others view their ceremonies as contesting these same values. Indeed, many do both. Since same-sex couples cannot marry legally, their motivations for altering the traditional wedding ceremony differ from those of heterosexual couples.

Same-Sex Ceremonies
as Acts of Accommodation

Although most of the lesbians and gay men in this study who had or were planning a commitment ceremony stated that they believed their ceremonies were about "creating something new," their personal expectations about being in a committed relationship often echoed more traditional norms. The act of having a commitment ceremony often reinforces traditional marriage norms in two primary ways. First, many same-sex couples uphold a number of conventional expectations about adult relationships. In particular, they endorse the assumptions that couples "should" both make a commitment to having a long-term relationship and be sexually monogamous. Like heterosexual weddings, same-sex ceremonies reinforce the ideology that marriage is the proper site for adult sexual relations. By focusing on commitment and monogamy, they invalidate other forms of sexual expression. As sociologist Emile Durkheim (1971) noted, rites of passage convey the "core values" of a society to ritual participants and observers. Like heterosexual weddings, same-sex ceremonies reinforce monogamy as a cultural ideal, if not always the practice of particular individuals.

Second, same-sex ceremonies are one strategy for claiming that being gay or lesbian is not all that different from being heterosexual. For some lesbians and gay men, having a ceremony may help them manage their "spoiled" identities (Goffman, 1963). According to sociologist Erving Goffman (1963), all stigmatized individuals struggle with integrating their self-perceptions as being "like" everyone else with society's judgment of them as "others." Same-sex ceremonies can help lesbians and gay men cope with this "other" categorization by stressing the similarities between gay and heterosexual relationships. Indeed, within gay communities, this strategy often is referred to derogatorily as "passing" or attempting to gain "heterosexual privilege." Whether a couple has a ceremony for this reason, same-sex ceremonies are one avenue for trying to become "insiders."

Same-Sex Ceremonies as Acts of Resistance

Although same-sex ceremonies can be interpreted as strategies of accommodation that situate lesbian and gay couples within mainstream heterosexual culture, paradoxically this accommodation is accomplished through strategies of resistance that challenge marriage norms. While same-sex ceremonies reinforce some values about marriage, they simultaneously subvert a number of other conventional ideologies. When two women or two men decide to celebrate their relationship, they are asserting that marriage does not necessarily entail one man and one woman. In addition, they do not assume that they "must" take on traditional male and female gender roles within their relationships or have children in order to be part of a "family."

As many feminist scholars have noted, resistance takes place on two levels (Abu-Lughod, 1990; E. Lewin, 1994). First, direct resistance can occur on the terrain of everyday life through actions that sabotage specific institutions. For example, lesbian and gay organizations, such as the Lambda Legal Defense and Education Fund, that want to legalize same-sex marriages are working to undermine the gendered basis of the institution of marriage. In the United States, state marriage laws explicitly assert or are interpreted to imply that marriage is an act that takes place between a woman and a man. By claiming the legal right to have a commitment or wedding ceremony, lesbians and gay men challenge the gender component of marriage as well as its underlying procreative function.

Second, resistance can take place on the level of consciousness. According to anthropologist Emily Martin (1987), in women's relation to the field of medicine "there are a great many ways that women express consciousness of their position and opposition to oppression" (p. 183). In her definition of resistance, Martin includes "refusing to accept a definition of oneself" and "refusing to act as requested or required" (p. 187).

In having a ceremony, lesbians and gay men participate in both of these types of conscious resistance. They refuse to accept the social construction of homosexuality as "abnormal" by claiming that the desire to marry is a "normal" aspiration for any two adults regardless of sexual identity. In addition, those who have ceremonies question the gendered basis of marriage. Two women or two men who "marry" subvert the belief that women and men take on separate but complementary roles within a marriage and overtly resist the notion that marriage functions to support specifically defined gender roles.

Recently anthropologists have begun to argue that rites of passage do not merely transmit the "core values" of a society, as Durkheim first suggested (Baumann, 1994). Rituals are spheres of "contradictory and contestable perspectives—participants having their own reasons, viewpoints, and motives, and in fact, [rituals] are made up as they go along."[1] Although participants and observers expect rituals to follow certain rules, they also have the ability to "reconstruct" rituals by changing the wording or performance of certain procedures. For example, heterosexual couples often decide on the precise wording and procedures for their wedding ceremonies and do not follow a "strict" ritual format. Over time, this process of reconstruction slowly alters the format of wedding rituals, resulting in a moderate form of cultural change.

In creating their ceremonies, however, lesbians and gay men shift the conventional meanings of the wedding ritual more overtly. They consciously seek to reformulate cultural values not only about marriage but about gender and homosexuality as well. As anthropologist Gerd Baumann (1994) notes, rituals may not only "speak to values basic to the culture. . . . They can speak as clearly and centrally to aspirations towards cultural change . . ." (p. 109). Same-sex ceremonies have a political dimension that is absent from heterosexual weddings. They challenge normative ideologies of both gender and homosexuality and "reconstruct" the very meaning of the wedding ritual, contributing to a more radical form of cultural change in marriage norms.

Analyses of same-sex ceremonies need to move beyond framing them in a simple dualistic fashion: as acts of assimilation or as acts of resistance. These ceremonies alter some cultural ideals while supporting other social norms at the same time. "Mixed" strategies of accommodation and resistance are commonly part of same-sex ceremonies. One respondent, David Gascon, remarked about the lesbian and gay ceremonies he had been to:

> To me a wedding is a sexual contract. The gay and lesbian commitment ceremonies I've seen have been sexual contracts, companionship contracts, but there also are political statements in them. They are more about, from my perspective, a commitment toward a person than an institution like marriage. Straight people are expected to be married, whereas the gay culture hasn't expected anybody to do anything. The commitment has more to do with taking control and creating our own world rather than fulfilling someone else's need for us to conform.

To examine this dualistic nature of same-sex ceremonies, the remainder of this chapter focuses on how the language used to name same-sex ceremonies both upholds and challenges traditional marriage norms. Like heterosexuals, lesbians and gay men make many choices in constructing their ceremonies. Unlike heterosexuals, however, they rarely choose only conventional customs.

Naming the Ceremony

According to authors Tess Ayers and Paul Brown (1994), one of the first steps in planning a ceremony is deciding what to call the event. There is little consensus, however, about what terms to use in naming same-sex ceremonies. Lesbians and gay men hold many divergent viewpoints and are even in conflict about this issue. While some are happy to use the term "wedding," others prefer less traditional phrases, such as "blessing ceremony," "joining," "holy union," or "commitment ceremony." A great deal of the controversy and debate revolves around language as a powerful symbol and political tool. Clearly, language is one avenue lesbians and gay men have for either accepting or contesting the social meanings of marriage. Sociologist Mark Steinberg (1994) recently noted that "language is the central vehicle through which meanings are produced and contested" (p. 512). Linguistic challenges to dominant belief systems are a form of resistance to oppression (Scott, 1990; and Steinberg, 1994). In the context of same-sex ceremonies, however, it is not so clear that struggles over language always represent resistance.

Although the lesbians and gay men in this study used a variety of different names to identify their ceremonies, they each had clear reasons for why they chose specific words. As discussed in chapter 4, for the purpose of analysis, same-sex ceremonies fell into two distinct categories: celebrations of relatively new commitments (between six months and four years) and celebrations of longer commitments (between ten and sixteen years). Most respondents who acknowledged a recent commitment selected phrases like "commitment ceremony" and "holy union" on their invitations. In comparison, other lesbians and gay men chose phrases that reflected their existing commitments, such as "recommitment ceremony" and "tenth-anniversary celebration." Regardless of the length of their relationship, however, most respondents did not use the term "wedding" to refer to their ceremonies on their invitations, nor did they verbally call their ceremonies weddings.

Why Not Use the Term "Wedding?"

The majority of lesbians and gay men who did not use "wedding" on their invitations gave six main reasons for not using the term. First, they stated that they wanted to differentiate their ceremonies from "traditional heterosexual weddings." Many respondents who celebrated newer commitments (less than five years) wanted to do something "distinctive." As Paula Hughes remarked: "My partner felt uncomfortable with calling it a wedding. I didn't care as much but we both wanted our ceremony to be different from a heterosexual wedding."

Many respondents used the phrase "commitment ceremony" to refer to their ceremonies.[2] This expression signaled that they were making a lifetime commitment. As Maria Siggia commented:

> We called our ceremony a "commitment ceremony" because that's what it was about for us. I suppose we didn't call it a "wedding" or "marriage ceremony" because we wanted to not feel like we were

copying the heterosexual model but more to feel that we were creating a ritual that was similar but separate from that. We wanted to distinguish it and at the same time make it clear that it was about commitment.

For many respondents the phrase "commitment ceremony" symbolized their inclusion in the ritual (but not the institution) of marriage.

Second, a few lesbians did not use the term "wedding" because they wanted to emphasize that they were celebrating existing commitments. They decided to combine observing anniversaries with some type of "formal" ritual or ceremony. According to Margaret Dubek:

We called ours a "tenth-anniversary celebration." On the invitations we said, "Celebrating ten years together." I was reluctant at the time to get into anything that either was too ceremonial or too mushy. But recently we were talking with friends and they said something about "your commitment ceremony." I said I guess it was. We were definitely aware when we were planning it that it wasn't going to be formal and that it was just going to be fun. But we did end up including things that were sweet and part of showing our commitment to other people.

The language these women used to identify their celebrations emphasized the length of their relationships. According to Esther Gould:

The wording in our invitation said something like "Come celebrate our Simcha [Hebrew for "happy event"], our joy, as we reaffirm our commitment to each other." The way we thought about it was that it would have to do with celebrating something that we had already created because we were really pissed off when people thought this was a new commitment.

For Beth Epstein, the term "wedding" also did not accurately describe what she and her partner wanted in a ceremony since they were not heterosexual and were already in a long-term relationship. As Beth commented:

I wanted our ceremony to be different. It was really clear that we were not a heterosexual couple getting married. We were doing something really different. I wanted that to be clear for myself and to everybody that came. We were very serious about what we called our ceremony, a "recommitment celebration," because we did it at twelve years.

All of these lesbians thought it was important to create their own names and rituals for their ceremonies. They wanted the name of the ceremony to reflect its meaning and significance. In particular, these ceremonies were not concerned with "making commitments." Instead, they were celebrations commemorating the duration of commitments that had been made many years before. For example, Melanie Obermeier and her partner decided to call their ceremony and tenth-anniversary celebration a "tryst." As Melanie recalled:

We called ours a "tryst." Tryst means trust [from the Old Norse *traust*]. It's got a lot to do with there being a trust between the two people and a commitment. We stole it from the book called *Ceremonies of the Heart* and the Zsuzzana Budapest book on women's rituals.[3]

When asked why they didn't call their celebration a wedding or commitment ceremony, Melanie replied:

We choose "tryst" instead of a wedding, which has connotations we didn't like and instead of "commitment ceremony," which seemed sort of redundant. We already had the commitment. We had already been together many years, and with "tryst" we tried to put a spiritual spin on the whole thing. That we were having a ritual thing. "Tryst" is much more ritualistic sounding than commitment ceremony. "Commitment ceremony" to me sounds like domestic partner. It sounds like domestic engineer, which is just a fancy name for a housewife.

Third, other lesbians and gay men stated that their desire to do "something different" stemmed from the "baggage" they felt was attached to heterosexual weddings. These restrictions included specific traditions, symbols, and expectations. According to Mike Finn, he and his partner, Gerald, called their ceremony an "exchange of vows" because the phrase highlighted their long-term commitment. As Mike stated:

> I like the commitment part of it 'cause it doesn't have the baggage that the word "wedding" does. I think it sets, not exactly limits, but at least sets parameters. There are so many traditions. I was a Catholic priest so I went to quite a few weddings. There are so many things that are expected by people at a ceremony that it's difficult to break out of it and still call it a wedding. I think it's almost better to dispense with that term and just call it something a little broader.

These lesbians and gay men discussed the specific customs they disliked, such as elaborate food, having an expensive reception, the giving of gifts, and throwing a garter belt or rice after the ceremony.

Some respondents also mentioned that the term "wedding" carried specific gender or religious constraints. As Martha Price noted, "The true definition of a wedding, you know, and the common concept is that it has to be between a man and a woman." Paula Hughes also commented, "'Wedding' simply brings to mind male and female, priests and religion—straight heterosexual weddings."

Fourth, some lesbians and gay men discussed their feelings of pain, grief, and anger over being excluded from the institution of marriage. Like Beth Epstein and Paula Hughes, Patrick Flemming replied that he and his partner, Joel, wanted to make their ceremony "their own." In addition, they did not use the term "wedding" because

> heterosexual society makes everyone feel like they have to get married or there is something wrong with them. I've watched all these straight people get all this positive regard and jubilation just for getting married and I knew I could never have that. It's so hurtful to gay people that it is hard to use the same word.

Some lesbians and gay men grew up with the goal of "getting married." According to Esther Gould, she first started to think about having a ceremony with her partner, Susan, at a time when all their heterosexual friends were getting married. Esther commented: "All of our straight couple friends got married. And it was incredibly painful to me. Everyone was so happy for them, everyone was giving them presents. And they were getting dresses. I was green in a way." Esther felt a great deal of anger and grief that she could not have a wedding, especially since it was one of her childhood dreams. She recounted:

> A therapist of mine, probably in 1983 or 1984, said to me, "You could have a wedding if you wanted. So and so did it." But I didn't really hear her then. At that point I was grieving about not having a wedding. . . . I think this had to do with my being a Southern girl and in some ways growing up and always wanting to have a wedding. Spending a lot of time as a child daydreaming with my mother about what my wedding would be like and what colors there would be and who would come.

Although Esther wanted to have a "wedding," she was extremely uncomfortable about using that term to describe her ceremony, and felt that doing so would weaken the legitimizing power of the ceremony. She wanted a word that would more aptly describe the life she and Susan had together. To Esther, using a different name would make the ceremony more authentic by showing that it was not "a pretend or quasi wedding."

Fifth, other lesbians and gay men based their decisions on how they believed heterosexuals and other gay people might react to the term "wedding." Kathleen O'Brien was worried more about what her friends might think of the language used to refer to the event than she was concerned about their reactions to the ceremony itself. She commented:

> If I am honest, I felt like what we were doing was sacred and I didn't want heterosexual people and our gay and lesbian friends to kind of snicker at the term. . . . I had a lot of fears of it being somehow made less of because of people's lack of support for it. Surprisingly, everyone was very supportive. But if we had called it a "wedding," I can pick out people who would have had a hard time with it.

Many respondents were aware of the debate over using the term "wedding" within the lesbian and gay communities. In a few cases, even partners did not totally agree with one another about this issue. Kathleen O'Brien and her partner, Valerie, had a ceremony four years after their relationship began. They officially decided to use the phrase "We invite you to join us in the union of our hearts and minds" on their invitations, which they based on an invitation quoted in the book *Ceremonies of the Heart*. According to Kathleen, however, Valerie was more comfortable than she was in referring to their ceremony as a wedding.

> We would refer to it, when talking to people or inviting people, as our "commitment ceremony." Interestingly, actually, Valerie would call it a "wedding." She would go back and forth, but she would use the term and I would not. I don't think that she has a whole lot of room for certain kinds of political opinions when she was just kind of going with the whole romantic idea of what was happening. I think things through too much.

Finally, a few respondents commented that they might have used the term "wedding" but the church or synagogue that sanctioned their ceremony had designated a specific name for same-sex unions. For example, the Metropolitan Community Church officially uses the phrase "holy union," and the Unitarian Universalist Church employs "services of union" and "holy union." After asking him why he and his partner Lenny referred to their ceremony as a "holy union," Randall Harris remarked:

> There were no personal reasons for not calling it a wedding. We called the ceremony a "holy union" because that is what the MCC called it. . . . I suppose at the time we referred to it as a "wedding." But ours was officially a "holy union." That is what they had on the certificate.

Overall, the reasons lesbians and gay men discussed for not using the word "wedding" stemmed from political convictions, early experiences, and religious beliefs. For many respondents, the word "wedding" either symbolized an oppressive institution or did not describe a union of two men or two women. In general, lesbians and gay men who did not use the term stressed how their relationships and ceremonies were "different" from heterosexual marriages. Many emphasized how language could be used as a form of resistance to traditional connotations of "marriage." Thus they believed it was important to develop a new language for naming same-sex ceremonies.

Why Call Same-Sex Ceremonies Weddings?

Although most of the lesbians and gay men in this study did not refer to their ceremonies as "weddings," some did speak of the power of using the term. Although he and his partner used the phrase "commitment ceremony," Patrick Flemming understood why other gay couples might make a different choice.

> The terms "wedding," "husband," and "wife" are so loaded that some people want to make new words, new names for things. I understand that. That's what Joel and I did. But there is power in using the old word and taking it over and saying it is ours too. I am getting "married." This is my "wedding."

Only two respondents called their ceremonies weddings on their invitations (although an additional four stated they were planning to have "weddings" in the next year). The two lesbians and the gay man who used the word "wedding" thought it described and conveyed the seriousness of their commitment. According to Tom Douglass, he and his partner, John, referred to their ceremony as a "wedding" because:

> the term "wedding" had a completeness to it. We weren't just two people getting together to live together for a while in an apartment. We understood that we were creating not only family but a home. The term "wedding" seemed to be the most accurate to describe what we were doing.

Tom thought that the phrase "commitment ceremony" just did not mean the same thing as "wedding."

It would not have had the same meaning to the two of us. I also believe that other people would have had a different perspective on what we were doing as well. We wanted everybody to understand specifically and exactly what we were thinking and what we were doing. We wanted to have a traditional ceremony so that other people could know how to operate within that.

For Tom, the term "wedding" was linked to both images and meanings that friends and family members could understand immediately. It was a word that did not need to be explained.

Similarly, Anna Blumberg and her partner, Carol, called their ceremony a "wedding" because they wanted their friends and family to understand that this partnership was important and different from previous relationships. As Anna explained:

> In our community people date. They move in together. They break up. They move out. It happens over and over. It felt really important for us to be able to say in a public way that this was different. Yes, we're dating, we're lovers, we're moving in together, but after that there is another whole level that is quantitatively different from anything that has gone on before for us. We wanted to celebrate that, not to just announce it, but really celebrate that with the people that were important to our lives.

While neither Tom nor Anna explicitly stated they used the term "wedding" for political reasons, they both believed it was important to take a positive stand in support of gay relationships. Rather than rejecting the word as being exclusively "heterosexual," both respondents wanted to claim its meaning for gay and lesbian couples. When I asked Anna if she and Carol had any political reasons for calling their ceremony a "wedding," she replied:

> I suppose so. If my primary relationship was with a man, I would not have gotten married. Because marriage is an option that is not open to me, I felt extra strongly that I really needed to do this because there

is no other way for people in my life to know that this is the kind of relationship that we have.

For Tom and John, the words "wedding," "marriage," and "husband" were a way to communicate to other people that their relationship was just as valid as a heterosexual marriage. As Tom stated:

> Since our "wedding," people understand that we are married. We call each other husband. Sometimes people have to have that explained. "Oh, if you call him the husband, are you the wife?" I explain, "No, this is a gay relationship. There is no woman, therefore there is no wife. There are two husbands." And that's been since '84, so we are coming up on our ninth anniversary.

By claiming the term "wedding," these two couples attempted both to gain the support of their family and friends and to confirm that gay couples have similar feelings and motivations for making lifetime commitments as heterosexual couples. While their reasons for having a ceremony were similar to respondents who had commitment ceremonies and holy unions, Tom and Anna wanted to make a different political statement by transforming the meaning of the term "wedding."

Use of the Term "Wedding" in Private Situations

Although Tom and Anna were the only respondents in this study officially to call their ceremonies a wedding, thirteen lesbians and gay men who celebrated recent commitments (less than five years) did use the term when talking more "privately" about their commitment ceremonies and holy unions. These respondents used the word "wedding" in more selective and personal circumstances, that fell into two categories: as a way to convey the meaning of their ceremonies to individuals who did not attend the ceremony and when talking with their partners, friends, or family who did attend the ceremony.

Some used "wedding" casually because they felt people could understand what the term meant. Like Tom and Anna, these respondents wanted to tap into people's unconscious "cognitive maps" about marriage.

"Cognitive maps" are shared cultural beliefs, symbols, and values. For example, Barbara Mercier first started dating her partner, Meriman, in the spring of 1991. After seeing one another for about six months, they decided to plan a "commitment ceremony" for the following summer. Although her partner did not like the word "wedding," Barbara used it when talking with heterosexual friends and colleagues.

> Meriman had a problem with the word "wedding." She didn't like calling it a "wedding." But I didn't really care what it was called. Actually, I would tend to call it a "commitment ceremony" with gay people, but I would call it a "wedding" when I was talking to straight people because I wanted them to understand that's what it meant to me. That this was like a wedding, how they would understand a wedding.

When asked why she didn't use the term "wedding" with gay people, Barbara replied, "I don't know. I guess because I haven't heard it used that much by gay people."

Clearly, many respondents were aware of the different opinions lesbians and gay men hold about using the terms "wedding" and "marriage" to refer to same-sex ceremonies. In order not to offend their lesbian and gay friends, some couples consciously choose not to use the term "wedding" on their invitations. For example, as Paula Hughes explained: "On the invitation we said it was a 'commitment ceremony,' but we also tell people we got married." Paula and Jenny had their ceremony a year and a half after becoming lovers. When asked why they decided against just saying "come to our wedding," Paula clarified:

> When we were doing the invitations, we were sitting at a table with other friends there. We were getting their input on it too, how exactly to phrase it and what to write. We agreed on calling it a "commitment ceremony." We did talk about it. Because we were sending invitations mostly to gay and lesbian and bisexual people, that's what we decided to call it.

While some respondents knew that other lesbians and gay men did not approve of these terms, they used "wedding" or "marriage" in more private circumstances in part because they symbolized a lifetime commitment.

Although most people expressed ambivalence about the word, some
respondents felt using "wedding" was a way to express the emotion and
feeling of their ceremonies with their partners, friends, and family. In
certain situations, they wanted to capitalize on the symbolic meaning of
the word. Their hesitancy to use the term with other gay men and
lesbians and at times heterosexuals, however, stemmed from their fears
of being ridiculed and their political concerns about adopting the term.

Conclusion

Paradoxically, for heterosexual as well as gay couples, rituals such as
wedding ceremonies both uphold dominant value systems and elicit
social change (Geertz, 1973). As the anthropologist Robbie Davis-Floyd
(1992) has noted, "entrenched belief and value systems are most
effectively altered through alterations in the rituals that enact them" (p.
17). Clearly, language is one avenue lesbians and gay men use to
transform the social meanings of the terms "wedding" and "marriage."

Indeed, this chapter points out that the language chosen to identify
a ceremony often reflects the participants' political goals. Lesbian and
gay couples who construct distinctive names for their ceremonies often
want to emphasize how they are "different" from heterosexual couples.
Many who adopt this strategy want to alter the structure of marriage
itself by changing its terminology. By using new terms, they can
highlight their "differences" from heterosexuals while claiming an equal
right to affirm their relationships. In contrast, lesbians and gay men who
choose to call their ceremonies "weddings" generally prefer to stress their
"similarities" to heterosexuals. This approach is based on the assumption
that collective use of the term "wedding" will support the legitimacy of
lesbian and gay relationships. These respondents believe they can
transform the social meanings of "marriage" by changing its definition.

Both the rejection and the acceptance of the term "wedding,"
however, have the potential to further the affirmation of lesbian and gay
identity, relationships, and civil rights. The language employed to

identify same-sex ceremonies can transform the social meanings of those terms. Yet the language and the ceremonies themselves will not revolutionize the way legal and economic rights are allocated to heterosexual couples and not to homosexual ones. Although having a "wedding," "commitment ceremony," or "anniversary celebration" will not change how legal rights are allocated, it can further the integration of lesbians and gay men into the institution of marriage.

Language, however, is only one avenue lesbians and gay have for either claiming inclusion in or rejecting the institution of marriage. In planning their actual ceremonies, the respondents in this study also considered how they personally and politically thought about the wedding ritual itself. Chapter 6 focuses on the specific rituals included in their ceremonies and examines how some elements that "fit" from heterosexual weddings are incorporated into ceremonies while other elements are rejected.

CHAPTER SIX

Church Bells
May Ring

Same-Sex Ceremonies
as Acts of Accommodation
and Resistance

I honestly don't remember who first suggested it. Well, actually
we talked about getting engaged first. We looked for rings, that
kind of thing. We thought it would be awhile before we got
married, and then we just got all excited about it. Next, we
talked with our friends about it, not "Do you think we should
get married?" but "When should we get married?"

—Paula Hughes

John was the one who asked me, "Will you marry me?" We
both knew that the term "marry" meant a lifetime commitment. So when I said, "Yes," that was when we decided okay, we
are not only going to feel married, we are going to *get* married.

—Tom Douglass

AS DISCUSSED IN CHAPTERS 4 AND 5, same-sex ceremonies can
include both acts of accommodation and acts of resistance. In planning
their rituals, lesbians and gay men borrow from traditional wedding

ceremonies, add their own rituals, and at times totally create their own types of services. Regardless of how they are structured, most same-sex ceremonies emphasize rituals of integration. In addition, like heterosexual weddings, they often include rituals of separation and transition.

According to anthropologist Victor Turner (1974), rituals of separation include behaviors that detach an individual from their established place in society. In traditional Western marriage rites, rituals of separation disconnect individuals from their previous position as single and sexually available. For example, getting engaged is one ritual that separates a couple from their old "single" status and marks the beginning of their new transitional status before "marriage." In comparison, rituals of transition are periods in which the "state of the ritual subject becomes ambiguous, neither here nor there, betwixt and between all fixed points of classification" (p. 232). While the act of getting engaged is a rite of separation, the betrothal period marks the couple's transitional status.

Rituals of Separation and Transition in Same-Sex Ceremonies

For lesbian and gay couples, rituals of separation and transition work in a similar fashion. Their purpose is to indicate the end of one relationship status and to signify the beginning of the passage to the next stage. As Riccardo Hernandez commented during his interview as he showed off his engagement ring, "Our engagement rings mean union. Together. We are together. I'm yours. You're mine. And if somebody looks at him, it means he's taken!"

All respondents who had a ceremony participated in some type of separation ritual prior to the actual event. For most couples, this ritual was fairly informal and entailed discussing whether to have a ceremony. According to Esther Gould, she and her partner discussed having a ceremony.

I think it was more like something we thought out loud about together. I'm not sure that one of us really suggested it. I think we took turns being more and less interested, more and less willing. But it was something that we both entertained.

Similarly, Patrick Flemming recalled:

> We both decided to have our ceremony. I don't remember that well why we decided to have it. We have friends, a lesbian couple, and they were having one. I think that got us thinking. Also we have straight friends who had been living together for ten years and they finally got married.

Most lesbians and gay men did not use the phrase "being engaged" for one main reason: They thought the phrase was inappropriate because they already lived with their partners and had made a commitment to their relationships. In general, they did not feel it was necessary to have a separate period of "engagement" to set them apart from couples who were merely dating. This separation had occurred when they decided to live together.

Getting Engaged

A small minority of respondents either proposed to their partners or were proposed to. The majority of these gay men and lesbians did not live with their partners when they decided to have a ceremony. Most, although not all, used the term "engaged" when talking about this time. For example, Lynn Ettleman got engaged to her partner after they had been dating for six months. As Lynn commented, they lived apart because they were "only engaged, after all!" "When I asked her to marry me, it just kind of came out and I was a little shocked that I asked her although my friends say to me, 'You've always been the marrying kind.' They've been telling me that for years." Randall Harris's partner, Lenny, also proposed to him when "they hadn't even been together yet for a year." As Randall laughingly recalled:

> I was a little surprised when he asked me to marry him. I was going to the Metropolitan Community Church and I felt he was probably

going to MCC because I was going. One day when I was in his kitchen and washing dishes he said, "Will you marry me?" I said, "What?" [Laughter] He just wanted me to do the dishes for him!

For lesbians and gay men who "got engaged," the words took on two different meanings. Being engaged had fairly traditional connotations for some. It symbolized their commitment and indicated to others the seriousness of their relationship. Chris Avery recalled when his partner first proposed to him.

> We were just sitting by Emerald Brook. He said, "Well, I think sometime I would really like to get married to you." I said, "Is this a proposal?" He thought about it and said, "Yes." So I said, "Yes, absolutely, I want to do the same." So that's how it happened.

When asked to elaborate on what it meant to be engaged, Chris replied that it marked a more serious level of commitment.

> The first thing that comes to mind is that it is an additional level of commitment, although we were committed before. It's a step toward being married, which to me is an even more public statement of our relationship. I guess it feels even tighter and more solid.

Getting engaged originated out of their spiritual convictions for many gay men. In fact, all of those who went through a "formal" type of proposal held strong religious or spiritual beliefs. Even if they were not currently active in a church or synagogue, most of these men commented on the importance of getting married with "God's blessing." According to Ben Fletcher, he first suggested having a ceremony to his partner, Greg, about a year after they met.

> I first mentioned having a ceremony to Greg. And he said that is exactly what he'd like to do too. I remember saying to him that I think we ought to do this right. To have a ceremony, do it before God. And once those words came out of my mouth, it was so right. . . . Greg later said it was like Judy Garland and Mickey Rooney!

In addition, a few gay men believed it was important to follow a traditional route to marriage even though they had been living together for some time. For James LaFleur and his partner, Jack, it was important that "God bless their union" even though they had lived together for over ten years. Although James first asked Jack to marry him, Jack responded by formally asking James's mother for his hand in marriage. As James recalled:

> He made my mother very happy. She was very happy. Matter of fact, Jack did the old tradition. He got on his knees and asked my mother for my hand. Actually, he asked both my sister and my mother. I really thought my sister wouldn't accept. But they love him, they adore him. My mother said, "Yes, I would like it." She told him that he didn't even have to ask because she adored him from the start. He could do no wrong in her eyes.

For other respondents, saying "I'm engaged" had more mixed connotations. They used the term "engaged" as a way to both appropriate and resist the symbolism and meanings of marriage. For example, although Chris Avery stated being engaged symbolized making a deeper commitment to his partner, he also believed engagement and marriage had political as well as personal implications.

> I think it is both personal and political. I feel like in our society sexuality is a political issue. Because people are given or denied rights based on their sexuality, it becomes a political issue. So I feel like it's personal, because dammit, I want to be treated just like any couple, and it's also political.

In general, lesbians were more likely than gay men to talk about how the term "engaged" carried both old-fashioned and new meanings. For Lynn Ettleman, getting engaged symbolized that she was making a lifetime commitment to her partner.

> It used to be, and I don't know in your experience, but in my experience, lesbians would get together and everyone would sit and

wait and say, "When are they going to break up?" And the reaction to using the word "engaged" was that people expect this is going to last your lifetime. I think having that intention put out from the people around you is really wonderful.

Lynn also believed that as a lesbian, she could alter the meaning of the word "engaged." When asked why she used that term and not some other word, Lynn replied, "There's a place in my heart that is touched by using the words that I grew up with, even though I am changing their context."

According to Lynn, using the term "engaged" was one way to undermine the assumption that two women or men can't "get married." For example, she discussed how her engagement changed the beliefs a friend's daughter held about marriage.

> Like a friend of mine's sixteen-year-old daughter. My friend found this book called *The Complete Jewish Wedding Planner*, and she gave it to me just as a joke. And my friend Susan said, "This is for Lynn." And her daughter said, "Lynn is not getting married." So Susan explained it. And her daughter said, "You are always changing the rules on me." That's what I think the difference is. We can use these words but we figure out what they mean for us.

To Lynn, being a lesbian automatically meant that she had to question the traditional meanings behind the words "engagement" and "marriage." While she believed that heterosexual couples did not have to question the traditional assumptions that go with getting married, lesbians were "forced to question everything."

Lesbians also were more likely than gay men to question the financial arrangements in a "marriage." As women, they articulated more awareness of not wanting to be or not having the economic means to be dependent on a spouse. For heterosexuals, in daily practice and in the law, marriage remains very much an economic institution, in which financial elements often are hidden or mystified by terms of love (Gerstel and Gross, 1989). For lesbians, however, these economic factors often are more explicit from the start. For example, Celeste Davis discussed how she and her partner, Grace, worked together on supporting their family financially and did not assume one partner would take financial care of the other.

> Since our marriage is not legal and our ceremony was called a holy union, I think in some way it has made us more consciously aware or more careful to look at the ways heterosexual couples are married. That they make all kinds of assumptions about things, that we don't get to do. Like, during the ceremony, I wanted to put on the table the mutual funds we were buying together. It made me realize the length that we had to go to make this thing possible! To do it together!

Although many lesbians and gay men use traditional words, such as "being engaged," to separate themselves from other "available" gay men and lesbians, both Lynn's and Celeste's comments suggest that these words have multiple meanings. For some lesbians and gay men, "being engaged" served as a fairly traditional marker of separation. For others, "getting engaged" also challenged the traditional assumption that marriage signifies the financial dependence of one partner on another. Thus the act of "getting engaged" can be a strategy that simultaneously supports and resists marriage norms.

Bachelor Parties

None of the lesbians and gay men in this study had a "traditional" bachelor party. Historically, bachelor parties have symbolized the last opportunity a man has to be "free" and "single" before getting married and "tied" to his wife. Indeed, bachelor parties primarily function to reinforce traditional masculine and feminine gender roles within heterosexual relationships. Given their heterosexist as well as sexist implications, it is not surprising that most lesbians and gay men did not have them.

One gay man, however, did go to a strip club after his "bridal party." In contrast to the custom of going out with one's male friends, James LaFleur celebrated with his girlfriends. As he laughingly recounted:

> I had a bridal party. My partner and his friend went out and had cigars. But after the party, my girlfriends took me to a strip joint. Oh,

> I had a lot of my friends there. They are all women. It was strictly all
> women plus my mother. They said, "Where do you want to go?" And
> I said, "Oh, I think I'll go see a male stripper."

When James discussed what happened, he replied:

> So that's where they took me and they hired this guy who was big and
> masculine who was dressed up as a cop to handcuff me, which he did.
> He came over and he was talking to me, ya know, "You're under
> arrest" type of thing. Then they got me up on the stage and the next
> thing I know he's got me handcuffed with my arms around him. . . .
> But I got back at them. I paid him to get my girlfriend who rigged it
> up and he handcuffed her to a pole and she literally pissed in her
> pants. She did. Really. She wet that floor. We had a good time.

Since James had been living with his partner for ten years, going to the
strip club with his girlfriends was more of a fun night out on the town
than a symbol of his impending loss of freedom. By using this symbol,
he not only replicated a tradition but transformed and even mocked it.

Rites of Integration

As suggested in chapter 4, lesbians and gay men often seek social
integration in their same-sex ceremonies. Rites of integration serve to
incorporate an individual or couple back into their community, clan, or
family (V. Turner, 1974; van Gennep, 1960). In marriage ceremonies,
incorporation rites consist of collective rituals that join the couple into
their new family or community group and union rituals that unite the
couple. Collective rituals include bridal showers and aspects of the
ceremony itself that focus on connecting the couple and their community. In contrast, union rituals focus specifically on strengthening the
couple's bond of commitment.

Although weddings can be civil or religious ceremonies in the
United States, most weddings are still sanctified by a religious authority
(Whyte, 1990). Regardless of what religious authority blesses the

marriage, similar practices occur in most "traditional" wedding ceremonies. According to psychologist F. Philip Rice (1993), typically:

> Four parties are represented in the service: the couple, the religious group (clergy), the state (witnesses), and the parents (usually the father). Each party to the marriage rite covenants with the other parties in fulfilling his or her obligations so that the marriage will be blessed "according to the ordinances of God and the laws of the state." The denomination, through the clergy, pledges God's grace, love and blessing. The man and the woman make vows to each other "in the presence of God and these witnesses." The state grants the marriage license once the laws have been fulfilled (the witnesses are present to see that the law is obeyed.) The parents (through the father) pledge to give up their daughter to her new husband, no longer coming between the bride and the groom. After giving the bride away, the father sits down beside his wife, leaving the couple standing together. (p. 208)

As the following accounts suggest, many lesbians and gay men wish both to co-opt and to resist this image of the traditional wedding ceremony.

Wedding/Bridal Showers

Historically, bridal showers have been rituals that help transfer commodities to a couple and integrate the bride into her new family role as a wife. In Western societies, bridal showers typically are planned by either the bridesmaid or female relatives of the bride. Traditional shower gifts, such as household appliances, sheets, and towels, clearly signify the expected gender roles of the married couple. Although today many heterosexual couples have joint "wedding showers," this gift-giving ritual remains centered on helping the couple set up their new household.

The majority of respondents who had a ceremony, however, did not have showers given for them. Only two lesbians and one gay man had coworkers or friends who gave them wedding showers. These friends and coworkers clearly understood that the couples were getting "married." For example, Celeste Davis's coworkers "naturally" assumed they should give her a wedding shower since she was having a "commitment ceremony." As Celeste recalled:

> There were a lot of things I never thought about before that were a big deal. Like the matter of my job. Everybody at my job came and they gave me a shower. It was incredible. It's not like these women were my best friends or anything. They just assumed you'd have a shower if you were getting married.

Celeste also described how her shower and ceremony dramatically changed her relationships with her straight coworkers.

> Even ones that knew that I was a dyke relate to me differently now. They say different things. They ask about Grace, plans in my life, more concern about my life, how things are going. It has a greater importance now than before. Part of what I think marriage does it places you in the context of family and relationships. I think that they saw me as being sort of this thing out here. Yes, I have children, but seeing my family and seeing me in the context of a broader community was very different.

By giving her a shower, Celeste's coworkers could categorize her and her partner, Grace, as "married" and therefore more "like" themselves. They could understand their relationship because they were "getting married." Celeste's shower clearly helped integrate her into her work community. As this experience suggests, lesbians and gay men can appropriate aspects of the wedding shower tradition without totally accepting its gendered principles.

Ceremony/Ritual Format

Given the gendered structure of traditional wedding ceremonies, it is not surprising that lesbians and gay men would struggle with how much of the customary wedding format they would want to include in their own ceremonies. While some were adamant about making their ceremonies as "traditional" as possible, most were determined to make their ceremonies unique. Similarly, many heterosexual couples alter the typical wedding format to fit their own needs. Today, it is not unusual for heterosexual couples to forgo having a conventional, religious wedding. Lesbians and gay men, however, often have political as well as personal reasons for altering the wedding ritual. Usually heterosexual couples do not use their weddings to make political statements about gender inequality or gay rights.

Only a few lesbians and gay men had fairly traditional, Christian ceremonies. For example, Randall Harris and his partner, Lenny, "had prayers, readings, hymns, songs, vows, blessings, exchange of rings, and communion" as part of their "holy union" ceremony. Similarly, Ben Fletcher and his partner, Greg, included religious readings and prayers in their ceremony. According to Ben, he and Greg had "a group prayer, scripture readings, a meditation, a short homily, vows, blessings, and the exchanging of the rings."

Most lesbians and gay men incorporated a mixture of "traditional" and "nontraditional" wedding practices into their ceremonies. In planning the format for their ceremonies, many altered the conventional wedding ritual to fit same-sex relationships. In particular, many changed the gendered aspects of certain Christian and Jewish rituals. For example, Tom Douglass and his partner, John, had a "customized version of the so-called traditional ceremony," changed to fit a gay relationship. As Tom recalled:

> As we began to plan what we were going to do, we both began to realize that some of the things from a traditional wedding ceremonial rite wouldn't work. For example, we knew best man and maid of honor wasn't going to work. So what we decided to do was to choose a best friend to stand up with us.

In planning the format of their ceremonies, many lesbians and gay men utilized both strategies of accommodation and resistance. For example, Beth Epstein discussed how she had to change the language of the Hebrew prayers in her "recommitment ceremony" to fit a lesbian relationship.

A friend did some blessings in Hebrew, and we blessed the candles. I had my Grandma Ruth's candlesticks that she gave me. I used those. We said a blessing for that. We blessed the challah and then we passed around several breads and everybody tore a piece off and ate some. We also blessed the wine. I also rewrote the prayers. Because I speak Hebrew somewhat, I changed the Hebrew language from the masculine to the feminine.

Similarly, Esther Gould and her partner decided to use a set of feminist blessings in their "tenth-anniversary ceremony." As Esther recalled:

We had beautiful blessings that had been written by a feminist, an incredible writer in the Jewish liturgical tradition. She sort of reconceptualized the Hebrew blessings and had rewritten them. So we had very beautiful blessings, not the traditional, patriarchal blessings. And we had everybody have a little card with these blessings on them because even Jews wouldn't necessarily know this form of the blessing and people made the blessings with us.

Beth and Esther also changed other gendered aspects of the traditional Jewish wedding ceremony. In their interviews, they both discussed the meaning of breaking a glass at the end of a Jewish wedding. Beth and her partner, Gina, "broke a glass . . . except usually the man breaks the glass, and we broke it together." As Beth explained, the breaking of the glass "symbolizes a few different things."

One is that even in the midst of our joy, supposedly we need to remember the destruction of the Temple which happened some years ago, and all the oppression and stuff. So that's that breaking is that taking away from the joy a little bit. The other interpretation I've heard is that it signifies a break with what's come before. We are going to just break and move on to some new place.

Esther Gould and her partner, Susan, decided not to break a glass at the end of their ceremony because they associated the ritual with male power. As Esther explained:

We didn't break a glass. I don't like that ritual. I think it's just so associated with male power. I know that the meanings have to do with remembering the destruction of the Temple and the moment of joy and also have to do with monogamy. It really bugged me and also I just don't like the idea of destructiveness. We picked up the glass and blessed the wine that remained in it, and we put it down gently. It was what we did instead of breaking it.

In addition to changing the gendered aspects of the wedding ritual, many lesbians and gay men added personal symbols from their relationships to their ceremonies. For example, Barbara Mercier and her partner, Meriman, used many traditional wedding practices in their "commitment ceremony."

> Some of the specifics of what we did were kind of more like a traditional wedding. I mean, some weren't at all, but some things were more like a traditional wedding. I wanted it to be that way, because those other folks get to do this so I want to be able to. We had little matchbooks. Rings, matchbooks. We also had a traditional wedding cake.

Barbara further explained, however, that they altered some things in order to give them a more personal meaning. Instead of having two women on their cake, Barbara and Meriman chose to have a moose and a cow on top. Barbara said, "Do you know Fred Small's music, the song about the moose and the cow? We had a moose and a cow on the top of our wedding cake. Other than that it looked exactly like a regular wedding cake." Small's song immortalized the newspaper story about a moose that fell "in love" with a cow one summer in Vermont. For Barbara and Meriman, these animals represented "enduring love," love that remains despite all the obstacles that get in its way.

As a way to personalize their ceremony, Tom Douglass and John followed the tradition of including something old, something new, something borrowed, something blue.[1] As Tom explained:

> We included something old, something new, something borrowed, something blue in the ceremony. John's sister brought along their

mother's wedding ring. Their mother died when John was about thirteen. So his sister had their mother's wedding ring. It didn't fit anywhere except past the first knuckle on his baby finger, but during the ceremony she brought it so that he could wear that. My best friend brought along a pendant, which is a favorite of his, so I wore that and it's visible in some of the photographs. So there was, I forget now exactly what was new, but we had some old things and some new things. So that whole saying, old, new, borrowed, and blue.

In addition to these personal mementos, Tom and John added symbols from gay culture to their ceremony. When asked what was blue in the ceremony, Tom replied:

> The blue were Levi's. They were not only the blue, but the 501s were traditionally, up until that point anyway, a symbol of the gay men's community. So we wore 501s. We had morning coats, tuxedo shirts with bow ties, boutonnieres, 501s. The upper part being the traditional wedding kind of thing. The 501s being the gay part of the thing.

A number of other couples also included symbols, readings, and music from lesbian and gay culture. For example, Maria Siggia and her partner, Linda, each read a poem by the lesbian poet Adrienne Rich in their "commitment ceremony." Patrick Flemming and his partner, Joel, included a number of songs written by or sung by gay men or lesbians. As Patrick recalled, their music included:

> a song Joel and I sang together sung by the St. Vincent's Gay Men's Chorus, which was written by Rogers and Hammerstein, called "We Kiss in the Shadow." We sang that together. Joel taught me how to do it. So that was fun. . . . Later one of our friends, I can't remember whether she played the music or she sang it, but she did a song by Holly Near called "Simply Love." Also, two friends of ours, a lesbian couple who had just had their commitment ceremony, one played the guitar and the other one sang "Darling I'm Glad That You Are Gay," by Betsy Rose.

All couples who had a commitment ritual incorporated symbols or traditions with personal meaning into their ceremonies.

A few lesbians also drew on wedding traditions outside of their own "religious" backgrounds in planning their ceremonies. For instance, five had a period of sharing in their ceremonies similar to what Quakers use in their marriage services. Although Beth Epstein and her partner had many Jewish traditions in their "recommitment ceremony," they also included a time for people at the ceremony to talk about the meaning of commitment. According to Beth:

> We had a section during the ceremony where we opened up a Quaker thing to just have people talk about commitment. We just asked people to speak about commitment to themselves, to each other, and to the community and to the world. What does commitment really mean? It was really lovely. I can barely remember what anybody said. It was all so touching. I was in tears from what each person said.

Similarly, Kathleen O'Brien and her partner, Valerie, included a time for people to speak during their "commitment ceremony": "There was also an opportunity for people who had come to share any feelings or wishes or anything they had. About six or seven people spoke, including both our mothers."

Borrowing from a Spanish wedding tradition, Barbara Mercier and her partner, Meriman, exchanged Mexican coins as part of their "commitment ceremony." The exchange of coins represented their financial commitment to one another. Barbara explained:

> Meriman lived in south Texas for seventeen years. She was doing community work there, right on the border. It is apparently a common tradition in a Mexican wedding, and of course they do it in a very patriarchal, heterosexual way, but one of the things they do in the wedding is that the man will give the woman some coins. It's a symbol of his commitment to financially support her. So what we did was we exchanged coins. She had some really big silver peso pieces. So we traded them with each other.

Maria Siggia and her partner also borrowed from a wedding tradition outside of their own culture. "I think I mentioned to you that the minister was a Chinese-American woman. So we had people sign this piece of silk, which apparently is a Chinese tradition, to sign their names on a piece of silk at the end. Sort of as witnesses."

Although most of these lesbians and gay men chose to include some aspects of the traditional Christian or Jewish wedding ceremonies, a few lesbians who had tenth-anniversary celebrations created their own, personal ceremonies. For example, Margaret Dubek and her partner invited about thirty friends to a buffet dinner and celebration. They had their ceremony after the meal was over. Margaret recalled:

> What we ended up doing for our little ceremony was, first of all, we had planned to have kind of a reminiscence of our relationship. We had this box full of items that we would pull out, like a kite. Here was our first joint purchase, and we would tell a story about that. A football for how we met. We just progressed through our relationship with different symbols. Just shared some stories with people. Showed our rings that we had bought four years ago. We gave other people an opportunity to talk too. Some people shared some things or made some toasts.

When asked if she and her partner had spoken more specifically about their commitment to each other, she replied:

> We each had written something for the other person that we hadn't shared with each other before that. So we recited that. It was along the lines of our appreciating each other and our hopes for the future. That kind of thing. Then we had music, which was very nice.

In planning their "tryst," Melanie Obermeier stated that she and her partner, Trish, also wanted to "create their own ceremony," a ritual that was serious but that didn't "buy into institutionalized marriage." Melanie explained their ceremony was not a political statement but one about their commitment to each other. According to Melanie, their "tryst" consisted mostly of goddess rites but included a few Jewish and Christian rituals as well.[2]

> Two of our best friends directed the ritual. One was the firekeeper and the other the chalice keeper. The ceremony was very grounded and naturalistic. First we burned sage and said the four blessings for the four goddess spirits. East, West, North, and South. Next, we were blessed with lavender oil. Then came the food blessing. We also said vows and jumped over a broom. The broom signified going into another reality. And we wrapped a wineglass in a napkin and Trish stomped on it to signify the insignificance of material things. Lastly, we had a bagpiper play "Amazing Grace" at the end.

By incorporating goddess rites into their ceremony, Melanie and Trish created a ritual that was woman-centered and resisted what they considered to be the "male-centered" dynamic of conventional weddings.

Location of Ceremony

Traditionally, marriage in the United States has been defined as both a legal and a religious institution. Since only a few liberal Protestant churches and Jewish synagogues sanction same-sex unions, it is not surprising that most lesbians and gay men did not have their ceremonies in a religious setting. In fact, 90 percent of the couples in this study held their ceremonies in their own homes, at a friend's house, or in a public building.

In a Church. A few respondents did have their ceremonies in liberal Protestant churches. These couples stressed the importance of belonging to a religious community. They had their ceremonies in a church because they wanted their union blessed by a religious authority and because they felt comfortable there. According to Celeste Davis:

> We had looked and talked about a lot of other places, and gone to different churches on different Sundays to check them out. See how we would be accepted and how our family would be received. We

kind of got a good response there and we both felt very intellectually and spiritually connected with the minister. Grace was raised Catholic and felt the Unitarian church was very welcoming. The philosophy was very welcome. We felt very much at home there.

Indeed, Celeste used the term "home" as a metaphor for her larger religious community.

Not in a Church or Synagogue. The respondents that did not have their ceremonies in a church or synagogue discussed two main reasons why they chose to have their ceremony somewhere else. Many said that either they or their partners did not believe in God. As Patrick Flemming stated: "I think because we don't believe in God. Neither of us do, so we were just being true to ourselves. If we believed in God, we would be involved in gay religious groups and would have had it at a church." Similarly, Tom Douglass remarked:

> John is self-identified as agnostic. I identify myself as spiritually a believer in Christ. However, there isn't any one organized religion within which I would feel comfortable enough to commit to membership. I can't morally give myself over to an organization who isn't going to support me. . . . Obviously, there are some that are coming along like the Metropolitan Community Church. But again, John wouldn't have felt comfortable. At the time when we were doing this, we both decided that organized religion wasn't pertinent to what we were doing.

Other respondents stated that although they had strong spiritual or religious beliefs, they felt excluded from the religious faiths they had been brought up in. According to Beth Epstein, she and her partner did not have their ceremony in a synagogue because as a lesbian she felt uncomfortable in most synagogues and her partner was not Jewish. As Beth recalled:

> I have felt very excluded from the synagogue until coming across the Jewish community here, which is an incredibly liberal place. It sure was unlike the synagogue of my childhood. But Gina would have

never been comfortable, so I had to consider that too. Even if I had any thoughts about it of me wanting it, she is so uncomfortable in a synagogue, so it just would have never worked. We had to pick something that felt comfortable to both of us.

A few individuals stated that they would have had their ceremony in a church but either their church would not allow it or they did not plan their ceremony in enough time to reserve the church. According to Luke Fontaine:

> At that time the rector, who was sympathetic toward gay and lesbian people, was not in the position where he felt comfortable performing services of holy union. . . . So I had it here at home because I couldn't have it at the church. If I couldn't have it in a church, I wanted it outside, and it's beautiful here. It's big enough, and I also felt that if I couldn't be married in a church I wanted to be married in a place that had some connection with us, and this is the home that my partner Ben grew up in.

And Paula Hughes remarked:

> First we thought about having it in maybe a church and having a female minister do the services, but we didn't plan it ahead of time enough to do that. I called the Unitarian church and I talked to a female minister. But she was booked for the next two months straight.

Respondents gave three reasons for having their ceremony in a private home or in public space rather than in a church or synagogue. In general, their decisions reflected their position as lesbians and gay men in American society. They felt they had to consider their comfort as well as their personal safety in choosing where to have their ceremony. Although many chose places that had some personal meaning to them, all felt that their decision on where to have their ceremony was informed by the level of homophobia in society in general.

First, many respondents discussed the level of comfort they felt in their own or their friends' homes. According to Margaret Dubek:

We really love our home and it's really an integral part of our relationship, and I think will be for a long time. So it's just a real comfortable place to be and a comfortable place for groups. We couldn't think of anywhere else where we would be more satisfied.

Similarly, Mike Finn replied:

The first answer is neutral territory. I'm Catholic and my partner is Jewish. But I also think that there is nothing more beautiful than being in the home you've created and developed together. That sounds a bit maudlin but I really mean it.

Other lesbians and gay men were even more explicit that they wanted a space that was safe and accepting. Esther Gould articulated this sentiment most strongly:

We had our ceremony in our home. We had the ceremony inside. I insisted on it because I was afraid of homophobic snipers. I mean that sort of teasing. But that was my hyperbolic language for it. But I was afraid I just didn't feel safe enough outside. I grew up in the South with a lot of violence and I knew I had to feel as comfortable as I could. So we had it in our home.

Patrick Flemming also wanted a space that was accepting. Patrick chose a church hall because it was a neutral and safe place in the community.

We had our ceremony in the community hall of a Unitarian church. It wasn't in the church. The Unitarians have a very neutral and accepting stance to the world, so that felt good. I don't think that there are that many community spaces that we could imagine having our ceremony. Where were we going to go? The Elks? The Foreign Vets? The American Legion? Those places are so male and so heterosexual. We would not have been comfortable there.

As these remarks make clear, even physical space is explicitly gendered and sexist in ways that excluded Patrick and his partner.

Maria Siggia also had her ceremony in a church space. Like Patrick, she did not choose this location for "official" recognition by a religious institution but rather because the Friends Meetinghouse was a safe and accepting place. Maria and her partner, Linda, rented time for their ceremony at a meetinghouse but did not request "to be married under the care of" the Quaker Meeting.[3] As Maria explained:

> Neither of us has a religious affiliation. While we thought of this as a ceremony having a spiritual aspect to it, we didn't think of it as religious. Neither of us goes to a church and that particular ritual wasn't anything either of us felt comfortable with. . . . I guess the meetinghouse came to mind because we wanted someplace simple and Linda was brought up a Quaker so it was easy to arrange.

As these accounts suggest, respondents' choices about where to have their ceremonies were based on personal preferences as well as on the rejection they felt as homosexuals.

Officiants

Just as the majority of respondents who had a ceremony did not have them in a church or synagogue, most individuals also did not ask a minister or rabbi to officiate. The ten individuals who did, however, had two main reasons for doing so. First, many had strong religious beliefs and felt it was important to be married "by a representative of God." Indeed, all of the respondents who had "holy union" ceremonies asked a minister to officiate their ceremonies. According to Ben Fletcher, "We wanted a religious authority to bless our union."

Second, most of these individuals wanted a minister or rabbi to "marry" them as well as to help orchestrate the ceremony. For Esther Gould and her partner, Susan, having a rabbi was important because of their spiritual beliefs and because it helped legitimize their ceremony in the eyes of their families. According to Esther: "The fact that we had a rabbi meant something to us and I think to the people there, certainly the Jewish people there. They felt like this was an acceptable Jewish form of the family, according to at least one Jewish authority."

For Kathleen O'Brien and her partner, Valerie, having a minister also was a way to help them make a statement that their ceremony was different from heterosexual weddings. They wanted their guests to be aware of the fact that lesbians and gay couples do not receive the same legal rights and benefits as married, heterosexual couples. According to Kathleen:

> We stood in the front of the church. Virginia [the minister] spoke about ceremonies of union and that this was not a wedding because it was not legally sanctioned. . . . After the vows, we had a signing and a witnessing of some of our documents. But again, Virginia explained that these are rights that are automatically passed on to heterosexuals couples when they say "I do" and are not given to lesbian and gay couples.

Maria Siggia and her partner asked a minister, who was a friend, to direct their ceremony. They wanted someone to "run the show" and did not ask her to officiate because of their spiritual beliefs:

> At a Quaker wedding there isn't anyone who officiates. People just exchange vows. But because that's not my background, what we settled on was a woman minister who I knew. She was Presbyterian by background and out here on sabbatical. She was a Chinese American woman and we asked her to officiate. But again not in a religious way or with references to God or whatever but just to officiate really.

Most respondents, however, asked a friend or group of friends to direct their ceremonies. They specifically did not want to have their rituals legitimized by a religious authority. Tom Douglass and his partner, John, asked

> a friend of ours who is, among other things, a wonderful gospel singer, to be our master of ceremonies. We told him we are not going to have this done in a church. We are not going to stand in front of a justice of the peace. We want you to have a special place by being master of ceremonies.

Many individuals discussed how not having a minister officiate their ceremonies made a political statement that gay relationships did not need religious or state recognition. As Patrick Flemming commented: "We officiated ourselves. It was a political thing. We don't need any official to tell us that it's okay for us to have a relationship. We've been having one in spite of the state for so many years." Thus, for some respondents, the choice of who officiated their ceremony was based on a strategy of resistance to religious wedding norms; for others it was based more on a strategy of accommodation to these same traditions.

Support People and Giving the "Bride/Groom" Away

Although it may be common for other lesbians and gay men, none of the respondents in this study had traditional bridesmaids and groomsmen. Most couples choose to have "support people" or "best friends" stand with them as witnesses. According to Randall Harris:

> We each had two people stand up for us. I think some of the ceremony blew their minds! Some parts were very religious, we even had communion, and I had not prepared them for that! I saw them sort of look at each other and look like they wondered what was going to happen next!

Similarly, Paula Hughes commented:

> Cheryl, Joyce, and Lee were our best friends, best people. I guess we wanted to choose people who were very important to us and that had supported us a lot in our lives. . . . We just wanted people directly in the ceremony that were very important to us.

These support people clearly represented the couple's "community." They did not represent the traditional gender segregation of the bride and groom. For Beth Epstein and her partner, Gina, it was very important to include individuals from their "chosen" family as representatives of their community in their ceremony. Beth explained:

We had chosen four people who were important people in various times in our lives to hold the four corners of the chuppah. So they were up in front doing that. The chuppah, you know the significance of that? It's like an open-sided house. So you are creating a home but it's open to your community. That's really nice. One of our friends wove it.

In addition, no one included the ritual of having the "father" symbolically give the "bride" away. Most respondents rejected the gender stereotypes inherent in this ritual. Instead, many couples had their support people walk with them into the service. Paula Hughes and her partner, Jenny, had their support people give them to each other. According to Paula, in their procession:

We had Maryenda, who did the ceremony, come up first. Cheryl, who was holding the rings, came out next. And then Lee and Jenny walked out together, arm in arm. Then Joyce and I came out after that. We walked down the stairs to the yard. When Lee and Jenny got down to the bottom of the stairs, they waited for Joyce and me, and then they handed Jenny and me to each other. We hooked arms and went into the circle and stood on the other side of table from where Maryenda and Cheryl were standing.

Tom Douglass and his partner, John, also proceeded with their "best friends" but chose to give themselves to each other. "I didn't have someone give me away. John didn't have someone give him away. We gave each other to each other." By rejecting the traditions of having the father give the "bride" away and of having "bridesmaids," these respondents were resisting the gender implications of these rituals. In this manner, they clearly utilized strategies of resistance by having "support people" participate in their ceremonies.

Ceremony/Wedding Cakes

Approximately one-third of the lesbians and gay men who had ceremonies had wedding cakes at their receptions. Although many do not ascribe any meaning to the cutting of the wedding cake, some believe it represents "the couple's plunge into new life," "the surrender of the bride's virginity," or "the first joint action of the married couple," although the exact meaning of cutting the wedding cake is difficult to pin down (Charsley, 1992). Indeed, the cake may be more of a convention than a tradition imbued with specific meaning. Thus people may decide to have a wedding cake at their ceremony because that is what others have done before them.

The respondents in this study did not have any concrete explanations for why they had wedding cakes, except that they wanted to have one. For some, the cake and its "cutting" took a fairly traditional form. James LaFleur and his partner, Jack, not only had a traditional three-tiered cake but also engaged in the ritual cake feeding at the end of their reception. As James recalled:

> We know some people who own a bakery. They gave us a cake with three layers. I have a Lincoln Town Car and we couldn't get it in my car. You should have seen it. I was banished to my sister's. My mother and I were going crazy trying to figure out how we were going to get it into the car. The cake had a staircase, ya know what a staircase is, with the candles all the way up the stairs? I'm like, this thing's going to go plop and I have to drive through rush hour, through the tunnel with this cake! We fed each other the cake, we've got pictures of that.

Barbara Mercier and her partner also had a traditional cake but, as was previously discussed, they put a moose and cow on the top.

> The cake with the moose and the cow. The woman who made the cake asked "What do you want me to put on the top?" I said, "You don't have to put anything on the top. We have something special we are going to put on the top. We are going to put a couple animals up there." She didn't miss a beat. She said, "A lot of people do that." Yes, sure. We played the song for people. We did our cake feeding.

Barbara commented they did the traditional feeding of the cake because "it was fun to get to do that. And I like cake. There is a piece of it in our freezer that we are saving for our first anniversary." Similarly, Melanie Obermeier and her partner had two carrot cakes that they cut after their "tryst." However, they put two female dolls on top of one of the cakes to symbolize their union. Thus, all the respondents who had a cake altered the traditional centerpiece from the bride and groom to items that reflected their personal relationships.

Tom Douglass and his partner didn't plan to have a cake but ended up feeding each other chocolate cream pie, thereby changing the customary "feeding of the cake" ritual to fit their relationship:

> We didn't plan it that way. However, it was one of those wonderful things that we kind of took psychically and said somebody brought this along because it was meant to be. Again it went along with the chocolate and the cream being the black and the white, us as the couple.

Rituals of Union

In addition to community rituals that focus on integrating a couple into their new families and communities, traditional marriage ceremonies also include rituals of union. These rituals of union focus directly on the couple's promises of commitment and faithfulness to one another. Most lesbians and gay men in this study included union rituals, such as exchanging vows and rings, in their ceremonies. This is not too surprising since most lesbians and gay men who have ceremonies do so in part to mark their commitment to their partners. In creating their vows and in exchanging rings, they utilized strategies of accommodation as individuals and couples. At the same time, their union rituals contained hints of resistance to the traditional meanings behind these rites.

Saying Vows

The ceremonies of all but one respondent included vows. A number of gay men and lesbians with strong religious beliefs exchanged fairly traditional vows. For example, Ben Fletcher and his partner said to each other the following promise:

In the name of God the Father and God's Son Jesus Christ, I give myself to be united with you from this day on, sharing my love and my life, my strengths and my weaknesses, my sorrows and my joys, my sickness and good health, my poverty and my riches, every failure and success—by the grace of God. I will love you, honor you, respect you with my whole being, to be always honest and truthful, and forsaking all other, to be faithful to you in mind, soul, and body for all the days of my life, until death divides us or until the coming of our Lord Jesus Christ. This is my solemn vow.

Similarly, Tom Douglass recalled:

Our friend [who officiated their ceremony] planned what he was going to say and went through some of the traditional things like for better or for worse, through sickness and in health, that kind of thing. But at the very end he said, "I now pronounce you each other's."

Although some lesbians and gay men followed a fairly traditional format for saying their vows, most created their own format. According to Patrick Flemming:

In the program, it says "Statements of Love and Commitment by Patrick and Joel." So that was when we each gave our speech. Joel read part of a letter he had written to me when we first started our relationship. He reflected back on that and how things had changed and stayed the same. I read a poem that I wrote for the day. It talked about him and our relationship. Then we gave each other rings. Everyone clapped. We said, "I commit myself to you."

As Barbara Mercier recalled:

Actually the way we did it, we had this scroll. We wrote this thing. It was all on one paper. It was not like I read to Meriman and then she read to me. We read it together. I'd read one line and she'd read the next. We read it to everybody sitting there. So we shared the vows.

For Barbara and Meriman, their vows also symbolized their connection to their community. Barbara explained:

> Actually, we wrote our vows out and wrote them down ahead of time. Then we signed them as part of the ceremony. The program. As part of the ceremony, we had the women that were there say, since we didn't have a priest or somebody like that, "Okay, you are married." It was an affirmation of the other people there that they were witnesses and that they were affirming the relationship. We had all of them sign it.

Overall, vows were rituals that asserted the couple's faithfulness to each other. In this sense, they were fairly traditional rituals of union. On the other hand, all of the lesbians and gay men who had ceremonies either wrote their own vows or changed the traditional vows to fit a same-sex couple. In addition, all had their officiants change the phrase "I now pronounce you husband and wife" to something else.

Exchanging Rings

Half of the lesbians and gay men exchanged rings as part of their ceremonies. For most of these respondents, the rings primarily were a symbol of commitment. In general, they exchanged rings with their partners for many of the same reasons heterosexual couples do, including indicating their commitment, and marking that they were "taken."

According to Maria Siggia, exchanging rings with her partner was important because the rings symbolized their promise to each other. She said, "They symbolize the commitment that we have made to each other and our love for each other and our pledging support and promising to be a sort of constant person in the other one's life." Similarly, Luke Fontaine stated: "We exchanged rings. Means that I'm his, that I'm committed to him. Not so much for eternity, it's forever for this life on earth, for as long as we're both alive."

Indeed, many lesbians and gay men commented that the rings were a statement about their relationships. According to Barbara Mercier:

For me, partly, it was like one of those things that it affirmed to me, and will continue to affirm to other people, that this is as serious a commitment as heterosexual couples make. Also just to have something that is always with me.

And as Ben Fletcher noted:

Actually because we're very traditional and very romantic. We love symbolism and that sort of stuff, not that it makes us any more married, or that it protects us when we're out socializing. It's a symbol. Sometimes I shake my head and scoff at weddings, straight weddings, and I see all the hocus pocus and that sort of bothers me. But I like the sort of traditional symbolism, the romanticism. It gives an outward symbol to other people. Not to show off the relationship, but it's another sign to the outside that it's serious.

Some lesbians and gay men mentioned that they exchanged rings in part as a marker of "being taken." For Paula Hughes:

I guess the rings were just another proof that we had gotten married. That if somebody that doesn't know me sees me and notices the ring, most likely would assume that I am taken. And I like that part of it because I think that chances are that if somebody sees the ring on Jenny, they'll be less likely to hit on her than if she wasn't wearing the ring. It kind of gives me a more secure feeling, which is probably kind of silly. But it does.

For Esther Gould, however, deciding to have rings as part of her "tenth-anniversary ceremony" was a difficult decision. As she explained: "We exchanged rings, we bought rings for each other but they don't look exactly the same. We came to the rings really late because we were so determined that we didn't want to mimic a heterosexual wedding." When asked why the decision was so difficult, Esther continued:

But then our rabbi asked us if we wanted to use rings and we said, "No." He said, "You must have something." So the rings. They

weren't a really big part of the ceremony for us but they have come
to be important. We didn't buy them and think about them with a
whole lot of elaborations. The way some couples do, ya know, design
them. My feeling about my ring is that it just is a concrete
connection, a tie to an experience of celebrating our commitment to
each other.

Although Esther and her partner initially resisted having rings, they
ultimately decided to incorporate them into their ceremony. Over time,
their rings came to symbolize their commitment to each other.

A few lesbians and gay men did not exchange "traditional" rings but
drew on their symbolism to construct the meaning of the jewelry they
exchanged. For example, Patrick Flemming and his partner decided to
exchange pinky rings because of their connection to gay culture.
According to Patrick:

> The rings symbolize our marriage, our commitment, however you
> want to put it. We talked a lot about which finger it would be on. We
> were thinking about having them on the finger that straight people
> have it on just to say our relationship is just as good as yours. But
> then we read a book about gay mythology and gay symbolism. It was
> by Judy Grahn, *Another Mother Tongue*. She talked about the pinky
> finger and how the pinky ring has been part of gay culture for years,
> and years, and years. We wanted to be part of that culture, that
> tradition, and get strength from it.

Drawing on the symbolism of their different racial identities, Tom
Douglass and his partner decided to exchange earrings with different
color pearls in them. According to Tom, the earrings

> had the same symbolism as a ring in a traditional, if traditional is the
> right word, marriage. They were a symbol of each of us giving the
> other something valuable, something that we cared about, and
> trusting that the other would accept it and consider it just as
> valuable and care for it. Specifically, I gave him a black pearl; he gave
> me a white pearl. I am Black; he is White. That symbolized, of

course, our relationship and the coming together of our two different cultures.

Clearly, both Tom and Patrick wanted to keep the symbolism behind the rings, but at the same time they changed it to fit their gay or racial identities. Thus they turned the traditional rite of exchanging rings into a form of resistance that asserted their own identities.

A number of lesbians initially were somewhat ambivalent about the traditional symbolism of wedding rings. Although Celeste Davis and her partner exchanged rings when they first got together, Celeste did not want to exchange gold bands as part of their "commitment ceremony." She explained:

> We exchanged rings early on in our relationship. Probably within the first year. . . . The first time we bought these rings that were somewhat matching in that mine had sapphires and hers had emeralds. So that it felt like it identified us as a couple yet somewhat different. It meant to me that we were a couple, hoping to build a long-term commitment.

Celeste's partner, Grace, however, wanted to exchange gold bands. According to Celeste:

> Actually during our ceremony, Grace really wanted a simple gold band, and I argued that we already had rings and that it was going to be too showy and too heterosexual and all that kind of stuff [to do in the ceremony]. It was more actually probably internalized homophobia that all of a sudden people would see me with a solid gold band and ask me questions. I [later] got over it. So for the fourth-year anniversary of us being together, I ended up getting us matching gold bands. So we exchanged rings twice.

When asked what the gold band now symbolized to her, Celeste replied:

> Now the gold band makes me feel married with all the kind of romanticized beliefs that I bring with me from my own childhood

and all the kind of nice stuff that I can tolerate about the heterosexual definition of marriage. The gold band says to the world that I am committed to somebody else. That I love someone else enough to do that and that someone else loves me enough to commit.

Beth Epstein also had mixed feelings about the symbolism of wedding rings. She explained:

When we first were planning it, we didn't want to do rings, because it just felt so heterosexual. It really felt like "I don't need to have this symbol on my finger to tell people this!" We were really against that. Then somehow it just started feeling like something I really wanted to do, mainly because of my work situation. I was really tired of people saying "Such a nice girl like you, how come you are not married?" It just got really difficult, so I thought "I really want a ring. I want people to know this."

Although Celeste and Beth did not incorporate rings into their ceremony, they later appropriated this traditional symbol into their relationship. Thus, for some respondents rings held conventional meanings of commitment at the same time they were a way to subvert the assumption that only heterosexual couples can marry.

Conclusion

As the experiences of the lesbians and gay men discussed in this chapter suggest, same-sex ceremonies are both shaped by and in turn have the potential to reshape the conventional meanings of the wedding ritual. Indeed, many stated that they thought they were creating something "new" by constructing their own ceremony. While their rituals incorporated some "traditional" aspects of the wedding ceremony, most respondents discussed how their ceremonies were not like heterosexual weddings.

Overall, respondents utilized strategies of both resistance and accommodation in altering the format of the traditional wedding ceremony to fit same-sex relationships or in creating new formats for their services. Paradoxically, however, same-sex ceremonies often question stereotypical gender norms but not mainstream sexual ideologies. Same-sex ceremonies defy lesbians' and gay men's exclusion from the institution of marriage but they also uphold the ideal that marriage is the appropriate site for sexual activity. In addition to the political nature of same-sex ceremonies themselves, many lesbians and gay men also commented on the importance of taking legal action to ensure their rights. As chapter 7 discusses, many lesbians and gay men now are advocating the legal right of same-sex couples to marry.

Same-Sex Marriages and Legal Issues

A Change Is Gonna Come

The Movement to Legalize Lesbian and Gay Marriage

What Ninia Baehr and Genora Dancel wanted was to make each other beneficiaries of their life insurance. When they tried, their native state of Hawaii told them they could not; they had to be married. And so the two women enlisted in what many believe will become the highest-profile lesbian and gay issue of the decade: They sued for the right to wed.
—Elaine Herscher, *San Francisco Chronicle*,
May 15, 1995

DURING THE LAST TEN YEARS, an increasing number of lesbian and gay couples have gone to court in order to obtain the legal right to marry.[1] Although some lesbians and gay men object to the idea of legalizing same-sex marriages, others, like Ninia Baehr and Genora Dancel, have begun to demand the social, legal, and economic benefits associated with being married. In order to examine attitudes toward the legalization of same-sex marriages and the benefits associated with it, this chapter focuses on four questions. First, do lesbians and gay men advocate the legalization of same-sex marriages, and if so, what are their reasons for doing so? Second, would some lesbians and gay men choose to get married if same-sex marriages were legalized? Third, do they think the legal right to marry should be a priority for lesbian and gay organizations? Last, what are the alternatives to legalizing marriage? Why do some lesbians and gay men advocate the passage of domestic partnership laws as an alternative to the legalization of same-sex marriages? Each of these questions speaks to the larger legal and political implications of what often is viewed as a personal bond. The fact that lesbians and gay men are denied the legal right to marry allows them to examine closely the specific economic and legal aspects of marriage.

Until recently, the legalization of same-sex marriages was not a priority for national lesbian and gay political organizations. During the 1970s many gay and lesbian activists and scholars decried the oppressive nature of marriage and advocated that it be abolished (Altman, 1979). Although three couples sued for the right to marry in the early 1970s, only two legal cases concerning the right of lesbian and gay couples to marry were brought before the courts in the United States between 1975 and 1989.[2]

In 1989, however, Craig Dean and his partner sued the District of Columbia for not granting them a marriage license. In part, Dean's highly publicized legal action reinstated an interest in pursuing the right to marry among some gay and lesbian activists. Subsequently, a number of national lesbian and gay organizations began discussing the pros and cons of focusing their resources on the right to legally marry. Staff members in the Lambda Legal Defense and Education Fund, the Human Rights Campaign Fund, and the National Lesbian and Gay Task Force debated among themselves and in public journals and magazines the political reasons for and against pushing for the legalization of same-sex marriages (Ettlebrick, 1989; Stoddard, 1989). In large part, this debate was led by staff attorneys at Lambda who first organized what is now called "The Marriage Project" to legalize lesbian and gay marriages.

Although activists continue to disagree over whether lesbian and gay political organizations should push for the right of same-sex couples to marry, the 1993 decision of the Hawaii State Supreme Court galvanized many large national lesbian and gay organizations to join

Lambda in placing the legalization of same-sex marriages at the top of their priority list. According to Evan Wolfson (1995), a senior staff attorney at Lambda and co-counsel for the plaintiffs in the *Baehr v. Lewin* case:

> Longtime activists who for ideological or tactical reasons would not have chosen to fight for marriage right now agree that we have no choice. Whichever metaphor you prefer—the train has left the station, the ship has set sail—we are almost certainly going to win the right to marry. . . . Numerous activists—including Lorri Jean of the L.A. Lesbian and Gay Center, Paula Ettelbrick of the Empire State Pride Agenda, Elizabeth Burch of the Human Rights Campaign Fund, and the ACLU's Matt Coles and David Davidson— have agreed with Lambda that whatever our past differences on whether or how to fight for the right to marry, it is time to focus on the task at hand. (p. 30)

Although many national lesbian and gay organizations consider the legalization of same-sex marriages to be a civil rights issue, for many right-wing conservatives the issue has become a symbol of the decline of American society. According to the Reverend Lou Sheldon of the Traditional Values Coalition: "This is a front-burner issue, because if you destroy the heterosexual ethic, then you are destroying a major pillar of Western civilization. If Hawaii moves forward on this issue, conservatives may push for an amendment striking down the 'full faith and credit' provision of the U.S. Constitution" (Herscher, 1995, p. A1).[3] In turn, these right-wing responses to the "possible" legalization of same-sex marriages have ignited activists to implore others to become more involved in the lesbian and gay marriage campaign. As Robert Bray, a staff member at the National Lesbian and Gay Task Force, warned, the legalization of same-sex marriages "is coming at us like a 3,000-ton locomotive. We can pretend it's not and risk another gays-in-the-military debacle, or we can educate ourselves and foster a discussion in our own community" (Hersher, 1995, p. A1). Although many national lesbian and gay organizations now are focusing their resources on the marriage issue, neither activists nor researchers have interviewed individ-

TABLE 7.1

SHOULD SAME-SEX MARRIAGES BE LEGALIZED?

	MALE	FEMALE	TOTAL
LEGALIZED	%	%	%
Yes	100	98	99
No	0	2	1
Total	N=45	N=45	N=90

uals about their viewpoints on this matter. The next section examines individual attitudes toward the legalization of same-sex marriages.

Should Same-Sex Marriages Be Legalized?

The overwhelming majority of lesbians and gay men interviewed for this book supported the legalization of same-sex marriages. (See table 7.1.) When asked, "In general, do you think that couples of the same-sex should have the legal right to marry in the United States?," eighty-nine respondents replied "Yes!" As Andrea Gorchov stated, "Gay and lesbian couples should have the same rights as heterosexual couples. The law should not discriminate on the basis of sexual orientation." Similarly, Connie Jones remarked, "We deserve the same rights. The only reason that same-sex marriages should not be allowed is if you fail your blood test!"

These respondents had four main reasons for their positions: legal, economic, emotional, and social. (See table 7.2.) First, all of these respondents commented that lesbians and gay men deserved the legal right to marry. They considered the issue to be a matter of equality. According to Deborah Cohen: "We are entitled to it. We are citizens of this country. We deserve the same rights as heterosexuals. Lesbian, gay, and heterosexual couples should all be treated the same by the government." Ben Fletcher also remarked, "Because straight people have the legal right, we should too. It's discriminatory and unethical to say that you have to be straight to have rights and to be accepted as a human being."

TABLE 7.2

REASONS FOR LEGALIZING SAME-SEX MARRIAGES

REASON	%	N
Should be a right	100	89
Legal and economic benefits	73	65
Strengthen commitment	12	11
Legitimize gay relationships	7	6

Second, the majority stated that lesbian and gay couples deserved the economic benefits of marriage; they should have the same "privileges" as married couples, such as access to a partner's health insurance, the right to make legal decisions for a partner, parental rights, immigration rights, and the right to inherit a spouse's property. Many even commented on "perceived" tax benefits. As Celeste Davis remarked, "Why not legalize same-sex marriages? We'd save on our taxes and have the same benefits as straight couples." David Gascon also replied that lesbians and gay men deserved the same entitlements. "You'd get the tax writeoff, the health benefits, and the family and bereavement leave. We are citizens just like everybody else. We vote. We pay taxes. We are part of society. We should have the same privileges."

Most respondents specifically highlighted the need for health insurance benefits and other legal rights granted to spouses. According to Chris Avery:

There are so many things that heterosexual couples who are married can have that gay couples don't. Mark has no health insurance. He could be on my health insurance if we were legally married. . . . And if somebody is in the hospital and in intensive care, only the immediate family can go and visit. If the relationship isn't recognized, a lover can't even visit his or her lover in the hospital. I think that is atrocious.

Similarly, Nancy Greenwood explained:

I am angry about how much money it costs me because I happen to be a lesbian and in a lesbian relationship than it would if I had married the guy I was engaged to in college. I can't have Cindy on my health insurance, which means she has gone without it for years. We can't afford to buy an individual policy for her.

When asked if she thought there were any other reasons to legalize same-sex marriages, Nancy continued:

All the legal stuff makes me wild. For instance, if something happens to me, if I am injured in some way, she would have a legal battle on her hands with my family over being my primary care provider even if we have a durable power of attorney. I do think that heterosexual marriages fulfill an important legal function that ought to be extended to gays and lesbians.

According to both Nancy and Chris, it is unfair that lesbians and gay men are denied the economic privileges and legal rights given to married heterosexual couples. In fact, many respondents commented on the importance of having the legal right to make decisions for a spouse who is mentally or physically unable to make their own decisions. In large part, respondents were aware of needing this right because of problems they themselves had experienced or had heard others discuss about visiting partners who were in the hospital with AIDS.

In addition, respondents commented on the legal problems faced by the lesbian couple Karen Thompson and Sharon Kowlaski during the 1980s. After Sharon was paralyzed in a car accident in the early 1980s, her partner was unable to become her legal guardian because they were not legally married.[4] For thousands of lesbians and gay men who heard about their story, Karen's and Sharon's legal situation highlighted the lack of rights lesbian and gay couples have in the United States (Thompson and Andrzejewski, 1988). Indeed, many respondents commented that same-sex marriages should be legalized in order to end this type of discrimination. As Peter Cole remarked:

> To be able to be married in a legal sense would end a lot of battles like the one the lesbian couple had where one woman ended up being confined to a bed and the other had no legal guardianship rights. Karen Thompson and Sharon Kowalski. It would end all that kind of thing.

Third, only a small proportion of respondents commented on the emotional aspects of marriage, stating that they thought legalized marriage would support lesbian and gay relationships by strengthening their bonds of commitment. As Brenda Wood commented, "I think legalization would help people get through hard times. It is easier to leave a relationship when it isn't formally recognized." Similarly, Juan Ortega replied: "Gay couples should have the right to marry because they have the same feelings as heterosexual couples. They are in love with each other. They want to make a deeper commitment. Marriage could help with that commitment."

A few respondents mentioned that the legalization of same-sex marriages might help legitimize and increase the acceptance of lesbian and gay relationships. As Conrad Gardner commented, "To be recognized as a legitimate relationship. It might break down some of those stereotypes about lesbian and gay relationships not lasting." Similarly, Alan Fischer replied: "To have a legal document would help straight people be more accepting of us. It would show that we are committed. I think that most people's perception of gay men is that we are promiscuous. If we were able to get married, we could show we are committed." Lori Morrison also thought that the right to marry would give same-sex relationships more legitimacy.

> For people who want them, it would give them legitimacy. It would legitimize their relationship. It would legitimize their choice of being lesbian or gay. It would take some of the stigma away. How can you be a pervert if you're in a legal marriage relationship with your partner?

Overall, these lesbians and gay men clearly stated that they should have the legal right to marry. Their views were based largely on a political strategy that advocates equal rights for lesbians and gay men. Given the emphasis of many social movements on rights claims over the past five decades, it is not surprising that lesbians and gay men would articulate a similar type of goal. A number of respondents, however, had mixed feelings about this endeavor. For example, seven stated that marriage should be a right but they ultimately did not want to base legal rights in the institution of marriage. As Colleen Ivy commented:

> As long as there is legal marriage for heterosexuals, there should be legal marriage for homosexual couples as well. I see that as a first step but I have trouble with legal marriage. It wouldn't be my ultimate goal. But it would be nice to see as a first step so we could get to something more ideal.

When asked to elaborate, Colleen continued:

> Well, I would like for there to be more commitment and no legal marriage for anybody! I have trouble with marriage because it means society defines your primary family. I know some people who define their primary family as say one female and two males or two females and one male. I would prefer to see something more like domestic partner registration that included homosexuals, bisexuals, and people that define their family as more than two adults.

Thus Colleen clearly articulated a right to marry but was also aware that this strategy would still exclude certain types of families from receiving legal rights or benefits.

In addition, David Gascon was concerned that legalized marriage would "require" lesbians and gay men to marry in order to be accepted.

> Yes. I think we're citizens just like everybody else. We vote. We pay taxes. We're part of society. We should have the same privileges. We obviously have the same responsibilities. But what bothers me is that I wouldn't want it to be another way of assimilating to an oppressive culture. "Oh, look! We're married, just like everybody else." So on a political level, I don't like it as a tactic of assimilation. I would hope

it wouldn't be like the greater heterosexual form of marriage, that's like "Well, you're having sex with this person, you must marry them and have this sexual contract and have this ownership over this person." From that level I don't like it.

Like Colleen, David discussed the right to marry but was leery of what he considered its possible negative outcomes.

Similarly, Eliza Schneider also commented on what might happen if same-sex marriages were legalized. She was not certain that the right to marry would end all discrimination against lesbians and gay men.

I think it is wrong that if we want to we can't be a married couple. By the government saying "Okay, you can get married," people will begin to think that our relationships are okay. But I'm not sure that would do the trick necessarily. The government, maybe thirty–forty years ago, said it was wrong to have segregation of schools, and it didn't suddenly make white people like black people. It still hasn't worked to a large extent, so I don't think marriage would necessarily make that happen. I also don't think anybody should feel that they should have to get married.

Thus, a number of respondents considered marriage to be a right but did not think it would change larger definitions of family, how benefits are given out in society, societal expectations, or discrimination.

Out of all the respondents, only one woman answered, "No, absolutely not!" when asked if lesbians and gay men should have the legal right to marry. As Cathy Newman vehemently argued:

I think that marriage itself should be abolished in the United States because marriage defines the property rights of men over women, the legal rights of men over women, and the behavior of men toward women. Marriage is an economic institution of property. . . . While I believe that men and women and gays and lesbians should all have the same rights, I think fighting for equal rights in marriage is a tactical error in the gay rights movement. What's going to happen is that only "good" gays who conform and get married will be accepted.

TABLE 7.3

WOULD YOU MARRY LEGALLY?

MARRY LEGALLY	MALE	FEMALE	TOTAL
	%	%	%
Yes	60	56	58
Maybe	22	27	24
No	18	16	17
Don't know	0	2	1
Total	N=45	N=45	N=90

According to Cathy, legal rights and economic benefits should be given to individuals instead of married couples. She believed both the tax and the health care systems should be reformed so that "there would be no benefit in being married." Thus she favored a political strategy that focused on changing the legal system to grant individual's rights instead of giving benefits to married couples.

Would You Marry if Same-Sex Marriages Were Legalized?

In order to understand their attitudes toward the institution of marriage, respondents were asked if they would marry if marriage laws were changed. While the majority of lesbians and gay men interviewed clearly supported the right of same-sex couples to marry, there was more reservation about whether they would personally choose to marry if marriage laws were changed. Overall, 58 percent of respondents stated they would get married, 24 percent commented they would consider getting married, 17 percent replied they would not get married, and 1 percent stated they did not know if they would marry legally (See table 7.3.)

Echoing the more abstract rationales for why marriage should be legalized, respondents who said they would marry legally articulated two reasons for why they would do so. First, most stated they would marry in order to receive the economic benefits and legal protections accorded married couples. As Margaret Dubek replied:

> I would go to city hall for the security. I would like to have the same benefits that married heterosexual people have, like holding property jointly and hospital visitation privileges. The kinds of things that are taken for granted for heterosexually married people.

Similarly, Barry Mullins stated:

> Right now my partner, Paul, is out of work. We can't have a family medical plan because where I work doesn't recognize same-sex relationships. If we were legally married, we could sign up for the family medical plan. It also would make it easier to get a family membership at the YMCA and things like that.

Peter Cole also would get married to allow his relationship with his partner, David, who is not a U.S. citizen, to continue. As Peter explained:

> Yes. The initial thing would be we wouldn't have to worry whether David could stay in the country. He would get a green card immediately. David only had the legal right to even come into the United States since last October. Until then it was illegal to visit the United States if you were gay, lesbian, or bisexual because the immigration service still considered you to have mental illness even though the American Associations of Psychiatrists and Psychologists both said no.

Overall, respondents would marry for the economic benefits and legal protections given married couples. Colleen Ivy clearly expressed this sentiment in her remarks: "Yes, but the only reason would be for the added legal protections. I don't think it would change our relationship in any way. It wouldn't make us feel more committed. So, it would be for purely legal reasons."

Second, a minority of these respondents stated they would marry for what they perceived as the personal aspects of marriage. In contrast to Colleen's remarks, they discussed how marriage would deepen their commitment and how it would provide recognition of their relationships by family and friends. They would marry because of their love for and commitment to their partners; they did not focus on the legal benefits of marriage. According to Mike Reilly:

> For a show of commitment and everything that goes with that. I think ultimately marriage is a show of love and commitment more than any of the other stuff that goes with that. Gay couples who have commitment ceremonies, they're not doing it for the "bennies." They're doing it for the love and commitment. So, that's why I would do it too.

As Julia Gomez also said: "I would get legally married if I met a woman I wanted to spend the rest of my life with. I think that making it legal would make the commitment and relationship last longer."

In addition to those who stated they would marry if it was legalized, other respondents commented they would consider getting married. They gave the same reasons for why they might do so as did those who said they would marry: economic benefits and legal rights. As Richard Hudson replied:

> Maybe for the legal and economic benefits, but not with any ceremony or anything. We would just sign the documents and do it. Makes wills easier, makes property distribution easier. But again for the legal/economic reasons. Not for the sentimental reasons.

Leslie Walker also discussed marrying for the benefits.

> I would consider it. There is something still about it that gives me the hebbie-gebbies. I don't know exactly what it is. The whole idea, the legal marriage and all the documents. That state-controlled thing. It would be in trade-off I guess to get the goodies you have to do it.

Some lesbians and gay men said that they might consider getting married if they were ready to make that kind of commitment. According to Brian Davies:

> I might, but not yet. Because I'm not at that point. But I might for some financial things like health insurance, home ownership, things like that. Just to announce to the community. The legal attachment is also a social declaration.

A few respondents stated they would get married in part to make their relationships more secure as well as to set up a household. According to Eliza Schneider:

> I think if we both wanted to get married, sure. We would have to talk about it. I guess because I think, and maybe this is a product of my upbringing and being a member of this society, deep down I do believe that there is something more permanent about a relationship when you actually go through some kind of ceremony. It doesn't have to be the whole production in a cathedral or something like the *Sound of Music* or anything like that but I really do believe that. Also we could get matching towels and all sorts of appliances and things. Gifts. I would definitely do it for that, and I would make sure that everybody would give me some sort of kitchen appliance because I love to cook.

In contrast to these two groups, a smaller group of respondents stated they would not get married. These lesbians and gay men had two reasons for their responses. First, the majority stated that they personally did not want to be part of the institution of marriage. According to Lori Morrison:

> No, I would never want to get married. Marriage is disgusting. It's just a bunch of hoopla. It isn't relevant to my life or relationship. Who would want to? It robs you of the opportunity to "freely" be involved in your relationship. If one of you decided that you don't want to be in it, it just makes it so much like being married to a man.

You have to disentangle yourself from the relationship, not only emotionally, but legally.

Similarly, Lynn Ettelman remarked:

I don't believe in supporting the state, so a legal marriage would be asking for sanction from the state. I wouldn't be interested in doing that. The state is something I would like to stay as far removed from as possible, which is not quite far enough when you own a house. I view the state as a group that benefits white men and that functions to support oppression. I have never seen a state that respects people.

Second, a few respondents commented that they really didn't think marriage would add anything to their relationships. As Sam Johnson commented: "I wouldn't want to get married. John and I have already lived together for twenty-five years, so I think it is a little too late. Getting legally married wouldn't change our relationship." In contrast to individuals who stated they would or might marry, these respondents were much more adamant about keeping the state out of their lives and relationships. Overall, they did not consider the "benefits" of marriage to be worth the costs.

A few people who originally said that they would not marry legally later qualified their initial responses. For example, Andrea Gorchov first replied, "Absolutely not!" but immediately stated:

Well, I have to back up on that, because if Eleanor could get on my health insurance, I would consider marrying her. But the only reason to get married would be health insurance. It really bugs me that I am a state employee and she doesn't get covered on my health insurance.

Similarly, Michael Sullivan replied:

No. Not go to the town hall and that sort of thing. Well, maybe if it meant getting health insurance or some legal reason why we had to do it, I would do it. But I feel this way about straight couples too. I don't think the state belongs in relationships. I'm a radical. For straight people, it's like you get married. You have these parties in the relationship, the husband, the wife, and the state. The state imposes all of these obligations of people that make it extremely difficult for them to function in the world. I believe people should have relationship agreements so that it should be clear what's going to happen when things break apart. But keep the state out of it!

Although these respondents did not want the state to intervene in their lives, they qualified their responses because they might marry for the economic and legal benefits of marriage.

Only one respondent stated she did not know whether she would marry legally. In general, however, she thought the legal institution of marriage had too many negative implications. According to Lucy Wallace:

I don't know if I would get legally married. Marriage is pretty rigidly defined by society, and not all of those definitions are for me. I think that the husband-and-wife roles have not changed all that much. I think that there is a big assumption that when you get married, you are going to have children. I think there are gender roles built into marriage, and I think they would spread over into same-sex relationships.

While many respondents indicated that they had problems with the institution of marriage, almost equal numbers stated they would or might consider getting married legally. Although age and birth cohort differentiated respondents' attitudes toward whether they would have a same-sex ceremony (discussed in chapter 4), they did not distinguish individuals' attitudes toward whether they would marry legally. This contrast may be related to the current emphasis in lesbian and gay politics on gaining civil rights. Thus respondents, regardless of age, might not choose to have a commitment ceremony but would marry legally to secure economic benefits and legal rights.

While most thought that marriage should be a right for all U.S. citizens regardless of their sexual identity, respondents were more hesitant about whether they would marry if given the legal option.

Although initially these responses seem contradictory, they are consistent with the discrimination lesbians and gay men face in this country. On one hand, lesbians and gay men continue to experience persecution at the hands of state authorities for being homosexual. Sodomy laws, police brutality, and recent court decisions that have denied lesbians and gay men the same parental rights as heterosexuals continue to highlight the negative features of state-sanctioned social control. Indeed, four respondents discussed their concerns that getting married would put their names on a list that would allow the government to "round up" lesbians and gay men. While this type of response may seem paranoid, it is an understandable, even rational response, given the government's not-too-distant discussion of quarantining people with HIV/AIDS in large containment camps.

On the other hand, lesbians and gay men are well aware that they need the state to protect and guarantee their rights. They recognize that the state as well as the legal system have worked in the past to expand individual's civil rights. Indeed, over the last ten years, nine states plus the District of Columbia have passed lesbian and gay civil rights bills and eight additional states have executive orders that prohibit discrimination on the basis of sexual orientation in public employment.[5] Subsequently, many respondents discussed the need for a national gay and lesbian civil rights law. Lesbians and gay men are caught between these two contradictory views because of the political and social context in which they find themselves today.

Should Marriage Be a Priority for National Lesbian and Gay Organizations?

While almost all respondents thought that lesbians and gay men should have the legal right to marry, fewer (albeit still a majority) thought that the legalization of same-sex marriage should be a priority for lesbian and gay political organizations. When asked "In your opinion, should the legalization of same-sex marriages be a priority for lesbian and gay organizations?," 69 percent of respondents answered "Yes," 29 percent

TABLE 7.4

SHOULD MARRIAGE BE A PRIORITY?

	MALE	FEMALE	TOTAL
PRIORITY	%	%	%
Yes	82	56	69
No	13	44	29
Maybe	4	0	2
Total	N=45	N=45	N=90

answered "No," and 2 percent answered "maybe." (See table 7.4.) The accounts of those who stated that legalizing marriage should be a priority focused heavily on the need to gain legal rights and social acceptance for lesbian and gay relationships. As Nancy Greenwood explained:

> Yes, it should be a priority. As I get older and my gay and lesbian friends get older, I begin to see more and more how great the potential for suffering is for us without legal protections for our relationships both financially and in terms of health care issues. When my parents were my age, they owned a home and had retirement plans. My father, who was the major wage earner, had in place insurance and other stuff to provide for the family if something happened to him. Society allowed him to do those things in a way that I can't do for Cindy.

Many of these respondents thought that organizations should push for legalizing same-sex marriages because it also would increase the social acceptance of lesbian and gay relationships. As Emily Atkinson commented:

> Yes, because I think it would be symbolic in our culture of accepting lesbian and gay relationships. If we had that symbol, it basically would reflect a change of attitudes toward our relationships in general. It also would give us equal legal standing and protection.

Similarly, Karl Hanks replied:

> Yes, legal recognition would have a lot to do with achieving social recognition. It would be the official stamp of approval. When these things happen it just means that a lot of prejudices are going to be less than they are now. There won't be as much fear and prejudice going around.

A few respondents specifically commented that the social recognition of lesbian and gay relationships would happen only if the law changed first. According to Cheryl Foley:

> Yes, I think it should be a priority. We can tell society that we are not strange but unless we are operating under the same rules we're still the bad stepchild. I think as a rule society knows on average we are not strange. My neighbor sees how I live. Your neighbor sees how you live. It's no secret, at least to my neighbors, that I'm a lesbian. So if we ask my neighbors what they thought, I don't think they would argue the point. . . . But on the other hand you take those same townies, like at this bar that I pop into to see people that I know. They don't like queers but I sit there time after time. I ask them do they like Cheryl Foley. They like Cheryl Foley but they don't like queers. So you've got to get the federal government to make it the law.

Deborah Cohen also said that the law could provide a model for individuals to follow.

> I think legalized marriages are a useful tool in educating people about their homophobia. It's almost like forced busing. You're not eliminating the racism, but you're at least providing equal opportunity under the law. I think that's what legalized marriages would do: offer some protection and equal opportunity. It is probably one of the most volatile issues around. It goes back to what weddings mean to heterosexuals. It's connected with religion, which views homosexuality as a sin. A lot of people who are really homophobic are going to

react negatively about this. It pushes people's buttons, but that is where we need to go.

The majority of these respondents, however, stated that legalizing same-sex marriages should be "a" priority but that other issues were equally or more important. Here again, many respondents stressed the need for a national lesbian and gay civil rights bill. As Peter Cole remarked:

> I think that marriage should be a high priority but the highest priority would be comprehensive civil rights law, which would make marriage legal. A civil rights law that said that there should be no law banning the rights of people based on sexual orientation. A civil rights bill would allow you to knock down any kind of marriage laws. If you have that law, then you can go from there to attack discrimination in all areas.

Similarly, Lucy Wallace replied:

> It should be one priority but it shouldn't be the priority. It should be something that gay and lesbian organizations are working for because if we don't, nobody else will. It's not going to be handed to us. Nobody is going to miraculously become enlightened and say, "Oh you know, we should be giving you the same rights as everybody else." We have to fight for them. But I don't think there should be one focus. There is so much that needs to get done like the overall human rights campaign, AIDS awareness, and outside issues that are not specifically lesbian or gay but are equally important, like women's rights and racial issues.

Thus even the majority of respondents who thought that legalizing same-sex marriages should be a priority of lesbian and gay organizations did not consider it to be the most important issue of discrimination facing lesbians and gay men.

In fact, 29 percent of respondents felt that legalization of same-sex marriages should not be an organizational priority. Among the accounts of those individuals who stated same-sex marriages should not be a priority, two main considerations stood out. First, the majority argued that other issues were much more important, including working against discrimination in housing and employment, antigay violence and gay bashing, gay and lesbian battering, working for a national gay and lesbian civil rights law, repealing state sodomy laws, lifting the military's ban on gay men and lesbians, and providing more education and awareness around HIV/AIDS. As Eric Warren commented:

> No. It is not an emergency. There are many things that are more pressing, like gay bashing. The violence is so horrible! I also think that something like an overall gay rights law would be a better way for us to go than working on specific issues. It's sort of like the civil rights law for black people. It established a climate, at least in terms of the law, in which you weren't supposed to discriminate.

Similarly, Julia Gomez replied:

> No. I think there are a lot more things that are of much greater priority than the legalization of same-sex marriages such as ending discrimination against gays and lesbians because of their sexual orientation. Passing the Gay Rights Bill. And with AIDS, when you think about it, it is more important to work on ending the epidemic. Getting a civil rights bill and ending discrimination will probably open the doors to the legalization of same-sex marriages.

Many respondents specifically mentioned violence aimed at lesbians and gay men by either strangers or their partners as an issue that needed to be addressed. As Deborah Leiberman commented:

> No. There's too much other stuff to do. Oh, Christ, just discrimination work and changing people's attitudes. Whether I can get married or not, in the long run I can't give two shits about it. I would be much happier if I didn't have to worry about getting attacked on

the streets. Marriage is a nice little goody, but it's like the icing on the cake, so to speak.

Linda Roberts also stated: "No. There are a lot of other important issues in the gay community that people don't realize, like gay and lesbian battering. That is the most important issue to me right now."

A few of these respondents also mentioned parental rights as a concern. According to Leslie Walker:

That's a good question. I guess part of me believes in the shotgun approach that everybody should be working on every front. But if someone forced me to prioritize, I would not put that at the top of my list. No, I think basic civil rights and protection from violence and things like that would be my first priority. Next, there is a whole cluster of family-related things like child custody and the right to have children, whether it's biological children or adopted children or foster children, that I consider to be important. More important than legalizing marriage.

Indeed, the wide range of issues discussed by these respondents highlights the difficulties many lesbian and gay organizations have in attempting to mobilize a constituency around one specific issue. As the recent dissolution of the national organization Queer Nation typified, sustaining collective action is difficult when individuals are focused on too many different issues.

A minority of respondents stated that marriage should not be a priority because it did not support the rights of single and nonmarried heterosexual couples. As Lynn Ettelman commented:

I would rather do things from the focus of each individual, of being able to maintain their civil rights, job opportunities, and freedom from oppression. This society is very couplistic and nonsupportive of single people. So I would hate to see the lesbian and gay movement support that mode. Marriage only gives support and respect to couples and I don't like that.

Respondents with this view considered other issues, such as civil rights, parental rights, and violence, to be more pressing concerns.

Overall, most people interviewed for this book stated that they felt the legalization of same-sex marriages should be a priority for lesbian and gay organizations. Gay men, however, were more likely than lesbians to state that legalizing gay marriages should be a priority; 82 percent of the gay men compared to 69 percent of the lesbians answered yes to this question. Since men have historically benefited from marriage more than women, gay men may be more concerned with gaining the economic benefits and legal privileges of marriage than lesbians. The legalization of same-sex marriages, however, is only one route lesbian and gay organizations have taken to secure the legal rights given married couples. The other is domestic partnership legislation.

Starting in the early 1980s, numerous lesbian and gay organizations across the country have worked to pass domestic partnership laws in their cities and towns. Although they vary in their scope, in general domestic partnership laws cover health insurance benefits and leave policies. As Nan Hunter (1991) has noted, domestic partnerships laws are contracts that are more liberal than marriage laws.

> Domestic partnerships cover only reciprocal obligations for basic support while the two individuals remain in the partnership. There is no implied agreement as to the ownership or division of property acquired during the term of the partnership, nor is there any basis for compelling one partner to support the other for any length of time, however short, after the partnership is dissolved. These laws thus go the farthest toward removing the state from regulation of intimate relationships. (pp. 24-25)

The following section examines attitudes toward whether domestic partnership legislation should be a priority for lesbian and gay organizations.

Should Domestic Partnership Legislation Be a Priority?

Overall, compared to those who thought marriage should be a priority, considerably more respondents emphasized the importance of domestic

TABLE 7.5

SHOULD DOMESTIC PARTNERSHIP
LEGISLATION BE A PRIORITY?

	MALE	FEMALE	TOTAL
PRIORITY	%	%	%
Yes	89	91	90
No	11	3	7
Don't Know	0	6	3
Total	N=45	N=45	N=90

partnerships. A full ninety percent of respondents stated that they thought domestic partnership laws should be a priority for lesbian and gay organizations. (See table 7.5.) These respondents articulated very similar reasons to those they emphasized when advocating marriage: the legal protections and social recognition given married couples. According to Lori Morrison:

> Well, because [domestic partnership laws] are important. A lot of times only one partner has a job that offers health insurance. Any other married couple could name that other person on their health insurance. If you've been living with somebody in a committed relationship just as long as someone who's supposedly gone through this sanctioned ceremony, then they should be able to take advantage of those little perks too. Also, family memberships to things like the Y or health clubs. Think about two lesbians that have had a baby together and are raising this child together and that they can't share each other's health insurance, can't join the health club, can't join the Y, can't take advantage of the same perks as people who are married to each other can. I think it's just antiquated. Society defined families in 1845 and never changed the definition.

Similarly, Michael Sullivan felt that domestic partnership laws should be passed:

Because of the benefits. It's not just strictly material benefits. I think that it also helps to give recognition to gay relationships and put them on an equal footing with straight relationships and so the people like my mother out there who have no way to relate to it, you know, there would be something out there.

Only 7 percent of respondents stated that domestic partnership legislation should not be a priority. These people stated either that lesbian and gay organizations should focus on passing a comprehensive lesbian and gay civil rights bill or that pushing for the legalization of marriage was more important. For example, as Martha Price commented, "Not a priority. I think the energy should be used for gay rights in general for single people." In addition, Theo Nelson commented:

No, because I think that it has to go all the way and that's because domestic partnership is only halfway there. I feel it's allowing us to be less grown up, less responsible than other people have to be in order to get by, and it's the same problem I have with other things, like relaxing standards for blacks to get into schools, it should be the same standards. What our parents really fought for was equality not a hand out or a lower standard.

Marriage As a Civil Right

The overall picture that emerges from these accounts and interviews is threefold. First, most lesbians and gay men believe that same-sex couples should have the right to marry legally in the United States. Their claims for inclusion in the institution of marriage are based in a language of rights. As Hunter (1991) has noted, arguments favoring same-sex marriages are organized around the body of rights discourse that has stemmed from the major civil rights movements of the last twenty-five years, including the lesbian and gay civil rights movement of the 1980s and 1990s.

Second, gay men seem to be more supportive of making same-sex marriages a priority for lesbian and gay organizations and were more interested in getting married than lesbians. Many of the gay men believed that enlarging the legal concept of marriage to include gay couples would alter society's views of gay relationships. In addition, they felt they would personally benefit from being able to marry since marriage would give them legal and economic advantages.

While lesbians also used a language of rights to argue for the legalization of same-sex marriages, they were more skeptical that such marriages would dramatically change society or benefit lesbians and gay men as a class or minority group. Although many acknowledged that marriage could provide them with economic and legal benefits, they also were more critical of gaining these benefits by marrying. Many of the lesbians based their critique of marriage on the language of the gay liberation and lesbian feminist movements of the 1970s. As Paula Ettelbrick (1989) has noted, the goals of lesbian feminism and gay liberation were to affirm lesbian and gay identity and culture and to celebrate the differences of lesbians and gay men from heterosexuals. A number of lesbians who stated they would not marry a woman argued that the legalization of same-sex marriages would not radically alter the structure of marriage. In fact, it would increase the stigma attached to any sexual activity outside the boundaries of heterosexual and homosexual marriages.

In many ways, the differences in lesbians' and gay men's attitudes toward marriage are consistent with the consequences of marriage for heterosexual women and men. As many feminist scholars have argued, among heterosexuals there is a "his" and "hers" marriage that are not equal (Gerstel and Gross, 1987). Often, men get more economic benefits than do women. Thus gay men's greater preference for marriage is a preference for an institution that favors men.

What are the social and political implications of lesbians' and gay men's attempts to change the institution of marriage? Efforts to legalize same-sex marriages through the courts do have the capacity to change how gender is used to structure of marriage. As Hunter (1991) has argued: "The legalization of lesbian and gay marriages would not directly shift the balance of power in heterosexual relationships. It could, however, alter the fundamental concept of the institution of marriage. Its potential is to disrupt both the gendered definition of marriage and the assumption that marriage is a form of socially, if not legally, prescribed hierarchy" (p. 16). At the same time, as the respondents suggest, the legalization of same-sex marriages simultaneously would alter how sexuality and identity are characterized. Thus the legalization of gay marriages has a radical potential to alter religious, social, and legal definitions of what a marriage is supposed to be.

There is a problem, however, in conceptualizing same-sex marriages only in terms of how they challenge the traditional gender distinctions inherent in marriage. While the right to marry would give lesbian and gay couples access to the same benefits and rights as married heterosexual couples, it would not change the basis of these rights in conventional couple relationships. As scholars in the Critical Legal Studies movement have suggested, the problem with rights claims is that they are easily co-opted by the political system and ultimately legitimize the authority of the legal system (Hunter, 1991). The extent to which the legalization of same-sex marriages ultimately would serve to reform or transform the institution of marriage is not easy to assess. However, some public support seems to exist for granting lesbians and gay men the rights associated with marriage. According to a 1989 Time/CNN poll, most respondents stated that lesbian and gay couples should be allowed to inherit each other's property (65 percent) and to receive medical and life insurance benefits from a partner's policy (54 percent)(Isaacson, 1989).

Despite their economic concessions, however, most people who responded to that poll also stated that same-sex marriages should not be legalized (69 percent). More recently, a USA TODAY/CNN/Gallup poll showed that only 27 percent of respondents thought same-sex marriages should be valid ("More Folks Say Gay is OK, But Most Oppose Marriage," 1996). This discrepancy in attitudes suggests that the public may distinguish between the granting of economic rights and the granting of what it considers moral rights. Previous research already has established that public attitudes are more negative toward the morality of homosexual relations than the rights of homosexuals (General Social Survey, 1998). Thus people also may oppose the legalization of same-sex marriages because they see marriage in moral terms rather than as a fundamental right.

In contrast, the lesbians and gay men in this book clearly emphasized the economic and legal aspects of marriage and did not focus on moral rights. In many ways the results suggest that because lesbians and gay men are denied the legal and economic benefits of marriage, they may be more likely to focus on these rights over and above the moral or even emotional aspects of marriage. Indeed, the people studied emphasized the belief that all individuals deserve the basic rights and freedoms allegedly guaranteed by the U.S. Constitution.

Conclusion

Lesbians and gay men are an integral part of the changing landscape of family life in the United States. Although they always have been part of so-called nuclear families (as spouses, parents, and children), the families they create with their own partners, children, and friends have become more visible outside of lesbian and gay communities over the last thirty years. This visibility largely has resulted from the political and legal steps they have taken to ensure their unions are accorded the same legal rights as married, heterosexual couples. Over the last twenty years many lesbians and gay men around the country have fought for increased family, parenting, and marriage rights for same-sex couples.

The accounts in this book highlight four important themes about marriage and family life in the United States today. First, what socially and legally constitutes "family" is continually (albeit slowly) being transformed. Changes in the structure of family are not new to the last few decades but have been in progress for over the last 150 years (Gordon, 1988). Clearly, the increasing inclusion of same-sex couples in the social and legal matrix of family life is one important aspect of this evolution.

Second, social definitions of marriage also are changing. In contrast to the breadwinner/homemaker ideal of the 1940s and 1950s, a new "companionate" model of marriage has emerged, which stresses that partners should provide each other with emotional intimacy, companionship, and sexual fulfillment (Reissman, 1990). Indeed, many lesbian and gay couples (although certainly not all) have adopted this model for their own relationships. Their relationships illustrate the potential for self-growth and long-term commitment as well as conflict in this new model of marriage.

Third, although marriage and family norms are changing, marriage remains a primary vehicle through which individuals form intimate relationships. Instead of rejecting marriage as some did in the 1970s and 1980s, today many lesbians and gay men are pushing for the right to be included in this institution. Contrary to the often-stated diatribe by the New Right that same-sex marriages would undermine the institution of marriage, most respondents believed that legal recognition of lesbian and gay unions would further strengthen the social, economic, and legal rights of all married couples (heterosexual, lesbian, or gay) over those of single individuals.

Finally, many individuals hold ambivalent or even contradictory views on the changes occurring in the institutions of marriage and family. Although women have gained more equality within marriage, husbands and wives continue to struggle over money, housework, and child care issues. Not surprisingly, many heterosexuals "remain torn by their reverence for the traditional nuclear family as it was, or seemed to be, and their acceptance of the 'new' forms of family in today's society" (Skolnick, 1991, p. 198).

The attitudes of lesbians and gay men toward family and marriage issues highlight the changes taking place in these institutions and the conflicting sentiments individuals have about them. While many respondents were critical of the institutions of marriage and family, the majority valued the ideals of love, commitment, monogamy, and family life. At the same time they were supportive of these so-called traditional values, they also argued that marriage and the family need to be redefined to reflect the families people actually create. Their attitudes both mirrored contemporary beliefs and critiqued these same expectations.

As part of the changing fabric of family life in the United States, lesbians and gay men clearly have a stake in how the institutions of marriage and family will be redefined in the future. Although the views of the people studied cannot be generalized to all lesbians and gay men, they do provide an important critique of modern ideals about intimate relationships. Clearly, the battle over who should and will be included in modern social, religious, and legal definitions of family and marriage will continue into the twenty-first century. Despite some legal setbacks, such as the passage of the Defense of Marriage Act by Congress in 1996, lesbians and gay men will continue to fight for and eventually win the battle for full equality.

Fieldwork
and Methods

THE INFORMATION IN THIS BOOK is based on materials gathered from ninety interviews conducted during the summers of 1993 and 1994 with adults (over age eighteen) who self-identified as lesbian, gay, or bisexual. It focuses on one piece of the larger debate over same-sex ceremonies by examining the attitudes and practices toward marriage among a group of lesbians and gay men living in Massachusetts. While their accounts do not represent the views of all lesbians and gay men, their narratives provide one picture of how some are altering the "traditional" boundaries of marriage and family life.

As indicated in appendix II, which contains tables enumerating respondents' sample characteristics, half were lesbians, and half were gay men. Approximately 24 percent of the respondents were Black, Latino, or Asian. In addition, out of the ninety lesbians and gay men interviewed, 19 percent were age eighteen to twenty-nine, thirty-seven percent were age thirty to thirty-nine, 37 percent were age forty to forty-nine, and 11 percent were age fifty to eighty-five. The respondents also had divergent class backgrounds as measured by occupation.

Although social class was not used as a criteria for choosing respondents, the final sample was evenly divided between middle-class and working-class lesbians and gay men. Social class background was defined by a person's occupation. As sociologist Harold Kerbo (1991) has noted, working-class occupations are "characterized by low skill level, lower education, and lower degree of complexity, as well as manual instead of non-manual labor" (p. 270). Approximately 49 percent of the respondents worked in low-paying blue-collar jobs (such as machine operators, truck drivers, service workers, or laborers). The remaining 51 percent of respondents worked in white-collar jobs (such as professionals, managers, or clerical workers).

Last, 78 percent of respondents were currently in a relationship. In a preliminary phone interview, respondents were asked if they were "currently in a primary relationship, that is, a relationship in which they thought of themselves as part of a couple and considered a specific woman or man to be a significant part of their lives." If they were, they also were asked if they had or were planning to have a commitment or union ceremony with their partners. Out of the lesbians and gay men who were currently in a significant relationship, 71 percent lived with their partners, 67 percent had been with their current partner three years or more, and 46 percent either had or were planning to have a ceremony with their partner. Thus the sample for this study heavily emphasizes the views of lesbians and gay men in significant relationships.

Since lesbians and gay men are a stigmatized and often hidden group, random samples are difficult to procure. Records of those who belong to organizations do exist, but these lists are biased toward more educated and affluent individuals who have an affinity for an organization's politics. In order to acquire a more diverse sample, respondents for the study were chosen using a snowball sampling technique, which entails asking contacted individuals to name other potential respondents. Snowball sampling is an ideal method for locating individuals who maintain a low profile (Biernacki and Waldorf, 1981).

Locating respondents is difficult in a group that is hidden and lacks specific criteria for membership (Weston, 1991). Most studies of lesbians and gay men have chosen respondents based on either self-definition or same-sex behavior. Choosing respondents based on either criterion, however, is problematic. Limiting a sample to individuals who self-identify as lesbian or gay potentially could bias a sample toward white, middle-class individuals. Although people from all class backgrounds and races identify as gay or lesbian, people of color and individuals from working-class backgrounds who are involved in same-sex activities often do not self-identify as gay or lesbian. As journalist Neil Miller (1989) suggests, for some black men "gay sex is just messing around; gay identity is a white concept that has no relevance" (p. 180). Therefore, a sample that selects individuals based only on self-definition would exclude women and men who are active in same-sex activities or relationships but do not identify with the labels "lesbian" or "gay."

Choosing respondents based only on same-sex behavior also is problematic. As sex researcher Alfred Kinsey and colleagues (1948) first noted in the 1940s, many people have sexual experiences with individuals of the same sex. Although more recent research by Edward Laumann and associates (1994) suggests that there may be fewer people who have homosexual experiences over the course of their lives than Kinsey reported, using sexual behavior as a sampling criterion remains problematic, because reported behavior could include individuals whose primary identification is heterosexual.[1]

Clearly, any criterion for the inclusion or exclusion of respondents has its limitations. Since the purpose of the study was to examine attitudes toward long-term relationships, the method of self-identification posed fewer problems. The sample was restricted to individuals who self-identified as gay or lesbian or who currently were in a primary relationship with a same-sex partner. Thus individuals who identified as bisexual were included only if they were currently in a same-sex relationship.

To begin the snowball sampling, referral chains were used. The phrase "referral chain" refers to the method of locating potential respondents by asking key individuals to provide referrals to other lesbians and gay men. Key individuals serve as entry points into the population. In this study, three major substantive concerns guided how these key individuals were chosen: gender, race, and education. In order to include a diverse set of respondents in the study, the first three interviews were conducted with a White college-educated gay man, a Black college-educated lesbian, and a Black high school–educated gay man. At the end of each interview, these people each provided referral lists of potential respondents.

From these initial referral lists and following ones, individuals were randomly chosen to call for preliminary phone interviews. These phone interviews provided demographic information on each individual's race, age, relationship situation, and ceremony status, information that subsequently was used to ensure that the sample included a diverse set of respondents.

During these phone interviews, all individuals were asked specifically to participate in the study; if they agreed, a date and time were set up for the interview. In total, 110 phone calls were made and 90 respondents were selected to interview. Only 3 individuals refused to participate.[2] In both the phone and the personal interviews, I made it clear to respondents that I was a lesbian. In general, this disclosure helped to establish a sense of trust and rapport with both the lesbians and the gay men in the study. As one woman commented over the phone, "I thought you probably were a lesbian but I'm relieved to know you are one." Although being a lesbian was not a criterion for conducting this study, it allowed me access to individuals who might not have been as open with a heterosexual interviewer.

All interviews were conducted in Massachusetts, and all respondents were state residents. State residents only were chosen for two reasons. First, this decision limited any potential bias that would arise from interviewing individuals living in states with different political climates. Massachusetts is well known for its liberal politics and relative openness to lesbian and gay issues. In November 1989 it became the second state in the country to pass a Lesbian and Gay Civil Rights Bill. In addition, the state has a history of lesbian and gay political organizing and several established lesbian and gay organizations (Kessler et al., 1988). Second, limited funds were available for travel, so traveling within the state's boundaries was economically feasible and convenient.

The interview schedule consisted of 177 questions ranging in scope from demographic questions to attitudes toward ceremonies, commitment, love, and sex. I developed the questionnaire by examining previous relationship studies that included lesbians and gay men, such as Blumstein and Schwartz's (1983) *American Couples*. While many questions were similar to those previously used, the majority were newly constructed since the goal of this study was to cover a topic that had not been extensively examined. Approximately three-fourths of the questions were open-ended and one-forth consisted of standardized response categories.

The length of each interview ranged on average from two to two and one-half hours. Most were conducted at the respondent's home or, in a few cases, at an office at Smith College (where I was teaching part time). The respondents were extremely generous with their time and made me feel very welcome in their homes. I really enjoyed meeting and talking with all of the individuals in the study. Each person's life story was fascinating. In fact, the most difficult part of the process was learning how to keep the respondent focused on the specific questions in my interview schedule. Many lesbians and gay men shared many intimate aspects of their lives, including their joys and sorrows. In fact, I initially was not prepared for the degree to which she served as a confidante for many individuals' deepest hurts, including rejection from parents, sexual frustrations, breakups with partners, sexual assault, rape, and child abuse.

Although there was a conscious effort to include a diverse range of respondents in the study, the sample has three main limitations. First, it contains a high percentage of individuals who have college degrees. Sixty-seven percent of respondents had a college degree compared to 33 percent who had a high school degree or less (See table AII.4.) Although approximately half of the respondents included worked in blue-collar or low-level service occupations, 29 percent of these individuals had a college degree. In part, this may reflect the availability of four-year educational institutions in the State of Massachusetts. Massachusetts currently has eighty-seven colleges and universities, which makes it the state with the highest per-capita number of four-year institutions in the country (National Center for Educational Statistics, p. 243; *Statistical Abstracts*, 1994, p. 27).

Second, the sample consists primarily of individuals under the age of fifty. (See table AII.3.) While lesbians and gay men over the age of fifty were deliberately sought out, the referral lists gathered from respondents contained few people in their fifties, sixties, and seventies. I had more difficulty finding lesbians and gay men who were over age fifty than anticipated. Although referral lists contained individuals who participated in an "older" lesbian and gay potluck group, the social networks of respondents either did not extend far beyond the group (which included anyone over the age of forty) or did not include many Massachusetts residents. All of the respondents interviewed in the study who were age fifty or over had extensive social networks that included lesbians and gay who were approximately their ages, but many lived in other states. This may reflect the fact that more than half of respondents who were over fifty had moved to Massachusetts to retire. Thus, the sample underrepresents the particular views of older lesbians and gay men.

This sample also included a high percentage of lesbians and gay men who had had commitment or union ceremonies. Out of the seventy respondents who were in a significant relationship with a same-sex partner, 46 percent had or were planning to have a commitment or union ceremony with their partner. (See tables AII.11 and AII.12.) Although same-sex ceremonies were a major focus of the study, the sample may contain a higher percentage of individuals who have had a ceremony than may be true for the larger lesbian and gay population. Thus, the results may indicate that lesbians and gay men value relationship ideals, such as commitment, more than is true for the larger gay population.

Last, it was much more difficult to locate gay men who had ceremonies than lesbians. Many respondents knew of lesbians who had had a same-sex ceremony but few were able to cite men who had. Indeed, it may be that more lesbians than gay men are having commitment and union ceremonies (E. Sullivan, 1991). In total, only ten gay men who had ceremonies were contacted through referral lists. Since it was important for analytical purposes to interview an equal number of lesbians and gay men who had had a ceremony, five additional gay men were contacted through churches and synagogues around the state. Unfortunately, the same difficulty arose from talking with rabbis, priests, and ministers that occurred with the original respondents— most knew of lesbian couples who had a ceremony but few knew any gay men. The best contact proved to be a minister at a Metropolitan Community Church who had conducted a number of union ceremonies for gay men over the past few years. Therefore, this sample may overrepresent gay men who have had commitment or union ceremonies witnessed by an MCC minister.

Demographic Characteristics of Sample

TABLE AII.1

SEXUAL IDENTITY

	FREQUENCY	PERCENT
Lesbian or bisexual	45	50.0
Gay man or bisexual	45	50.0
Total	90	100.0

TABLE AII.2

RACE

	FREQUENCY	PERCENT
White	68	75.6
Black	12	13.3
Latino	8	8.8
Asian	2	2.2
Total	90	100.0

TABLE AII.3

AGE

	FREQUENCY	PERCENT
18–29	17	18.9
30–39	33	36.7
40–49	30	33.3
50–85	10	11.1
Total	90	100.0

TABLE AII.4

HIGHEST GRADE IN SCHOOL

	FREQUENCY	PERCENT
High School or Less	30	33.3
Some College or More	60	66.6
Total	90	100.0

TABLE AII.5

OCCUPATION

	FREQUENCY	PERCENT
Professional	28	31.1
Manager	18	20.0
Clerical	4	4.4
Craftsman	9	10.0
Operatives	10	11.2
Transport	3	3.3
Service	18	20.0
Total	90	100.0

TABLE AII.6

INCOME

	FREQUENCY	PERCENT
$19,999 or Less	45	50.0
$20,000 or More	45	50.0
Total	90	100.0

TABLE AII.7

PREVIOUS HETEROSEXUAL MARRIAGE

	FREQUENCY	PERCENT
Yes	27	30.0
No	63	70.0
Total	90	100.0

TABLE AII.8

CHILDREN

	FREQUENCY	PERCENT
Yes	14	15.6
No	76	84.4
Total	90	100.0

TABLE AII.9.

CURRENT RELIGIOUS BELIEFS

	FREQUENCY	PERCENT
None	36	40.0
Protestant	18	20.0
Catholic	4	4.4
Jewish	8	8.9
Spiritual	19	21.1
Other	5	5.6
Total	90	100.0

TABLE AII.10

RELIGION RAISED

	FREQUENCY	PERCENT
None	11	12.2
Protestant	37	41.1
Catholic	34	37.8
Jewish	8	8.9
Total	90	100.0

TABLE AII.11

RELATIONSHIP STATUS

	FREQUENCY	PERCENT
In Couple	70	77.8
Single	20	22.2
Total	90	100.0

The following tables refer only to individuals in a significant relationship.

TABLE AII.12

HAD/PLANNING A CEREMONY WITH CURRENT PARTNER

	FREQUENCY	PERCENT
Yes	32	45.7
No	38	54.3
Total	70	100.0

TABLE AII.13

LENGTH OF CURRENT RELATIONSHIP

	FREQUENCY	PERCENT
2 years or less	23	32.9
3–7 years	21	30.0
8 years or more	26	37.1
Total	70	100.0

TABLE AII.14

LIVE WITH PARTNER

	FREQUENCY	PERCENT
Yes	50	71.4
No	20	28.6
Total	70	100.0

NOTES

Preface

1. The AIDS Coalition to Unleash Power (ACT UP) was organized in the early 1980s as a direct action organization to promote lesbian and gay liberation. While some ACT UP chapters primarily focus on AIDS treatment issues, others take a more multi-issue approach (Vaid, 1995).
2. In her book *All Our Kin*, Stack (1974) coined the phrase "fictive kin" to refer to friends who are treated as blood relatives. As Weston (1991) notes, however, the phrase has lost credibility in the social sciences. It implies that nonbiological families are only "substitutes" and undermines the legitimacy of these relationships. Weston argues that kinship ideologies should be viewed as "historical transformations rather than derivatives of other sorts of kinship relations" (p. 106). She suggests use of the phrase "chosen families" to describe these types of relationships.
3. Many lesbians and gay men, however, personally hold essentialist views of homosexuality (S. Epstein, 1987). It is important to note here that the fourth edition of the *Publication Manual of the American Psychological Association* (1994) states that "sexual orientation currently is the preferred term [by lesbians and gay men] and is to be used unless the implication of choice is intentional" (p. 51).

Chapter One

1. The Daughters of Bilitis was the first lesbian organization in the United States and began in the 1950s.
2. Three other legal cases concerning the legal right to marry also took place in the 1970s. These cases took place in Arizona in January 1975, Colorado in March 1975, and Chicago in 1976 (Ayers and Brown, 1994, p. 15; Butler, 1990, p. 36).
3. According to a personal phone conversation with Zerilli, the Universal Fellowship of Metropolitan Community Churches is planning another wedding ceremony to take place prior to the Millennium March on Washington for Equality in April, 2000. Information about "The Wedding: Now More Than Ever" and the millennium march can be found at the following website: www.ufmcc.com.
4. During the 1960s ministers involved in the Council on Religion and the Homosexual also performed "covenant" ceremonies for lesbian and gay couples (Ayers and Brown, 1994, p. 14).
5. Some of these cities are San Francisco, Berkeley, West Hollywood, Santa Cruz, and Los Angeles, California; Takoma Park, Maryland; Seattle, Washington; Madison, Wisconsin; Ithaca, New York; and Minneapolis, Minnesota.

6. In *Marvin v. Marvin* (1976), Justice Tobriner of the Supreme Court of California ruled that "the fact that a man and a woman live together without marriage, and engage in a sexual relationship, does not in itself invalidate agreements between them relating to their earnings, property, or expenses" (Areen, 1978, p. 736).

7. See *Brashi v. Stahl Associates;* and *Group House of Port Washington, Inc. v. Board of Zoning and Appeals for the Town of North Hempstead.*

8. See "A Right to Care," 1985; Murdoch, 1988; Thompson and Andrzejewski, 1988.

9. Text of speech taken from a talk given by Craig Dean at the University of Massachusetts–Amherst on April 21, 1992.

Chapter Two

1. As historian Martha May (1987) has noted, the family wage "as an ideology presented a particular arrangement of family work roles as socially desirable" (p. 11). The family wage ideal was based on the notion that husbands should be able to support their families financially so that their wives could stay at home.

2. Twenty percent or more of respondents mentioned these qualities.

3. Honesty was ranked first out of a choice of six traits. The other five attributes included in Laner's (1977) study were affectionate, intelligent, good-looking, has a sense of humor, and has money.

4. The top five most frequently mentioned qualities were: (1) Good, open communication, (2) support and caring, (3) tolerance, flexibility, and understanding, (4) honesty, and (5) commitment (Cancian, 1987, p. 41).

5. This stereotype stems from research that has emphasized the amount of sexual contacts gay men have over the course of their lives (Bell and Weinberg, 1978; Blumstein and Schwartz, 1983). Although many studies have shown that lesbians on average do have sex less frequently than gay men, previous research has not examined the value lesbians and gay men place on physical attraction and sexual intimacy in their long-term relationships.

6. In the early 1970s Radicalesbians attempted to define lesbianism as more than sexuality. As historian Alice Echols (1989) noted, they redefined "lesbianism as primarily a political choice" and argued it is was sexist to define lesbianism "simply by sex" (p. 216). Other lesbian feminists also attempted to define lesbianism as being different from the heterosexual pattern of male dominance. To these women, lesbianism involved "sensuality rather than sexuality, communication rather then conquest" (p. 217). As Sue Katz, a Boston author, wrote: "For me, coming out meant an end to sex. . . . Our sexuality may or may not include genital experience" (quoted in Echols, 1989, p. 217-218).

7. In this study, however, the length of time respondents had been in their current relationship was not significantly related to the amount of sex they had with their partner over the previous year. But not surprisingly, the eight lesbians and gay men who mentioned sexual problems did have sex less frequently with their partners than other respondents.

8. According to psychologists Letitia Anne Peplau and Steve Gordon (1985), women often define the term "communication" as meaning sharing one's feelings while for men it often refers to sharing information. One explanation for these differences stresses communication styles. Researcher Deborah Tannen (1990) feels women and men define communication in different ways because they grow up in different cultures and learn very different styles of communication. Men communicate "as individuals in a hierarchical social order in which they are either one-up or one down" (p. 24). They view conversations as negotiations in which they try to acquire status by gaining the upper hand and maintaining their independence. In contrast, women communicate as "individuals in a network of connections" (p. 25). For women, conversations are negotiations for intimacy, support, and connection. Thus women and men constantly struggle with each other in conversations because they approach communication with radically different goals.

Chapter Three

1. See Becker, 1960; Burke and Reitzes, 1991; Kanter, 1968; and Stryker and Serpe, 1982.
2. See de Waal, 1989; Rosenblatt, 1977; Scanzoni and Arnett, 1987; and Spanier, 1976.
3. See Bellah et al., 1985; Bernard, 1982; and Swidler, 1980.
4. See Rosenblatt, 1977; Spanier, 1976; and Scanzoni and Arnett, 1987.
5. See Fincham and Bradbury, 1987; Fowers, 1991; Grey-Little and Burks, 1983; and Peplau, Pedesky, and Hamilton, 1982.
6. The phrase "shiny toys" was Kathleen's euphemism for other women.

Chapter Four

1. This does not mean that no lesbians and gay men had "public" ceremonies. In fact, some Black lesbians and gay men in Harlem had highly visible same-sex ceremonies during the 1920s (Ayers and Brown, 1994). Same-sex ceremonies that included public witnesses, however, were uncommon until the 1970s and 1980s.
2. Among the respondents, no ceremonies took between five and nine years after a couple had gotten together.
3. The term "Lesbianville" was coined by the *National Enquirer* to refer to the town of Northampton, Massachusetts (1992, p. 8; Kelliher, 1991, p. 1).
4. The phrase "chosen families" was adopted from Kath Weston, who used it to refer to the families lesbians and gay men create. Members of chosen families can include friends, blood relatives, and children (Weston, 1991).
5. Harvey Milk was the first openly gay city supervisor to be elected to office in San Francisco. He was a city supervisor from June 1977 until his assassination in November 1978 (Adam, 1987).

Chapter Five

1. Gerholm quoted in Parkin, 1994, p. 13.
2. One lesbian couple used the phrase "We invite you to join us in the union of our hearts and lives together," which is derived from a phrase cited in *Ceremonies of the Heart* by Becky Butler (1990) on their invitations but used the words "commitment ceremony" when talking to or inviting guests. The original phrase was "Please join us in a celebration as proclaim the unity of our hearts and our lives together" (p. 192).
3. See Butler (1990) and Budapest (1989).

Chapter Six

1. One traditional marriage custom in the United States is that the bride wear something old, new, borrowed, and blue. The "old" symbolizes the strength and durability of the marriage; the "new" represents the couple's new life together; the "borrowed" implies the bride will be as happy as other women who have been married; and the "blue" denotes fertility.
2. This couple based their trysting ceremony on Goddess rituals taken from the Wicca (or witchcraft) tradition. As Butler (1990) noted, the women's spirituality movement has provided avenues for some women to reenvision the Judeo-Christian tradition and others to reclaim Goddess worship and witchcraft. In particular, the writers Starhawk (1982) and Zsuzsanna Budapest (1989) have elaborated on the feminist meanings of Wiccian beliefs. The term "tryst" means trust; its use is explained in Budapest's *Holy Book of Women's Mysteries*.
3. To have an official Quaker marriage, a couple (gay or heterosexual) must apply to the Friends Meeting House where they would like to have the ceremony for recognition and approval before the marriage can take place. This process is called "arriving at clearness" and often the couple is requested to meet with a clearness committee (Ayers and Brown, 1994, pp. 115-116).

Chapter Seven

1. See *Dean v. District of Columbia.*
2. See *Jones v. Hallahan, Baker v. Nelson,* and *Singer v. Hara.* In two other cases, gay men had commitment ceremonies and then sought to be recognized as married couples. These cases were *Adams v. Howertown,* and *McConnell v. Nooner.*
3. The "full faith and credit" provision ensures that every state recognizes the laws of all other states. This provision is particularly important in the case of marriage, since every state has its own marriage laws. This provision was struck down in 1996 when the Defense of Marriage Act was passed by Congress.
4. The Minnesota State Court initially assigned Sharon's father as her legal guardian. After an eight-year court battle, the state did overturn its ruling. This reversal,

however, came about only because of the Kowalskis' refusal to care adequately for their daughter (Thompson and Andrzejewski, 1988).

5. The following states have laws or executive orders prohibiting discrimination on the basis of sexual orientation in public employment: California (executive order—1979); Colorado (executive order—1990); Connecticut (law—1991); District of Columbia (law—1977); Hawaii (law—1991); Illinois (executive order—1995); Maryland (executive order—1996); Massachusetts (law—1989); Minnesota (law—1993); New Hampshire (law—1998); New Jersey (law—1992); New York (executive order—1994); Ohio (executive order—1992); Pennsylvania (executive order—1988); Rhode Island (law—1995); Vermont (law—1993); and Wisconsin (law—19xx). Only Connecticut, Massachusetts, Vermont, Washington, D.C., and Wisconsin have comprehensive laws that prohibit sexual discrimination in private and public employment, education, housing, credit, and union practices. For in-depth information on the scope of these civil rights laws, see Jane Goldschmidt (1998).

Appendix I

1. The prevalence of homosexuality is a debated issue. According to Laumann et al. (1994), in the past there has been a general consensus that approximately 10 percent of the population "identifies" as gay or lesbian. They argue, however, that the actual prevalence of homosexuality is much lower and suggest that approximately 1.5 percent of women and 3 percent of men in the United States identify as homosexual.

2. All three individuals who did not want to participate in the study were lesbians. One women explained that she was "just too busy studying" for a professional exam. Two other women, however, refused because they were skeptical of my intentions as a social researcher. One women stated that she felt research usually hurt more than it helped lesbians in general.

BIBLIOGRAPHY

Abu-Lughod, Lila. 1990. "The Romance of Resistance: Tracing Transformations of Power Through Bedouin Women," *American Ethnologist* 17(1):41-55.

Adam, Barry. 1987. *The Rise of a Gay and Lesbian Movement.* Boston: G. K. Hall and Company.

Adams v. Howertown, 673 F.2d 1036 (9th Cir. 1982).

Adams, Kathryn and Audrey Landers. 1978. "Sex Differences in Dominance Relationships," *Sex Roles* 4(2):215-223.

"A Legal Fiction?"1989, July 18. *The Wall Street Journal,* p. A22.

Allen, Clifford. 1957. "When Homosexuals Marry," *Sexology* (February):416-420.

Altman, Dennis. 1982. *The Homosexualization of America.* Boston: Beacon Press.

———. 1979. *Coming Out in the Seventies.* Boston: Alyson.

Altman, Irwin and Dalmas Taylor. 1973. *Social Penetration: The Development of Interpersonal Relations.* New York: Holt, Rinehart, and Winston.

American Psychological Association. 1994. *Publication Manual of the American Psychological Association, 4th ed.* Washington, D.C.: APA.

Areen, Judith. 1978. *Family Law: Case and Methods.* New York: The Foundation Press.

"A Right to Care," 1985. *MS* (September):21.

Atkinson, Jean. 1987. "Gender Roles in Marriage and the Family," *Journal of Family Issues* 8(1):5-41.

Atkinson, Jean and Ted Huston. 1984. "Sex Role Orientation and Division of Labor in Early Marriage." *Journal of Personality and Social Psychology* 41(February):330-345.

Ayers, Tess and Paul Brown. 1994. *The Essential Guide to Lesbian and Gay Weddings.* New York: HarperCollins.

Ayvasian, Andrea. 1987. "Rethinking Marriage." *Friends Journal* (October).

Baird, Robert and Stuart Rosenbaum. 1997. *Same-Sex Marriage: The Moral and Legal Debate.* New York: Prometheus Books.

Baehr v. Lewin, 74 Haw. 530, 852 P.2d 44 (1993).

Baehr v. Miike, 950 P.2d. 1234 (Haw. 1997).

Baker v. Nelson, 291 Minn. 310, 191 N.W.2d 185, appeal dismissed 409 U.S. 810 (1971).

Bane, Mary Jo. 1976. *Here to Stay: American Families in the Twentieth Century.* New York: Basic Books.

Barker, Diana Leonard. 1978. "A Proper Wedding." In Marie Corbin (ed.), *The Couple,* pp. 56-77. New York: Penguin Books.

Barrett, Michele. 1986. *Women's Oppression Today.* London: Verso.

Barrett, Michele and Mary McIntosh. 1982. *The Anti-Social Family.* London: Verso Editions.

Basheda, Valerie. 1989, July 7. "Domestic Partnership Ordinance Stalls," *Los Angeles Times,* Sec. I, p. 3.

Bauer, Gary. 1994, November 18. "Don't Forget Family Issues," *The Wall Street Journal,* p. A18.

Baumann, Gerd. 1994. "Ritual Implicates 'Others': Rereading Durkheim in a Plural Society." In Daniel de Coppet (ed.), *Understanding Rituals,* pp. 97-116. New York: Routledge.

Becker, Howard. 1960. "Notes on the Concept of Commitment," *American Journal of Sociology* 66(July):32-40.

Beigel, Hugo. 1948. "Romantic Love," *American Sociological Review* 16(June):326-334.

Bell, Alan and Martin Weinberg. 1978. *Homosexualities: A Study of Diversity Among Women and Men.* New York: Simon and Schuster.

Bellah, Robert, Richard Madsen, William Sullivan, Ann Swidler, and Steven Tipton. 1985. *Habits of the Heart: Individualism and Commitment in American Life.* New York: Harper & Row.

Benkov, Laura. 1994. *Reinventing the Family.* New York: Crown.

Bennett, Neil, Ann Blanc, and David Bloom. 1988. "Commitment and the Modern Union: Assessing the Link Between Premarital Cohabitation and Subsequent Marital Stability," *American Sociological Review* 53(February):127-138.

Berke, Richard. 1995, January 22. "Christian Right Embraces Republican 'Contract.'" *The New York Times*, p. E2.

Berger, Brigitte and Peter Berger. 1984. *The War Over the Family: Capturing the Middle Ground.* New York: Anchor Press.

Berger, Raymond. 1990. "Men Together: Understanding the Gay Couple," *Journal of Homosexuality* 19(3):31-49.

―――. 1982. *Gay and Gray: The Older Homosexual Man.* Boston: Alyson.

Berk, Richard and Sarah Fenstermaker Berk. 1979. *Labor and Leisure at Home: Content and Organization of the Household Day.* Beverly Hills, CA: Sage.

Bernard, Jessie. 1982. *The Future of Marriage* (2nd ed.). New Haven, CT: Yale University Press.

Bernstein, Robert. 1990, June 26. "Family Values and Gay Rights," *New York Times*, p. A23.

Berscheid, Ellen and Elaine Walster. 1974. "A Little Bit About Love." In Ted Huston (ed.), *Foundations of Interpersonal Attraction*, pp. 356-379. New York: Academic Press.

Biernacki, Patrick and Dan Waldorf. 1981. "Snowball Sampling: Problems and Techniques of Chain Referral Sampling," *Sociological Methods and Research* 10(2):141-163.

Bishop, Katherine. 1989, May 31. "San Francisco Grants Recognition to Couples Who Aren't Married," *The New York Times*, p. A17.

Blattner, Jane. 1981. "The Supreme Court's Intermediate Equal Protection Decision: Five Imperfect Models of Constitutional Equality," *Hastings Constitutional Law Quarterly* 8:777, 780-800.

Blau, Peter. 1964. *Exchange and Power in Social Life.* New York: John Wiley & Sons.

Blumberg, Grace. 1985. "New Model of Marriage and Divorce: Significant Legal Developments in the Last Decade." In Kingsley Davis (ed.), *Contemporary Marriage*, pp. 349-372. New York, Russell Sage.

Blumstein, Philip and Pepper Schwartz. 1983. *American Couples: Money, Work, Sex.* New York: William Morrow and Company.

Borgatta, Edgar and Marie Borgatta. 1992. *Encyclopedia of Sociology.* New York: Macmillan.

Borrello, Gloria and Bruce Thompson. 1988. "A Replication Bootstrap Analysis of the Structure Underlying Perceptions of Stereotypic Love," *Journal of General Psychology* 116(3):317-327.

Boswell, John. 1994. *Same-Sex Unions in Premodern Europe.* New York: Villard.

————. 1980. *Christianity, Social Tolerance, and Homosexuality.* Chicago: University of Chicago Press.

Bowers v. Hardwick, 106 S.Ct. 2841, 2843-44 (1986).

Braschi v. Stahl Associates, 543 N.E.2d 49 (N.Y.1989).

Braverman, Harry. 1974. *Labor Monopoly Capital: The Degradation of Work in The 20th Century.* New York: Monthly Review Press.

Briskin, Linda. 1990. "Identity Politics and the Hierarchy of Oppression," *Feminist Review,* 35(Summer):102-108.

Buchanan, Jane. 1985. "Same-Sex Marriage: The Linchpin Issue," *University of Dayton Law Review,* 10:541, 549-570.

Budapest, Zsuzsanna. 1989. *Holy Book of Women's Mysteries.* England: Wingbow Press.

Bumpass, Larry and James Sweet. 1989. "National Estimates of Cohabitation," *Demography* 26(4):615-625.

Burgess, Ernest and Harvey Locke. 1953. *The Family.* New York: American Book.

Burke, Peter and Donald Reitzes. 1991. "An Identity Approach to Commitment," *Social Psychology Quarterly* 54(3):239-251.

Burkett v. Zablocki, 54 F.R.D. 626 (E.D. Wis. 1972).

Butler, Becky. 1990. *Ceremonies of the Heart: Celebrating Lesbian Unions.* Seattle: The Seal Press.

Calhoun, Craig. 1993. "New Social Movements of the Early Nineteenth Century," *Social Science History* 17(3):385-427.

Camerer, Colin. 1994. "Gifts as Economic Signals and Social Symbols," *American Journal of Sociology* 94(Supplement):S180-S214.

Cancian, Francesca. 1987. *Love in America: Gender and Self-Development.* New York: Cambridge University Press.

————. 1986. "Love and Power: Types of Marriage in the U.S." *Urban Anthropology* 15(3-4):215-243.

————. 1985. "Gender Politics: Love and Power in the Private and Public Spheres." In Alice Rossi (ed.), *Gender and The Life Course,* pp. 253-264. New York: Aldine Publishing.

Cardell, Mona, Stephen Finn, and Jeanne Marecek. 1981. "Sex-Role Identity, Sex-Role Behavior, and Satisfaction in Heterosexual, Lesbian, and Gay Male Couples," *Psychology of Women Quarterly* 5(3):488-494.

Carl, Douglas. 1986. "Acquired Immune Deficiency Syndrome: A Preliminary Examination of the Effects on Gay Couples and Coupling," *Journal of Marital and Family Therapy* 12(3):241-247.

Cate, Rodney, Ted Huston, and John Nesselroade. 1986. "Premarital Relationships: Toward the Identification of Alternative Pathways to Marriage," *Journal of Social and Clinical Psychology* 4(1):3-22.

Charsley, Simon. 1992. "What Does a Wedding Cake Mean?" *New Society* 3(July):11-14.

Cherry, Kittredge and James Mitulski. 1990, February 28. "Committed Couples in the Gay Community," *The Christian Century,* pp. 218-220.

Chodorow, Nancy. 1978. *The Reproduction of Mothering: Psychoanalysis and the Sociology of Gender.* Berkeley: University of California Press.

Chow, Robert. 1989, May 23. "S.F. Supervisors OK 'Domestic Partner Law," *Los Angeles Times,* Sec. I, p. 3.

Clark, Margaret and Judson Mills. 1979. "Interpersonal Attraction in Exchange and Communal Relationships," *Journal of Personality and Social Psychology* 37(1):12-24.

Cleek, Margaret and Allan Pearson. 1985. "Perceived Causes of Divorce: An Analysis of Interrelationships," *Journal of Marriage and the Family* 47(1):179-183.

Clunis, Merilee and G. Dorsey Green. *Lesbian Couples.* Seattle: The Seal Press, 1988.

Cochran, Susan and Letitia Anne Peplau. 1985. *Value Orientations in Heterosexual Relationships.* Psychology of Women Quarterly, 9, 477-488.

Collier, Jane, Michelle Rosaldo, and Sylvia Yanagisako. 1982. "Is There a Family? New Anthropological Views." In Barrie Thorne and Marilyn Yalom (eds.), *Rethinking the Family: Some Feminist Questions,* pp. 25-39. New York: Longman Press.

Commonweal. 1997. "Marriage's True Ends." In Andrew Sullivan (ed.), *Same-Sex Marriage: Pro and Con,* pp. 54-57. New York: Vintage.

Contrada, Fred. 1991, June 23. "Starting a Family with Two Mothers," *Sunday Republican,* p. B1.

Cronan, Sheila. 1984. "Marriage." In Alison Jagger and Paula Rothenberg (eds.), *Feminist Frameworks,* pp. 240-244. New York: McGraw-Hill Book Company.

Cullen, Jane. 1979a. "Fundamental Interests and the Question of Same-Sex Marriage," *Tulsa Law Journal,* 15:141, 154-162.

———. 1979b. "Homosexual Right to Marry: A Constitutional Test and a Legislative Solution," *University of Pennsylvania Law Review,* 128:193, 210-212.

Current Population Reports. 1998. "Table B. Families by Type, Race, and Hispanic Origin, and Selected Characteristics: 1997," p. 4. http://www.census.gov/prod/ 3/ 98pubs/p20-509.pdf.

Dailey, Dennis. 1979. "Adjustment of Heterosexual and Homosexual Couples in Pairing Relationships: An Exploratory Study," *Journal of Sex Research* 15(2):143-157.

———. 1977. "Legitimacy and Permanence in the Gay Relationship: Some Intervention Alternatives," *Journal of Social Welfare* 4:81-88.

Davis, Kingsley. 1985. "The Future of Marriage," In Kingsley Davis (ed.), *Contemporary Marriage,* pp. 25-52. New York: Russell Sage Foundation.

Davis-Floyd, Robbie. 1992. *Birth as an American Right of Passage.* Berkeley: University of California Press.

Dean, Craig. 1991, October 28. "Legalize Gay Marriage," *New York Times,* p. A19.

———. 1994. "Gay Marriage: A Civil Right," *Journal of Homosexuality* 27(3-4):111-115.

Dean v. Dictrict of Columbia, 653 A.2d 307(D.C. App. 1995).

Degler, Carl. 1980. *At Odds: Women and the Family in America from the Revolution to the Present.* New York: Oxford Press.

Delmar, Rosalind. 1986. "What Is Feminism?" In Juliet Mitchell and Ann Oakly (eds.), *What Is Feminism?* pp. 8-33. New York: Pantheon Books.

D'Emilio, John. 1989. "Gay Politics and Community in San Francisco Since World War II." In Martin Duberman, Martha Vicinus, and George Chauncey, Jr. (eds.), *Hidden from History: Reclaiming the Gay and Lesbian Past,* pp. 456-476. New York: Meridian.

———. 1983. *Sexual Politics, Sexual Communities: The Making of a Homosexual Minority in the United States, 1940-1970.* Chicago: University of Chicago Press.

D'Emilio, John and Estelle Freedman. 1988. *Intimate Matters: A History of Sexuality in America.* New York: Harper & Row.

Delphy, Christine. 1984. *Close to Home: A Materialist Analysis of Women's Oppression.* Amherst: University of Massachusetts Press.

Demos, John. 1970. *A Little Commonwealth: Family Life in Plymouth Colony.* New York: Oxford University Press.

Derlega, Valerie, Bonnie Durham, Barbara Gockel, and David Sholis. 1981. "Sex Differences in Self-Disclosure: Effects of Topic Content, Friendship, and Partner's Sex," *Sex Roles* 7(4):433-447.

DeVault, Marjorie. 1991. *Feeding the Family: The Social Organization of Caring as Gendered Work.* Chicago: University of Chicago Press.

de Waal, Martha. 1989. "Aspects of a Cohort of Married Couples' Commitment to Marriage: Results of an Exploratory Study," *South African Journal of Sociology* 20(3):195-199.

Dion, Kenneth and Karen Dion. 1973. "Correlates of Romantic Love," *Journal of Consulting and Clinical Psychology* 41:51-56.

Donzelot, Jacques. 1979. *The Policing of Families.* New York: Pantheon Books.

Doudna, Christine. 1983. "American Couples: Surprising New Finds," *MS* (November):116-119.

Duberman, Martin, Martha Vicinus, and George Chauncey, Jr. (eds.). 1989. *Hidden from History: Reclaiming the Gay and Lesbian Past.* New York: Meridian.

Duffy, Sally and Caryl Rusbult. 1985-86. "Satisfaction and Commitment in Homosexual and Heterosexual Relationships," *Journal of Homosexuality* 12(2):1-23.

Dullea, George. 1988, February 7."Gay Couples' Wish to Adopt Grows, Along with Increasing Resistance," *New York Times*, p. 26.

Dunlap, David. 1996a, January 21. "Gay Images. Once Kept Out, Are Big Time," *New York Times*, sec. 1, p. 29.

Dunlap, David. 1996b, May 9. "Congressional Bills Withhold Sanction of Same-Sex Unions," *New York Times*, p. B15.

Dunlap, Mary. 1983, April 9. "Are We Legal Yet? A Lesbian Attorney Examines Our Current Legal Status and Looks at Some Key Cases," *Gay Community News*,

Durkheim, Emile. 1971. *The Elementary Forms of Religious Life.* London: George Allen and Unwin.

Echols, Alice. 1989. *Daring to be Bad: Radical Feminism in America 1967-1975.* Minneapolis: University of Minnesota Press.

Eisenstein, Zillah. 1988. *The Female Body and the Law.* Berkeley: University of California Press.

Elise, Dianne. 1986. "Lesbian Couples: The Implications of Sex Differences in Separation-Individuation," *Psychotherapy* 23 (Summer):305-310.

Elliot, Faith Robertson. 1986. *The Family: Change or Continuity.* Atlantic Highlands, NJ: Humanities Press International.

Ellis, Havelock. 1905. *Studies in the Psychology of Sex.* New York: Random House.

Engels, Friedrich. 1972. *The Origin of the Family, Private Property and the State.* New York: Pathfinders Press.

Epstein, Barbara. 1991. *Political Protest and Cultural Revolution.* Berkeley: University of California Press, 1991.

Epstein, Steven. 1987. "Gay Politics, Ethnic Identity: The Limits of Social Constructionism," *Socialist Review* (93/94):9-54.

Escoffier, Jeffry. 1985. "Sexual Revolution and the Politics of Gay Identity," *Socialist Review* (82/83):119-153.

Eskridge, William Jr. 1996. *From Sexual Liberty to Civilized Commitment: The Case for Same-Sex Marriage.* New York: The Free Press.

Ettlebrick, Paula. 1989. "Since When Is Marriage a Path to Liberation?" *OUT/LOOK* 2(2)(Fall): 14-17.

Faber, Nancy. 1979, July 9. "Lesbians Madeline Isaacson and Sandy Schuster Find 'Marriage' Happy but Hardly Untroubled," *People* 12(2).

Faderman, Lillian. 1991. *Odd Girls and Twilight Lovers.* New York: Penguin.

———. 1981. *Surpassing the Love of Men.* New York: William Morrow.

Falbo, Toni and Letitia Anne Peplau. 1980. "Power Strategies in Intimate Relationships," *Journal of Personality and Social Psychology* 38(4):618-628.

Ferdinand, Pamela. 2000, February 6. "Vermonters Rise to Sort Out Law on Marriage," *The Washington Post,* p. A3.

Ferstenberg, Frank and Graham Spanier. 1984. *Recycling the Family: Remarriage After Divorce.* Beverly Hills: Sage.

Fincham, Frank and Thomas Bradbury. 1987. "The Assessment of Marital Quality: A Reevaluation," *Journal of Marriage and the Family* 49 (November):797-809.

Findlen, Barbara. 1987. "Gay Marriage: Lifting the Bans," *MS* (February):29.

Fineman, Martha and Nancy Thomadsen (eds.). 1991. *At the Boundaries of Law: Feminism and Legal Theory.* New York: Routledge.

Firestone, Shulamith. 1970. *The Dialectic of Sex: The Case for the Feminist Revolution.* New York: Bantam Books.

Fishman, Pamela. 1978. "Interaction: The Work Women Do." *Social Problems,* 25, 397-406.

Fiske, Marjorie. 1980. "Changing Hierarchies of Commitment in Adulthood." In Neil Smelser and Erik Erikson (eds.), *Themes of Work and Love in Adulthood,* pp. 238-264. Cambridge, MA: Harvard University Press.

Fitzpatrick, M. 1988. "Approaches to Marital Interaction." In P. Noller and M. Fitzpatrick (eds.), *Perspectives on Marital Interaction,* pp. 1-28. Philadelphia: Multilingual Matters.

"Five of Today's Families." 1989, August 31. *The New York Times,* p. C6.

Foucault, Michel. 1978. *The History of Sexuality.* New York: Vintage.

Fowers, Blaine. 1991. "His and Her Marriage: A Multivariate Study of Gender and Marital Satisfaction," *Sex Roles* 24(3/4):209-221.

Friedman, Alissa. 1987/88. "The Necessity for State Recognition of Same-Sex Marriage," *Berkeley Women's Law Journal* 3:134-170.

Fromm, Erik. 1956. *The Art of Loving.* New York: Harper.

Frye, Marilyn. 1981. *The Politics of Reality: Essays on Feminist Theory.* Freedom, CA: The Crossing Press.

Gadlin, Howard. 1977. "Private Lives and Public Order: A Critical View of the History of Intimate Relations in the United States." In George Levinger and Harold Raush (eds.), *Close Relationships: Perspectives on the Meaning of Intimacy,* pp. 33-72. Amherst: University of Massachusetts Press.

Gagnon, John and William Simon (eds.). 1973. *The Sexual Scene.* New York: Dutton.

Gallagher, John. 2000, February 29. "Wedded to equality," *The Advocate,* pp. 33-37.

———. 1996, July 23. "Love and War," *The Advocate,* pp. 22-28.

Garcia, Dawn. 1989, March 8. "S. F. Effort to Develop Policy on Unmarried Couple's Rights," *San Francisco Chronicle.*

Geertz, Clifford. 1973. *The Interpretation of Cultures.* New York: Basic Books.

General Social Survey, 1998. *Codebook.* http://gort.ucsd.edu/gss/.

Gerholm, Tomas. 1988. "On Ritual: A Postmodern View," *Ethnos* 53(3/4):190-203.

Gerstel, Naomi and Sally Gallagher. 1994. "Caring for Kith and Kin: Gender, Employment, and the Privatization of Care," *Social Problems* 4(1):519-539.

Gerstel, Naomi and Harriet Engel Gross. 1989. "Women and the American Family: Continuity and Change." In Jo Freeman (ed.), *Women: A Feminist Perspective,* pp. 89-120. Mountain View, CA: Mayfield Publishing Company.

———. 1987. "Introduction and Overview." In Naomi Gerstel and Harriet Engel Gross (eds.) *Families and Work,* pp. 1-22. Philadelphia: Temple University Press.

———. 1984. *Commuter Marriage: A Study of Work and Family.* New York: Guilford Press.

Giele, Janet Zollinger. 1976. "Changing Sex Roles and the Future of Marriage." In Henry Grunebaum and Jacob Christ (eds.), *Contemporary Marriage,* pp. 69-85. Boston: Little, Brown and Company.

Gillingham, Maya. 1989. "Marriage in Lesbian and Gay Communities." Unpublished ms, University of Massachusetts.

Glendon, Mary Ann. 1989. *The Transformation of Family Law: State, Law, and Family in the United States and Western Europe.* Chicago: University of Chicago Press.

Glezer, Helen. 1991. "Cohabitation," *Family Matters* 30 (December):24-27.

Goethals, George, Robert Steele, and Gwen Broude. 1976. "Theories and Research on Marriage: A Review and Some New Directions." In Henry Grunebaum and Jacob Christ (eds.), *Contemporary Marriage,* pp. 229-273. Boston: Little, Brown and Company.

Goffman, Erving. 1963. *Stigma.* Englewood Cliffs, NJ: Prentice-Hall.

Goldberg, Carey. 2000, December 21. "Vermont High Court Backs Rights of Same-Sex Couples." http://www.nytimes.com/yr/mo/day/news/national/vt-gay-marriage.html.

Goldschmidt, Jane. 1998. "Gay Lesbian, Bisexual, and Transgender Civil Rights Laws in the U.S." Washington, D.C.: Policy Institute of the National Gay and Lesbian Task Force. http://www.ngltf.org.

Goode, William. 1971. *The Contemporary American Family.* Chicago: Quadrangle Books.

———. 1959. "The Theoretical Importance of Love," *American Sociological Review* 24(1):38-47.

Goodman, Ellen. 1989, June 24. "It's Love (!) And It's Legal," *Washington Post,* p. A27.

Goody, Jack. 1977. "Against Ritual: Loosely Structured Thoughts on a Loosely Defined Topic." In Sally Moore and Barbara Myerhoff (eds.), *Secular Ritual,* pp. 25-35. Amsterdam: Van Gorcum.

Gordon, Linda (ed.). 1990. *Women, the State, and Welfare.* Madison: University of Wisconsin Press.

———. 1988. *Heroes of Their Own Lives.* New York: Penguin.

Gould, Roger. 1972. "The Phases of Adult Life: A Study in Developmental Psychology," *American Journal of Psychiatry* 129(5):521-531.

Grahn, Judy. 1990. *Another Mother Tongue: Gay Words, Gay Worlds.* Boston: Beacon Press.

Grant, Linda, Katherine Ward, Donald Brown, and William Moore. 1987. "Development of Work and Family Commitments," *Journal of Family Issues* 8(2):176-198.

Greenberg, David. 1988. *The Construction of Homosexuality.* Chicago: University of Chicago Press.

Greig, Michael. 1970, July 15. "Lesbian Partners and Gay Married Life," *San Francisco Chronicle.*

Greven, Philip. 1983. "Family Structure in Seventeenth Century Andover, Massachusetts." In Michael Gordon (ed.), *The American Family in Historical Perspective*, pp. 136-154. New York: St. Martin's Press.

Grey-Little, Bernadette and Nancy Burks. 1983. "Power and Satisfaction in Marriage: A Review and Critique," *Psychological Bulletin* 93:513-538.

Griswold, Robert. 1988. "Sexual Cruelty and the Case for Divorce in Victorian America." In Norval Glenn and Marion Coleman (eds.), *Family Relations: A Reader*, pp. 54- 66. Chicago: The Dorsey Press.

Griswold v. Connecticut, 381 U.S. 479,484 (1965).

Gross, Jane. 1994, April 25. "After a Ruling, Hawaii Weighs Gay Marriages," *New York Times*, pp. A1 and B8.

Group House of Port Washington, Inc. v. Board of Zoning and Appeals for the Town of North Hempstead, 45 N.Y.2.d 266; 380 N.E. 2d 207 (NY 1978).

Gutis, Philip. 1989a, April 27. "How to Define a Family: Gay Tenant Fights Eviction," *New York Times*, pp. B1 and B2.

———. 1989b, November 5. "Small Steps Toward Acceptance Renew Debate On Gay Marriage," *New York Sunday Times*, p. E24.

———. 1989c, November 7. "Gay Teachers Sue for Benefits for Longtime Companions," *New York Times*, p. B2.

Gutman, Herbert. 1976. *The Black Family in Slavery and Freedom, 1750-1925.* New York: Pantheon Books.

Hagedorn, Ann and Amy Cocker Marcus. 1990, August 24. "AT&T Is Sued For Not Paying Benefit to Deceased Employee's Unmarried Partner," *Wall Street Journal*, p. B6.

———. 1989, September 8. "Case in California Could Expand Legal Definition of Parenthood," *Wall Street Journal*, p. B10.

Hager, Philip. 1987, June 25. "Appeals Court Rejects Homosexual's Distress Suit," *Los Angeles Times*, Sec. I, p. 3.

Halperin, David. 1990. *One Hundred Years of Homosexuality and Other Essays on Greek Love.* New York: Routledge.

Hansen, T. L. 1972. "Minnesota Marriage Statue Does Not Permit Marriage Between Two Persons of the Same Sex and Does Not Violate Constitutionally Protected Rights," *Drake Law Review* 22(1):206-212.

Hareven, Tamara. 1986. "American Families in Transition: Historical Perspectives on Change." In Arlene Skolnick and J. Skolnick (eds.), *Family in Transition*, pp. 40- 58. Boston: Little, Brown and Company.

Harper, Charles and Kevin Leicht. 1984. "Religious Awakenings and Status Politics: Sources of Support for the New Religious Right," *Sociological Analysis* 45(4):339-353.

Harry, Joseph. 1984. *Gay Couples.* New York: Praeger.

———. 1977. "Marriage Among Gay Males: The Separation of Intimacy and Sex." In Scott McNall (ed.), *The Sociological Perspective: Introductory Readings*, pp. 330-340. Boston: Little, Brown and Company.

Harry, Joseph and Robert Lovely. 1979. "Gay Marriages and Communities of Sexual Orientation," *Alternative Lifestyles* 2(2):177-200.

Hartmann, Heidi. 1981. "The Unhappy Marriage of Marxism and Feminism: Toward a More Progressive Union." In Lydia Sargent (ed.), *Women and Revolution,* pp. 1-41. Boston: South End Press.

Harvard Law Review. 1990. *Sexual Orientation and the Law.* Cambridge, MA: Harvard University Press.

Hatfield, Elaine. 1988. "Passionate and Companionate Love." In Robert Sternberg and Michael Barnes (eds.), *The Psychology of Love,* pp. 191-217. New Haven, CT: Yale University Press.

Hatkoff, Terry. and Thomas Laswell. 1979. "Male-Female Similarities and Differences in Conceptualizing Love." In Mark Cook and Glenn Wilson (eds.), *Love and Attraction,* pp. 221-227. Oxford: Pergamon Press.

"Hawaii Court Rules Against Same-Sex Couples." 1999, December 11. *The Washington Post,* p. A07.

Hendrick, Clyde and Susan Hendrick. 1992. *Romantic Love.* Newbury Park, CA: Sage.

———. 1986. "A Theory and Method of Love," *Journal of Personality and Social Psychology* 50(2):392-402.

Hendrick, Susan, Clyde Hendrick, and Nancy Adler. 1988. "Romantic Relationships: Love, Satisfaction, and Staying Together," *Journal of Personality and Social Psychology* 54(6):980-988.

Hendrick, Clyde, Susan Hendrick, Franklin Foote, and Michelle Slapion-Foote. 1984. "Do Women and Men Love Differently?" *Journal of Social and Personal Relationships* 1(1984):177-195.

Hendrick, Susan, Clyde Hendrick, Michelle Slapion-Foote, and Franklin Foote. 1985. "Gender Differences in Sexual Attitudes," *Journal of Personality and Social Psychology* 48(6):1630-1642.

Herscher, Elaine. 1995, May 15. "When Marriage is a Tough Proposal: Women's Suit at Heart of Debate Over Same Sex Unions," *San Francisco Chronicle,* p. A1.

Hill, Charles, Zick Rubin, and Letitia Anne Peplau. 1976. "Breakups Before Marriage: The End of 103 Affairs," *Journal of Social Issues* 32(1):147-168.

Hill, Charles, Zick Rubin, Letitia Anne Peplau, and Susan Willard. 1979. "The Volunteer Couple: Sex Differences, Couple Commitment, and Participation in Research on Interpersonal Relationships," *Social Psychology Quarterly* 42(4):415-420.

Hochschild, Arlie. 1989. *The Second Shift.* New York: Viking.

Hocquenghem, Guy. 1978. *Homosexual Desire.* London: Allison and Busby.

Hodson, Randy and Teresa Sullivan. 1995. *The Social Organization of Work.* Belmont, CA: Wadsworth.

Holmes, J. and J. Rempel. 1989. "Trust in Close Relationships." In Clyde Hendrick (ed.), *Close Relationships,* pp. 187-220. Newbury Park, CA: Sage.

"Homosexuals' Suit Seeks Marriage License." 1990, November 27. *New York Times,* p. A19.

hooks, bell. 1989. *Talking Back: Thinking Feminist, Thinking Black.* Boston: South End Press.

Horn, Patricia. 1992. "To Love and to Cherish," In Michael Kimmel and Michael Messner (eds.), *Men's Lives,* pp. 515-521. New York: Macmillan.

———. 1991. "Fringe Benefits for Gay Spouses," *Dollar and Sense* (December):10-11, 22.

Huber, J, C. Rexroat, and G. Spitze. 1978. "A Crucible of Opinion on Women's Status: ERA in Illinois," *Social Forces* 57(December):549-565.

Human Rights Campaign. 1997. "A Basic Human Right: Talking About Gay Marriage." http://www.hrcusa.org/issues/marriage/guide.html.

Humphries, Jane. 1977. "The Working Class Family, Women's Liberation, and Class Struggle: The Case of Nineteenth Century British History," *Review of Radical Political Economics* 9(Fall):25-42.

———. 1971. "Class Struggle and the Persistence of the Working Class Family," *Cambridge Journal of Economics* 1:241-58.

Humphreys, Laud. 1970. *Tearoom Trade: Impersonal Sex in Public Places.* New York: Aldine De Gruyter.

Hunter, Nan. 1991. "Marriage, Law, and Gender: A Feminist Inquiry," *Law and Sexuality* 1(Summer):9-30.

Ingram, John. 1984. "A Constitutional Critique of Restrictions on the Right to Marry: Why Fred Can't Marry George," *Journal of Constitutional Law* 10:46-50.

Isaacson, Walter. 1989, November 20. "Should Gays Have Marriage Rights?" *Time*, pp. 101-102.

Jackson-Paris, Rod and Bob Jackson-Paris. 1994. *Straight from the Heart: A Love Story.* New York: Time Warner.

Jagger, Alison. 1983. *Feminist Politics and Human Nature.* Totowa, NJ: Rowman and Allanheld.

Jay, Karla and Allen Young. 1979. *The Gay Report.* New York: Summit Books.

Johnson, Michael. 1973. "Commitment: A Conceptual Structure and Empirical Application," *Sociological Quarterly* 14(Summer):395-406.

Johnson, Susan. 1990. *Staying Power: Long Term Lesbian Couples.* Tallahassee, FA: The Naiad Press.

Jones, Jacqueline. 1985. *Labor of Love, Labor of Sorrow: Black Women, Work, and the Family from Slavery to the Present.* New York: Vintage Books.

Jones v. Hallahan, 501 S.W.2d 588 (Ky. Ct. App 1973).

Kanter, Rosabeth. 1968. "Commitment and Social Organization: A Study of Commitment Mechanisms in Utopian Communities," *American Sociological Review* 33(4):499-517.

Katz, Jonathan. 1976. *Gay American History.* New York: Harper & Row.

Kay, Herma Hill. 1988. *Sex-Based Discrimination.* St. Paul, MN: West Publishing, 1988.

Kelley, Harold. 1983. "Love and Commitment." In Harold Kelley et al. (eds.), *Close Relationships*, pp. 265-314. New York: W. H. Freeman and Company.

Kelliher, Judith. 1992, April 14. "Enquiring Minds Wanted to Know," *Daily Hampshire Gazette*, p. 1.

Kennedy, Elizabeth and Madeline Davis. 1993. *Boots of Leather, Slippers of Gold: The History of a Lesbian Community.* New York: Routledge.

Kerbo, Harold. 1991. *Social Stratification and Inequality.* New York: McGraw-Hill.

Kessler, Larry, Ann Silvia, David Aronstein, and Cynthia Patton. 1988. "A Call to Action: A Community Responds," *New England Journal of Public Policy* (Winter/Spring):441-454.

Kilpatrick, James. 1989, January 14. "Humpty-Dumpty on Gay Rights," *Washington Post*, p. A23.

Kinsey, Alfred, Wardell Pomeroy, and Clyde Martin. 1948. *Sexual Behavior in the Human Male.* Philadelphia: W. B. Saunders Co.

Kitzinger, Celia. 1987. *The Social Construction of Lesbianism.* London: Sage.

Klepfisz, Irena. 1989. "Jewish Progressives and the Jewish Community," *Tikkun* 4(May-June):83-85.

Knight, Robert. 1998. "Gay Marriage: Hawaii's Assault on Matrimony." http://www.frc.org/frc/fampol/fp96bhs.html.

———. 1997. "How Domestic Partnerships and 'Gay Marriage Threaten the Family,'" In Robert Baird and Stuart Rosenbaum (eds.), *Same-Sex Marriage: The Moral and Legal Debate*, pp. 108-12. New York: Prometheus Books.

Koepke, Leslie, Jan Hare, and Patricia Moran. 1992. "Relationship Quality in a Sample of Lesbian Couples with Children and Child-Free Lesbian Couples," *Family Relations* 41:224-229.

Kolb, William. 1948. "Sociologically Established Norms and Democratic Values," *Social Forces* 26(May):451-456.

Kort, Michele. 2000, February 29. "Proposing Marriage . . . in full," *The Advocate*, p. 35.

Kosterlitz, Julie. 1988, April 16. "Family Cries," *National Journal*, pp. 994-999.

Kurdeck, Lawrence. 1991. "Correlates of Relationship Satisfaction in Cohabiting Gay and Lesbian Couples: Integration of Contextual, Investment, and Problem-Solving Models," *Journal of Personality and Social Psychology* 61(6):910-922.

———. 1988. "Relationship Quality of Gay and Lesbian Cohabiting Couples," *Journal of Homosexuality* 15(3/4):93-118.

———. 1987. "Sex Role Self Schema and Psychological Adjustment in Coupled Homosexual and Heterosexual Men and Women," *Sex Roles* 17(9/10):549-232.

Kurdeck, Lawrence and Patrick Schmitt. 1987a. "Partner Homogamy in Married, Heterosexual Cohabiting, Gay, and Lesbian Couples," *Journal of Sex Research* 23(2):212-232.

———. 1987b. "Perceived Emotional Support from Family and Friends in Members of Homosexual, Married, and Heterosexual Cohabitating Couples," *Journal of Homosexuality* 14(3/4):57-68.

Lambda Legal Defense and Education Fund. 1998. "1998 Anti-Marriage Bills Status." http://www.lambdalegal.org/cgi-bin/pages/documents/record?record=51.

———. 1990, September. *Domestic Partnership: Issues and Legislation.* New York: Lambda Family Relationships Project.

Lambert, Wade. 1989, July 7. "Unmarried Couples Get Protection of New York's Rent-Control Law," *Wall Street Journal*, p. B4.

Lamphere, Louise. 1987. *From Working Daughters to Working Mothers: Factory Women in Massachusetts.* Albany: State University of New York Press.

Laner, Mary. 1977. "Permanent Partner Priorities: Gay and Straight," *Journal of Homosexuality* 3(1):21-39.

LaRossa, Ralph. 1988. "Renewing Our Faith in Qualitative Research," *Journal of Contemporary Ethnography* 17(3):243-260.

Lasch, Christopher. 1977. *Haven in a Heartless World.* New York: Basic Books.

Lauer, Robert and Sarah Kerr. 1990. "The Long-Term Marriage: Perceptions of Stability and Satisfaction," *International Journal of Aging and Human Development* 31(3):189-195.

Laumann, Edward, Robert Michael, John Gagnon, and Stuart Michaels. 1994. *The Social Organization of Sexuality: Sexual Practices in the United States.* Chicago: University of Chicago Press.

Lee, John. 1991. "Can We Talk? Can We Really Talk? Communication as a Key Factor in the Maturing Homosexual Couple," *Journal of Homosexuality* 20(2):143-155.

———. 1973. *Colours of Love.* Toronto: New Press.

222   FROM THIS DAY FORWARD

Lehr, Valerie. 1994. "Queer Politics in the 1990s: Identity and Issues," *New Political Science* 30/31(Summer/Fall):55-76.

Lewin, Ellen. 1994. "Negotiating Lesbian Motherhood: The Dialectics of Resistance and Accommodation." In Evelyn Glenn, Grace Chang, and Linda Forcey (eds.), *Mothering: Ideology, Experience, and Agency,* pp. 333-353. New York: Routledge.

Lewin, Tamar. 1990, September 21. "Suit Over Death Benefits Asks, What Is a Family?" *New York Times,* p. A1.

Lochhead, Carolyn. 1996, July 12. "Senate Battle On Restricting Gay Marriages," *The San Francisco Chronicle,* p. A3.

Loiacana, Darryl. 1989. "Gay Identity Issues Among Black Americans: Racism, Homophobia, and the Need for Validation," *Journal of Counseling and Development* 68:21-25.

Loisel, Laurie. 1988a, August 24. "Gay Couples Lack Rights," *Daily Hampshire Gazette.*
———. 1988b, August 24. "Homosexual Weddings: Religious Groups Take Different Stands," *Daily Hampshire Gazette.*

Longcope, Kay. 1991, March 4. "Gay Couples Fight for Spousal Rights," *Boston Globe,* p. 38.

Lorber, Judith. 1994. *Paradoxes of Gender.* New Haven, CT: Yale University Press.

Lorde, Audre. 1984. *Sister Outsider: Essays and Speeches.* Trumnansburg, NY: The Crossing Press.

Lovece, Frank. 1994. May 1. "Out of the Closet and Onto the Tube," *FanFare,* pp. 20-22.

Loving v. Virginia, 388 U.S. 1 (1967).

Lund, Mary. 1985. "The Development of Investment and Commitment Scales for Predicting Continuity of Personal Relationships," *Journal of Social and Personal Relationships* 2(1985):3-23.

Lynes, Tony. 1989, September 8. "Unfair Shares," *New Statesman and Society,* 2:28.

MacKinnon, Catherine. 1987. *Feminism Unmodified: Discourses on Life and Law.* Cambridge, MA: Harvard University Press.

Malinowski, Bronislaw. 1922. *Argonauts of the Western Pacific.* London: Routledge and Kegan Paul.

Mansbridge, Jane. 1986. *Why We Lost the ERA.* Chicago: University of Chicago Press.

Marcus, Amy Docker. 1990, September 18. "Technological, Social Changes May Spur Courts to Widen Definition of Parenthood," *Wall Street Journal,* pp. B1 and B8.

Marecek, Jeanne, Stephen Finn, and Mona Cardell. 1982. "Gender Roles in the Relationships of Lesbians and Gay Men," *Journal of Homosexuality* 8(2):45-49.

Marriage Project Hawaii. 2000. "December 1999 Update for Marriage Project-Hawaii." http://members.tripod.com/mphawaii/milestones.htm.

Martin, Del and Phyllis Lyon. 1991. *Lesbian/Woman* (20th anniversary ed.). Volcano, CA: Volcano Press.

Martin, Emily. 1987. *The Women in the Body: A Cultural Analysis of Reproduction.* Boston: Beacon Press.

Marvin v. Marvin, 18 Cal.3d 660 (1976).

Mathews, Jay. 1990, August 23. "Liberal Metropolis Balks at Redefining Family," *Washington Post,* p. A3.

Matthaei, Julie. 1982. *An Economic History of Women in America.* New York: Schocken Books.

Mattison, Andrew and David McWhirter. 1987. "Male Couples: The Beginning Years," *Journal of Social Work and Human Sexuality* 5(2):67-78.

Maupin, Armistead. 1994, January 9. "A Line that Commercial TV Won't Cross: The Networks Have Learned to Tolerate Gay Male Characters but Only PBS Lets Them Kiss," *New York Times,* p. H29.

May, Martha. 1987. "The Historical Problem of the Family Wage: The Ford Motor Company and the Five Dollar Day." In Naomi Gerstel and Harriet Engel Gross (eds.), *Families and Work,* pp. 111-131. Philadelphia: Temple University Press.

May, Rollo. 1975. "A Preface to Love." In Ashley Montagu (ed.), *The Practice of Love,* pp. 114-119. Englewood Cliffs, NJ: Prentice-Hall.

————. 1953. *Man's Search for Himself.* New York: W. W. Norton.

McBride, Martha and Shirley Emerson. 1989. "Group Work with Women Who Were Molested as Children," *Journal for Specialists in Group Work* 14(1):25-33.

McConnell v. Nooner, 547 F.2d 54 (8th Cir. 1976).

McGoldrick, Monica. 1988. "The Joining of Families Through Marriage: The New Couple." In Betty Carter and Monica McGoldrick (eds.), *The Changing Family Life Cycle: A Framework for Family Therapy* (2nd ed.), pp. 209-233 New York: Gardner Press.

McGuire, Meredith. 1981. *Religion: The Social Context.* Belmont, CA: Wadsworth Publishing Company, 1981.

McHale, Susan and Ted Huston. 1984. "Men and Women as Parents: Sex Role Orientations, Employment, and Parental Roles," *Child Development* 55(August):1349-1361.

McWhitter, David and Andrew Mattison. 1984. *The Male Couple: How Relationships Develop.* Englewood Cliffs, NJ: Prentice-Hall.

Mellucci, Alberto. 1988. "Getting Involved: Identity and Mobilization in Social Movements," *International Social Movements Research* 1:329-328.

Mendola, Mary. 1980. *The Mendola Report: A New Look at Gay Couples.* New York: Crown.

Miller, Neil. 1989. *In Search of Gay America.* New York: Harper & Row.

Millet, Kate. 1970. *Sexual Politics.* New York: Doubleday.

Millward, Christine. 1991. "What Marriage Means to Young Adults in the 1990s," *Family Matters* 29(August):26-28.

Mintz, Steven and Susan Kellogg. 1988. *Domestic Revolutions: A Social History of American Family Life.* New York: The Free Press.

Modell, John. "Historical Reflections on American Marriage." In Kingsley Davis (ed.), *Contemporary Marriage,* pp. 181-196. New York: Russell Sage Foundation.

Mohr, Richard. 1988. *Gays/Justice: A Study of Ethics and the Law.* New York: Columbia University Press.

Montgomery, Barbara. 1988. "Quality Communication in Personal Relationships." In S. Duck (ed.), *Handbook of Personal Relationships,* pp. 343-359. New York: John Wiley & Sons.

Moore, Gwen and Allen Whitt. 1992. "Introduction." *Research in Politics and Society* 4:xi-xxi.

Moore, Sally and Barbara Myerhoff. 1977. *Secular Ritual.* Amsterdam: Van Gorcum.

Moran, Janis. 1975. "I Do, I Do . . . Loophole Links Lesbians in Legal Marriage," *MS* 4(5):19.

"More Folks Say Gay is OK, But Most Oppose Marriages." 1996, March 19. *USA TODAY,* p. 3A.

Munro, Brenda and Gerald Adams. 1978. "Love American Style: A Test of Role Structure Theory on Changes in Attitudes Toward Love," *Human Relations* 31(3):215-228.

Murdoch, Joyce. 1988, August 5. "Fighting for Control of a Loved One," *Washington Post*, pp. A1 and A8.

Myricks, Noel and Roger Rubin. 1995. "Legalizing Gay and Lesbian Marriages: Trends and Policy Implications," *American Journal of Family Law* 9:35-44.

National Center for Education Statistics. 1994. *Digest of Education Statistics.* Washington, D.C.: U.S. Department of Education, Office of Education Research and Improvement, NCES 94-115, p. 243.

National Danish Organization for Gays and Lesbians. 1990. "The Complete List of Countries Where Lesbians and Gay Men Legally Can Get Married," *Outlook* 3(1)(Summer):81.

Nealon, Chris. 1990, October 27. "Fighting for Domestic Partnerships," *Gay Community News*, pp. 1 and 6.

Nicholson, Linda. 1986. *Gender and History: The Limits of Social Theory in the Age of the Family.* New York: Columbia University Press.

Nickel, Jeffrey. 1991, February 11-17. "Going to the Chapel," *Gay Community News*, p. 8.

Norton, Arthur and Jeanne Morman. 1987. "Current Trends in Marriage and Divorce Among American Women," *Journal of Marriage and the Family* 49:3-14.

O'Connor, John. 1994, November 23. "In TV Entertainment, a Heightened Gay Presence," *New York Times*, p. 86.

O'Neill v. Dent (1973), 364 F.Supp. 565.

Orkin, Susan Moller. 1989. *Justice, Gender, and the Family.* New York: Basic Books.

OUT/LOOK. 1989. "Questions for Couples: The Results" (Summer):86.

Oxford Latin Dictionary. 1982. "Intimus." New York: Oxford University Press.

Pankhurst, Jerry and Sharon Houseknecht. 1986. "The Family, Politics, and Religion in the 1980s: In Fear of the New Individualism." In Arlene Skolnick and Jerome Skolnick (eds.), *Family in Transition* (5th ed.), pp. 576-598. Boston: Little, Brown and Company.

Parkin, David. 1994. "Ritual as Spatial Direction and Bodily Division." In Daniel de Coppet (ed.), *Understanding Rituals*, pp. 9-25. New York: Routledge.

Parsons, Talcott. 1949. *Essays in Sociological Theory.* Glencoe, IL: The Free Press.

Parsons, Talcott and Robert Bales. 1955. *Family, Socialization, and Interaction Process.* Glencoe, IL: Free Press.

Patton, Cindy. 1985. *Sex and Germs: The Politics of AIDS.* Boston: South End Press.

Pearlman, Sarah. 1989. "Distancing and Connectedness: Impact on Couple Formation in Lesbian Relationships," *Women and Therapy* 8(1 and 2):77-88.

Peplau, Letitia Anne. 1982. "Research on Homosexual Couples," *Journal of Homosexuality* 8(2):3-8.

Peplau, Letitia Anne and Susan Cochran. 1981. "Value Orientations in the Intimate Relationships of Gay Men," *Journal of Homosexuality* 6(3):1-19.

Peplau, Letitia Anne, Susan Cochran, Karen Rook, and Christine Padesky. 1978. "Loving Women: Attachment and Autonomy in Lesbian Relationships," *Journal of Social Issues* 34(3):7-27.

Peplau, Letitia Anne and Steven Gordon. 1991. "The Intimate Relationships of Lesbian and Gay Men." In John Edwards and David Demos (eds.), *Marriage and Family in Transition*, pp. 479-496. Boston: Allyn and Bacon.

————. 1985. "Women and Men in Love: Gender Differences in Close Heterosexual Relationships." In Virginia O'Leary, Rhoda Kessler Unger, and Barbara Strudler (eds.), *Women, Gender, and Social Psychology,* pp. 257-291. Hillsdale, NJ: Lawrence Erlbaum Associates.

Peplau, Letitia Anne, Christine Padesky, and Mykol Hamilton. 1982. "Satisfaction in Lesbian Relationships," *Journal of Homosexuality* 8(2):23-35.

Peplau, Letitia Anne, Zick Rubin, and Charles Hill. 1977. "Sexual Intimacy in Dating Relationships," *Journal of Social Issues* 33(2):86-109.

Pies, Cheri. 1987. "Lesbians Choosing Children: The Use of Social Group Work and Maintaining and Strengthening the Primary Relationship," *Journal of Social Work and Human Sexuality* 5(2):79-88.

Plummer, Ken. 1978. "Men in Love: Observations on Male Homosexual Couples." In Marie Corbin (ed.), *The Couple,* pp. 173-220. New York: Penguin Books.

Poverny, Linda and Wilbur Finch. 1988. "Gay and Lesbian Domestic Partnerships: Expanding the Definition of Family," *Social Casework* 69(February):116-121.

Radsken, Jill. 1998, August 31. "New-Fashioned Families—Helping Gay Couples Make Babies the Contractual Way," *The Boston Herald,* p. 39.

Rankin, Deborah. 1987, June 7. "Living Together in Sickness and Health," *New York Sunday Times,* p. F13.

Raphael, Sharon and Mina Robinson. 1980. "The Older Lesbian: Love Relationships and Friendship Patterns," *Alternative Lifestyles* 3(2):207-229.

Rapp, Rayna. 1982. "Family and Class in Contemporary America: Noted Toward and Understanding of Ideology." In Barrie Thorne and Marilyn Yalom (eds.), *Rethinking the Family: Some Feminist Questions,* pp. 168-187. New York: Longman Press.

Raspberry, William. 1997, April 25. "Families in Peril: A Long-Running Drama," *The Washington Post,* p. A27.

Rauch, Jonathan. 1996, May 6. "For Better or Worse? The Case for Gay (and Straight Marriage)," *The New Republic,* pp. 18-23.

Reedy, Margaret, James Birren, and K. Warner Schaie. 1981. "Sex Differences in Satisfying Love Relationships Across the Adult Life Span," *Human Development* 24(1):52-56.

Reilly, Mary Ellen and Jean Lynch. 1990. "Power-Sharing in Lesbian Partnerships," *Journal of Homosexuality* 19(3):1-30.

Reisman, Barbara and Pepper Schwartz. 1989. *Gender in Intimate Relationships.* Belmont, CA: Wadsworth Publishing.

Reissman, C. 1990. *Divorce Talk: Women and Men Make Sense of Personal Relationships.* New Brunswick, NJ: Rutgers University Press.

Rhode, Deborah. 1989. *Justice and Gender.* Cambridge, MA: Harvard University Press.

Rice, F. Philip. 1993. *Intimate Relationships, Marriages, and Families.* Mountain View, CA: Mayfield Publishing.

Rich, Adrienne. 1984. "Compulsory Heterosexuality and Lesbian Existence." In Alison Jagger and Paula Rothenberg (eds.), *Feminist Frameworks,* pp. 311-314. New York: McGraw-Hill Book Company.

Roberts, Janine. 1988. "Setting the Frame: Definitions, Functions, and Typologies of Rituals." In Evan Imber-Black, Janine Roberts, and Richard Whiting (eds.), *Rituals in Families and Family Therapy,* pp. 3-27. New York: Norton.

Rosen, David. 1991. "What Is Family? Nature, Culture, and the Law," *Marriage and Family Review* 17(1-2):29-43.

Rosenblatt, Paul. 1977. "Needed Research on Commitment in Marriage." In George Levinger and Harold Raush (eds.), *Close Relationships: Perspectives on the Meaning of Intimacy,* pp. 73-86. Amherst: University of Massachusetts Press.

Roth, Sally. 1985. "Psychotherapy with Lesbian Couples: Individual Issues, Female Socialization, and the Social Context," *Journal of Marriage and Family Therapy* 11(3):273-286.

Rubin, Lilian. 1983. *Intimate Strangers.* New York: Harper and Row.

Rubin, Zick. 1983. "From Liking to Loving: Patterns of Attraction in Dating Relationships." In Ted Huston (ed.), *Foundations of Interpersonal Attraction,* pp. 383-400. New York: Academic Press.

———. 1973. *Liking and Loving: An Invitation to Social Psychology.* New York: Holt, Rinehart, and Winston.

———. 1970. "Measurement of Romantic Love," *Journal of Personality and Social Psychology* 16(2):265-273.

Rubin, Zick, Charles Hill, Letitia Anne Peplau, and Christine Dunkel-Schetter. 1980. "Self-Disclosure in Dating Couples: Sex Roles and the Ethic of Openness," *Journal of Marriage and the Family* (May):305-317.

Rubin, Zick, Letitia Anne Peplau, and Charles Hill. 1981. "Loving and Leaving: Sex Differences in Romantic Attachments," *Sex Roles* 7(8):821-835.

Rule, Shelia. 1989, October 2. "Rights for Gay Couples in Denmark," *New York Times.*

Rusbult, Caryl. 1993. "A Longitudinal Test of The Investment Model: The Development (and Deterioration) of Satisfaction and Commitment in Heterosexual Involvements," *Journal of Personality and Social Psychology* 45(1):101-117.

———. 1980. "Commitment and Satisfaction in Romantic Associations: A Test of the Investment Model," *Journal of Experimental Social Psychology* 16:172-186.

Rusbult, Caryl, Dennis Johnson, and Gregory Morrow. 1986. "Predicting Satisfaction and Commitment in Adult Romantic Involvements: An Assessment of the Generalizability of the Investment Model," *Social Psychology Quarterly* 49(1):81-89.

Ryan, Mary. 1981. *Cradle of the Middle Class: The Family in Oneida County, New York, 1790-1865.* New York: Cambridge University Press.

Santas, Gerasimos. 1988. *Plato and Freud: Two Theories of Love.* New York: Basil Blackwell.

Scanzoni, John. 1982. *Sexual Bargaining: Power Politics in the American Marriage.* Chicago: University of Chicago Press.

Scanzoni, John and Cynthia Arnett. 1987. "Enlarging the Understanding of Marital Commitment via Religious Devoutness, Gender Role Preferences, and Locus of Marital Control," *Journal of Family Issues* 8(1):136-156.

Schmitt, Eric. 1996, June 13. "Panel to Pass Bill to Let States Refuse to Recognize Gay Marriage," *New York Times,* p. A15.

Schwartz, Barry. 1967. "The Social Psychology of the Gift," *American Journal of Sociology* 73:1-11.

Scott, Alan. 1990. *Ideology and Social Movements.* London: Unwin Hyman.

Seddon, Terri. 1990. "Social Justice in Hard Times: From 'Equality of Opportunity' to 'Fairness and Efficiency,'" *Discourse* 11(1):21-42.

Senak, Mark. 1987. "The Lesbian and Gay Community." In Harlon Dalton and Scott Burris (eds.), *AIDS and the Law: A Guide for the Public,* pp. 290-300. New Haven, CT: Yale University Press.

Shafer, Siegrid. 1977. "Sociosexual Behavior in Male and Female Homosexuals: A Study in Sex Differences," *Archives of Sexual Behavior* 6(5):355-365.

Sherman, Suzanne. 1992. *Lesbian and Gay Marriage*. Philadelphia: Temple University Press.

Shulman, Alix. 1984. "A Marriage Agreement." In Alison Jagger and Paula Rothenberg (eds.), *Feminist Frameworks*, pp. 224-227. New York: McGraw-Hill Book Company.

Silverstein, Charles. 1981. *Man to Man: Gay Couples in America*. New York: William Morrow and Co.

Singer v. Hara, 11 Wash App 247, 522 P.2d 1187 (1974).

Skolnick, Arlene. 1991. *Embattled Paradise*. New York: HarperCollins.

Skolnick, Arlene and Jerome Skolnick. 1986. "Introduction: Family in Transition." In Arlene Skolnick and Jerome Skolnick (eds.), *Family in Transition*, pp. 1-18. Boston: Little, Brown and Company.

Slater, Suzanne. 1995. *The Lesbian Family Life Cycle*. New York: The Free Press.

Slator, Suzanne and Julie Mencher. 1991. "The Lesbian Family Life Cycle: A Contextual Approach," *American Journal of Orthopsychiatry* 61(3):372-382.

Smart, Carol. 1989. *Feminism and the Power of the Law*. New York: Routledge.

Smith, Daniel. 1973. "Parental Power and Marriage Patterns: An Analysis of Historical Trends in Hingham, Massachusetts," *Journal of Marriage and the Family* 35 (August):219-228.

"Something Borrowed, Something Pink." 1989, June 3. *The Economist*, p. 30.

Spada, James. 1979. *The Spada Report: The Newest Survey of Gay Male Sexuality*. New York: Signet.

Spanier, Graham. 1985. "Cohabitation in the 1980s: Recent Changes in the United States." In Kingsley Davis (ed.), *Contemporary Marriage*, pp. 91-112. New York: Russell Sage Foundation.

———. 1976. "Measuring the Dyadic Adjustment: New Scales for Assessing the Quality of Marriage and Similar Dyads," *Journal of Marriage and the Family* 38(February):15-30.

Spence, J. T. and R. Helmick. 1978. *Masculinity and Femininity*. Austin: University of Texas Press.

Spence, Michael. 1974. *Market Signaling*. Cambridge, MA: Harvard University Press.

Spong, John. 1988, July 31. "Sex and Sin: The Case for Blessing Divorce, Gay Couples, and Cohabitation," *Washington Post*, pp. C1 and C4.

Stacey, Judith. 1996. *In the Name of the Family: Rethinking Family Values in the Postmodern Age*. Boston: Beacon Press.

———. 1990. *Brave New Families*. New York: Basic Books.

———. 1986. "Are Feminists Afraid to Leave Home? The Challenge of Profamily Feminism." In Juliet Mitchell and Ann Oakley (eds.), *What Is Feminism?*, pp. 208-237. New York: Pantheon Books.

Stack, Carol. 1974. *All Our Kin: Strategies for Survival in a Black Community*. New York: Harper & Row.

Stafford, Laura and Daniel Canary. 1991. "Maintenance Strategies and Romantic Relationship Type, Gender and Relational Characteristics," *Journal of Social and Personal Relationships* 8:217-242.

Starhawk. 1982. *Dreaming the Dark: Magic, Sex, and Politics*. Boston: Beacon Press.

Statistical Abstracts. 1997a. "No. 68. Households, 1980-1996, and Persons in Households, 1996, by Type of Household and Presence of Children." U.S. Bureau of the Census. Lanham, MD: Bernan Press, p. 60.

————. 1997b. "No. 149. Divorce and Annulments—Duration of Marriage, Age at Divorce and Children Involved: 1970-1990." U.S. Bureau of the Census. Lanham, MD: Bernan Press, p. 106.

————. 1994. "No. 26. Resident Population—States: 1970 to 1993." U.S. Bureau of the Census. Lanham, MD: Bernan Press, p.27.

Steck, Loren et al. 1982. "Care, Need, and Conceptions of Love," *Journal of Personality and Social Psychology* 43(3):481-491.

Steinberg, Marc. 1994. "The Dialogue of Struggle: The Contest over Ideological Boundaries in the Case of the London Silk Weavers in the Early Nineteenth Century," *Social Science History* 18(4):505-541.

Sternberg, Robert. 1986. "A Triangular Theory of Love," *Psychological Review* 93(2):119-135.

Sternberg, Robert and Susan Grajek. 1984. "The Nature of Love," *Journal of Personality and Social Psychology* 47(2):312-329.

Stoddard, Thomas. 1989. "Why Gay People Should Seek the Right to Marry," *OUT/ LOOK* 2(2)(Fall):9-13.

"Strange Town Where Men Aren't Wanted." 1992, April 21. *National Enquirer,* p. 8.

Stryker, Sheldon and Richard Serpe. 1982. "Commitment, Identity Salience, and Role Behavior." In W. Ickes and E. Knowles (eds.), *Personality, Roles, and Social Behavior,* pp. 199-218. New York: Springer-Verlag.

Sullivan, Andrew (ed.). 1997. *Same-Sex Marriage: Pro and Con.* New York: Vintage Books.

————. 1996. *Virtually Normal: An Argument About Homosexuality.* New York: Vintage Books.

————. 1989, August 28. "Here Comes the Groom: A (Conservative) Case for Gay Marriage," *The New Republic,* pp. 20 and 22.

Sullivan, Elizabeth. 1991. "Lesbian Commitment Ceremonies: A Contextual Understanding," unpublished master's thesis. Smith College School for Social Work, Northampton, MA.

Surra, Catherine et al. 1988. "The Association Between Reasons for Commitment and the Development and Outcome of Marital Relationships," *Journal of Social and Personal Relationships* 5:47-63.

Swenson, Clifford, Ron Eskew, and Karen Kohlepp. 1981. "Stage of Family Life Cycle, Ego Development, and the Marriage Relationship," *Journal of Marriage and the Family* 43(4):841-853.

Swidler, Ann. 1980. "Love and Adulthood in American Culture." In Neil Smelser and Erik Erikson (eds.), *Themes of Work and Love in Adulthood,* pp. 120-147. Cambridge, MA: Harvard University Press.

Tambiah, Stanley. 1985. *Culture, Thought, and Social Action: An Anthropological Perspective.* Cambridge, MA: Harvard University Press.

Tannen, Deborah. 1990. *You Just Don't Understand.* New York: Ballantine Books.

Tessna, Tina. 1989. *Gay Relationships: For Men and Women.* Los Angeles: Jeremy Tarcher.

Testa, Ronald, Bill Kinder, and Gail Ironson. 1987. "Heterosexual Bias in the Perception of Loving Relationships of Gay Males and Lesbians." *Journal of Sex Research* 23:163-72.

Thompson, Karen and Julie Andrzejewski. 1988. *Why Can't Sharon Come Home?* San Francisco: Spinsters/Aunt Lute.

Thorne, Barrie. 1982. "Feminist Rethinking of the Family: An Overview." In Barrie Thorne and Marilyn Yalom (eds.), *Rethinking the Family: Some Feminist Questions,* pp. 1-24. New York: Longman Press.

Thorne, Barrie and Marilyn Yalom (eds.). 1982. *Rethinking the Family: Some Feminist Questions.* New York: Longman Press.

Timmons, Stuart. 1990. *The Trouble with Harry.* Boston: Alyson Press.

Toner, Robin. 1995, March 30. "G.O.P. Mobilizes for Contract Deadline: Concern that Public Not Overlook a Revolution," *The New York Times,* p. A21.

Tong, Rosemarie. 1984. *Women, Sex, and the Law.* Totowa, NJ: Rowman and Allenheld.

Turner, Ralph. 1976. "The Real Self: From Institution to Impulse," *American Journal of Sociology* 81:789-1,016.

Turner, Terence. 1977. "Transformation, Hierarchy, and Transcendence: A Reformulation of Van Gennep's Model of the Structure of Rites de Passage." In Sally Moore and Barbara Myerhoff (eds.), *Secular Ritual,* pp. 53-70. Amsterdam: Van Gorcum.

Turner, Victor. 1977. "Variations on the Theme of Liminality." In Sally Moore and Barbara Myerhoff (eds.), *Secular Ritual,* pp. 36-52. Amsterdam: Van Gorcum.

———. 1974. *Dramas, Fields, and Metaphors: Symbolic Action in Human Society.* Ithaca, NY: Cornell University Press.

———. 1973. *The Ritual Process: Structure and Anti-Structure.* Chicago: Aldine.

van Gelder, Lawrence. 1979, February 27. "Termination of Alimony to Lesbian Adds to Legal Debate," *New York Times.*

van Gennep, Arnold. 1960. *The Rites of Passage.* London: Routledge and Kegan Paul.

Vannoy, Dana. 1991. "Social Differentiation, Contemporary Marriage, and Human Development," *Journal of Family Issues* 12(3):251-267.

Vargo, Sue. 1987. "The Effects of Women's Socialization on Lesbian Couples." In Boston Lesbian Psychologies Collective (ed.),. *Lesbian Psychologies: Explorations and Challenges,* pp. 161-173. Chicago: University of Chicago Press.

Waller, Willard. 1938. *The Family.* New York: Dryden.

Walster, Elaine and William Walster. 1978. *A New Look at Love.* Reading, MA: Addison-Wesley.

Weeks, Jeffrey. 1977. *Coming Out: Homosexual Politics in Britain, From the Nineteenth Century to the Present.* London: Quartet Books.

Weitzman. Lenore. 1985. *The Divorce Revolution: The Unexpected Social and Economic Consequences of Divorce.* New York: The Free Press.

Welter, Barbara. 1983. "Cult of True Womanhood: 1820-1860." In Michael Gordon (ed.), *The American Family in Social-Historical Perspective,* pp. 372-392. New York: St. Martin's Press.

Weston, Kath. 1991. *Families We Choose: Lesbians, Gays, Kinship.* New York: Columbia University Press.

"What Is Family?" 1989, July 13. *The Washington Post,* p. A22.

"What's a Family? 1989, July 8. *The New York Times,* p. 25.

Whyte, Martin King. 1990. *Dating, Mating and Marriage.* New York: Aldine de Gruyter.

Wilson, Bradford. 1980. "Clinton, The Courts, and Social Policy," *Society* 31(3):64-68.

Wilson, Suzanne. 1991, March 15-21. "The Lesbian Baby Boom: Is Society Ready?" *Hampshire Life Magazine,* pp. 8-12.

Wittig, Monique. 1985. "The Mark of Gender," *Feminist Issues* 5(2):3-12.

————. 1981. "One Is Not Born a Woman," *Feminist Issues* 1(2):47-54.
————. 1980. "The Straight Mind," *Feminist Issues* 1(1):103-111.
Wolfson, Evan. 1995. "Altered States," *10 Percent* (May/June):28-30.
Yen, Marianne. 1989, July 7. "Court Adds Gay Couples to Definition of Family," *Washington Post*, p. A3.
Zaretsky, Eli. 1976. *Capitalism, The Family, and Personal Life*. New York: Harper & Row.

INDEX

Abbott, Toni, 37
ACT UP (AIDS Coalition to Unleash
    Power), xv, 205
Adam, Barry, 62
adoption rights, xv
Advocate, 13
AIDS, xv. *See also* HIV/AIDS
AIDS Memorial Quilt, xv
anniversary celebrations, 75, 80-81
Arnett, Cynthia, 48
Atkinson, Emily, 99, 177
autonomy, 38
Avery, Christopher, 25, 128, 129, 165,
    166
Ayers, Tess, 111

bachelor parties, 131-2
Baehr, Ninia, 161
Baehr v. Lewin, xvii-xviii, 6-8, 10, 161,
    162-3
Baehr v. Miike, 7
Baker v. Nelson, 17-18, 24
ban on military service, xvi
Barr, Bob, 8
Barry, Theresa, 60
Baumann, Gerd, 110
Becker, Howard, 47, 49
Belew, Judith Ann, 17
Bellah, Robert, 48
Berger, Raymond, 80
Bernard, Jessie: *The Future of Marriage,*
    48
Blumberg, Anna, 37, 53, 86, 91, 104,
    105, 119-20
Blumstein, Philip, 35
    American Couples, 79, 195
Boswell, John: *Same-Sex Unions in Pre-
    modern Europe,* 20
Bray, Robert, 163
breast cancer, xvi

bridal showers. *See* showers, wedding/
    bridal
Briggs, John, 18
Britt, Harry, 21
Brown, Ken, 14
Brown, Paul, 111
Burch, Elizabeth, 163
Bush, George, xv
butch/femme roles, 15
Butler, Becky, 16, 23
    Ceremonies of the Heart, 117, 208

cakes, ceremony/wedding, 148-50
Cancian, Francesca, 32, 35
Chang, Lisa, 51
children, 42, 53
Chodorow, Nancy, 52
Christian Coalition, xv
civil rights, xvii-xviii, 16, 163, 179,
    184-7
Clinton, Bill, xv, 9
Cochran, Susan, 32, 35
cognitive maps, 120-1
Cohen, Deborah, 164, 178-9
Cole, Peter, 166-7, 171, 179
Coles, Matt, 163
coming out, xiv, 4, 64, 77, 81, 97
commitment, 45-68
    and age differences, 61-64
    and being married, 56-61
    and feminism, 64-66
    and gender differences, 51-53
    length of, 53-56
    living together, 55
    meanings of, 49-51
commitment ceremonies. *See* same-sex
    ceremonies
commitment mechanisms, 66
Commonweal, 40
communication, 29-31, 38-40
community, xviii-xix, 92-96

conservative politics, 22-23. *See also* Republican Party
Couples, INC., 19
cult of domesticity, 27

Daily, Dennis, 66
Dancel, Genora, 161
Dateline, 4
Daughters of Bilitis, 17, 205
Davidson, David, 163
Davies, Brian, 31, 97, 173
Davis, Celeste, 58, 76, 130-1, 133-4, 141, 155, 156, 165
Davis-Floyd, Robbie, 122
Dean, Craig, 23-24, 162
Defense of Marriage Act (DOMA), xviii, 8-9, 189
discrimination, xiv, xvi
Divine, Francis, 31
divorce rate, 45
Domestic Partnership Legislation, 20-21, 182-4
Douglass, Tom, 57, 81, 85-86, 87, 95-96, 118-20, 125, 135, 137-8, 142-3, 146, 148, 150, 151, 154-5
drag, 14
Dubek, Margaret, 79, 83, 113, 140, 143, 171
Duffy, Sally, 47
Dufour, Teresa, 86-87
Durkheim, Emile, 108, 110
D'Emilio, John, 26

Echols, Alice, 206
Ellen, 3, 4
engagement, 127-31
Episcopal Church, 20
Epstein, Beth, 61, 75, 80, 87, 96, 113, 115, 135, 136, 139, 142, 147-8, 156
Eskridge, William, 41
essentialism, xix, 205
Ettelbrick, Paula, 163, 185

Ettelman, Lynn, 61, 127, 129-30, 174, 181
Evans, Wainright, 28

family, 11, 16
creation of, 82-89, 91
crisis of, 46
definition of, 20, 21, 89-92, 187
economy, 27
nuclear, 11, 13, 187
postmodern, 12
rights, 5
values, 6
Family Research Council, 7, 40
feminism, xiv, xvii, 18, 61, 64, 185, 206
femme. *See* butch/femme roles
Finn, Mike, 115, 144
Fischer, Alan, 167
Flemming, Patrick, 49, 58, 75, 81, 84, 88, 90, 105, 115, 118, 127, 138, 144, 147, 151, 154
Fletcher, Ben, 94, 128, 135, 145, 150-1, 153, 164
Foley, Cheryl, 100, 178
Fontaine, Luke, 49, 50, 77, 83, 143, 152
Frank, Barney, 9
Freedman, Estelle, 26
Freud, Sigmund, 43
Friends, 3, 4
Fromm, Erich: *The Art of Loving,* 38

Gardner, Conrad, 30, 32, 57, 107, 167
Gascon, David, 111, 165, 168-9
Gatland, Pamela, 50
gay, use of the term, xviii
gender differences, 51-53
gender roles, 47, 110
Gill, Patrick, 23-24
goddess rituals, 15, 141, 208
Goffman, Erving, 108
Gomez, Julia, 36, 172, 180

Gorchov, Andrea, 31, 53, 57, 99-100, 164, 174
Gordon, Linda, 11
Gordon, Steve, 207
Gould, Esther, 81, 85-86, 88, 89-90, 113, 115-6, 126, 136, 144, 145, 153-4
Grahn, Judy: *Another Mother Tongue,* 154
Greenwood, Nancy, 91-2, 165-6, 177
Gross, Jane, 24

Hanks, Karl, 178
Harris, Randall, 75, 93, 117, 127, 135, 147
hate crimes, xv
Hawaii. *See Baehr v. Lewin; Baehr v. Miike*
Heckman, Neva Joy, 17
Hendrick, Clyde, 34, 39
Hendrick, Susan, 34, 39
Hernandez, Ricardo, 29, 61, 126
Herscher, Elaine, 161
HIV/AIDS, xiv, xvi, 19, 22, 52, 176. *See also* AIDS
homophobia, xiii, xviii, 66
homosexual, use of the term, xviii
honesty, 31-32
Hudson, Richard, 63, 71, 99, 172
Hughes, Paula, 25, 58, 112, 115, 121, 125, 143, 147, 148, 153
Human Rights Campaign Fund, 8, 162
Hunter, Nan, 10, 16, 182, 185

interdependence, 38
intimacy, 43
investments, 51
IRS protest (1993), xvii, 19. *See also* Millennium March on Washington for Equality (2000); National March on Washington for Lesbian and Gay Rights (1987); National March on Washington

for Lesbian, Gay, and Bisexual Rights and Liberation (1993)
Ivy, Colleen, 98, 168, 171

Jean, Lorri, 163
Johnson, Kristen, 59, 79, 80, 84
Johnson, Sam, 174
Johnson, Susan, 80
Jones, Connie, 164
Jones v. Hallahan, 17
Junkin, J. Carey, 19

Kanter, Elizabeth, 47
Katz, Sue, 206
Kerbo, Harold, 191
Kinsey, Alfred, 193
Knight, Robert, 7, 40
Kowalski, Sharon, 22, 166, 208-9

LaFleur, James, 129, 131-2, 149
Lambda Legal Defense and Education Fund, 109, 162-3
Lamphere, Louise, 107
Laner, Mary, 31
Laumann, Edward, 193
legalization of same-sex marriages, 6, 16-19, 161-89. *See also Baehr v. Lewin;* Defense of Marriage Act; Domestic Partnership Legislation; marriage rights
lesbian, use of the term, xviii-xix
Levinson, Steven, 7
Lewin, Ellen, 107
Lieberman, Deborah, 37, 59, 97, 180
Lindsay, Ben, 28
Loulan, Joanne: *Lesbian Sex,* 33
love, 25-44
    and commitment, 43-44
    definition of, 43
    and eros, 43
    modern conceptions of, 26-29
    qualities of a good relationship, 29-38

romantic, 28
Loving v. Virginia, xviii, 9, 17
Lyon, Phyllis, 17

Mad About You, 3
marriage
    as antithesis of gay identity, 12,
        60-61
    arranged, 26
    colonial, 26
    companionate, 28, 40, 187
    definition of, 9-10, 23, 40
    democratic, 40, 41
    laws, 10, 109
    modern conceptions of, 26-29
    use of the term, 56, 61, 63-66,
        121, 122
Marriage Project, 162
marriage rights, xv, xvi, 5, 16, 42. See
    also legalization of same-sex mar-
    riages
Martin, Del, 17
Martin, Emily, 109
Martin, Harry, 55, 64
Maxwell, Terry, 45
May, Martha, 206
May, Rollo, 43
McConnell, Michael, 17
McGoldrick, Monica, 67
Melrose Place, 3
Mendola, Mary, 66
Mercier, Barbara, 94, 121, 137, 139,
    149, 151-3
Methodist Church, 20
Metropolitan Community Church, 18,
    117, 196
Milk, Harvey, 80, 207
Millennium March on Washington for
    Equality (2000), 205
Miller, Jackie, 37
Miller, Neil, 193
Minneapolis Star Tribune, 106
monogamy, 52, 53, 108

Morrison, Lori, 15, 35, 98, 167, 173,
    183
motherhood, 107
Mullins, Barry, 32, 34, 59, 171

National Lesbian and Gay Task Force,
    162, 163
National March on Washington for
    Lesbian and Gay Rights (1987),
    xiii, xiv, 18
National March on Washington for
    Lesbian, Gay, and Bisexual Rights
    and Liberation (1993), xv, 19
Nelson, Theo, 60, 184
New Republic, 42
Newman, Cathy, 32, 96-97, 169-70
Nickles, Don, 8
Northern Exposure, 3, 4

Obermeier, Melanie, 37, 76, 78, 79,
    81, 114, 140, 150
O'Brien, Kathleen, 52, 57, 75, 76, 88,
    116-7, 146
O'Neill, Michael, 55
On Our Backs, 33
Oprah, 3
Ortega, Juan, 167

parenting rights, xv, xvi, 21
Partners Magazine, 106
Peplau, Letitia Anne, 32, 35, 207
Perry, Troy, 17, 19, 20
Phillips, Samuel, 34, 45, 60, 99
physical attraction, 32-33
Plato, 43
Porter, Russell, 63
Price, Martha, 30, 115, 184
procreation, 26

Quaker Church, 20
Queer Nation, 181

Radicalesbians, 33, 206
Rauch, Jonathan, 41

referral chain, 193
Reilly, Mike, 39, 98, 172
religion, 5, 20, 37, 48, 76-7, 128, 132,
    136, 139, 141-7, 150-1. *See also*
    specific churches
Republican Party, 46
Rice, F. Philip, 133
Rich, Adrienne, 138
    "Compulsory Heterosexuality
    and Lesbian Existence," xix
Richards, Matthew, 51
Rickerby, Brian, 14
rituals, 58, 126, 150-6
Roberts, Linda, 181
Roseanne, 3, 4
Rosenblatt, Paul, 48, 55
Rubin, Zick, 38
Rusbult, Caryl, 47

Sally Jessy Raphael, 3
same-sex ceremonies, xix, 72
    as acts of accommodation, 106-9
    as acts of resistance, 106-11
    and age difference, 101-2
    and building community, 92-96
    and creation of family, 82-89
    and definitions of family, 89-92
    motivations for having, 74-82
    naming of, 111-22
    and previous heterosexual mari-
    tal status, 102-3
    reasons for future, 96-99
    as rites of passage, 73-74
San Francisco Chronicle, 17
Scanzoni, John, 48
Schneider, Eliza, 169, 173
Schwartz, Pepper, 35
    American Couples, 79, 194
separate spheres, doctrine of, 27
sexual activity, 27, 33, 52
sexual identity, use of the phrase, xix
sexual orientation, use of the phrase,
    xix
Sheldon, Lou, 163

showers, wedding/bridal, 133-4
Siggia, Maria, 71, 78, 83, 93, 95, 112,
    138, 140, 145, 146, 152
Singer v. Hara, 17, 18
Sisters, 3
social constructionism, xix
sodomy laws, xiv-xv
Sprinkle, Annie: "Post Porn Modern-
    ist," 33
Stacey, Judith, 12, 106
Stack, Carol: *All Our Kin*, 205
Steinberg, Mark, 111
Stonewall Inn riot, 64
Sullivan, Andrew: *Virtually Normal*, 42
Sullivan, Elizabeth, 94
Sullivan, Michael, 174-5, 183-4

Tanner, Deborah, 207
television, 3-4
Thompson, Karen, 22, 166
Thompson-Kowalski guardianship
    case, 19, 22. *See also* Kowalski,
    Sharon; Thompson, Karen
Traditional Values Coalition, 163
trust, 33-34, 36-38
Turner, Terence, 73
Turner, Victor, 126
20/20, 4

Unitarian Universalist Society, 20, 117
United Church of Christ, 20
Universal Fellowship of Metropolitan
    Community Churches, 19, 20,
    205

van Gennep, Arnold, 73
violence, xv, xvi, 18

Walker, Leslie, 33, 172, 181
Wallace, Lucy, 175, 179
Warner, Steve, 4, 9
Warren, Eric, 180
wedding
    cakes, 148-50

as cultural symbol, 4
showers, 133-4
use of the term, xix, 106, 113,
   115-22
See also anniversary celebration;
   marriage; same-sex ceremonies
Weinberg, Sarah, 61
Weston, Kath, 62, 82, 205, 207

Wheeler, Walter, 19
Wolfson, Evan, 163
women's movement, 16
Wood, Brenda, 34, 64, 167

Young, Ray, 100

Zaleski, Harold, 98
Zerilli, Frank, 19